"A deep spiritual well": eighteenth-century Evangelicals & their legacy—

ESSAYS *in* HONOUR *of*
GRANT A. GORDON

Edited by
Michael A. G. Azad Haykin

Grant & Margaret Gordon
at Old South Presbyterian Church,
Newburyport, MA, where George Whitefield is buried.

"A deep spiritual well": *eighteenth-century Evangelicals &*
their legacy—Essays in honour of Grant A. Gordon

Edited by Michael A. G. Azad Haykin

© 2025

Heritage Seminary Press

Design and Layout: Dustin Benge

Paperback: 978-1-77484-170-9
eBook: 978-1-77484-169-3

Contents

	List of contributors	9
	Preface *Michael A. G. Azad Haykin*	11
1	Grant A. Gordon: A biographical sketch *Stephen Gordon*	15
2	John Newton's letters to Thomas and Sophia Ring *Marylynn Rouse*	23

PART I: ENGLISH EVANGELICAL BAPTISTS

3	"Clothed in white raiment": A sermonic reflection by Benjamin Beddome *Michael A.G. Azad Haykin*	31
4	Pastoral usefulness: Retrieving wisdom from the letters of Benjamin Beddome *Yuta Seki*	41
5	Was he prone to wander? Robert Robinson (1735-1790) *Bruce Hindmarsh*	63
6	From theology to praxis: Theological renewal in eighteenth-century Particular Baptist life and the formation of the Baptist Missionary Society *Peter J. Morden*	73

PART II: THE RYLANDS

7	"Spiritual friendship is the union of souls": The ecclesiology of John Collett Ryland *Garrett M. Walden*	93
8	"Sing on, Blest Pilgrim!": The hymns of John Ryland, Jr. (1753–1825) *Ryan Griffith*	125

9	Forty years of friendship: The letters of John Ryland, Jr. to John Sutcliff *Lon Graham*	145
10	Faith and practice: Setting the "invisible" Lord "ever before me" *Keith Alan Tillman*	163
11	Herman Witsius Ryland (1759-1838) & the evangelical conversion narrative *Christopher W. Crocker*	189

PART III: EVANGELICAL ISSUES

12	Slavery, the slave trade, and Christians' theology *Ian Shaw*	207
13	In what sense was Canada a Christian land after the American Revolution? *Mark Noll*	231
14	Pastoral vision: George MacDonald & his *Thomas Wingfold, Curate* *Jonathan N. Cleland*	245
15	"Can a Chinaman become a Christian?": World Christianity and Evangelicalism—An historian's reflection *Baiyu Andrew Song*	259

LIST OF CONTRIBUTORS

Jonathan N. Cleland is an Adjunct Professor at Heritage College & Seminary and Director of NEXT (Young Adult) Ministries at Grandview Church, Kitchener, ON.

Christopher W. Crocker is the Pastor of Markdale Baptist Church, ON, and Professor of Church History, Toronto Baptist Seminary, ON.

Stephen Gordon is the son of Grant Gordon. He lives in Toronto with his wife Janelle and two boys. They are actively involved in their home church of Little Trinity Anglican.

Lon Graham is the Vice President at New Mexico Baptist Children's Home and Family Ministries and a Senior Research Fellow at the International Baptist Theological Study Centre.

Ryan Griffith is Dean of the Classical Christian Honors College and Associate Professor at the University of Northwestern—St Paul (MN). He also serves as a Senior Fellow at the Andrew Fuller Center for Baptist Studies.

Michael A. G. Azad Haykin serves as Professor of Church History and Biblical Spirituality at The Southern Baptist Theological Seminary and is the Director of the Andrew Fuller Center for Baptist Studies whose main office is on the Southern campus.

Bruce Hindmarsh, DPhil (Oxon), FRHistS, is the James M. Houston Professor of Spiritual Theology and Professor of the History of Christianity at Regent College, Vancouver, BC.

Peter Morden is Principal of Bristol Baptist College, England, and the author of several works on Baptist history, including the *Life and Thought of Andrew Fuller* (Paternoster, 2015).

Mark Noll, emeritus Professor of History (University of Notre Dame), is the author of *What Happened to Christian Canada?*

Marylynn Rouse is CEO of The John Newton Project, www.johnnewton.org, a registered charity seeking to publish and circulate previously unpublished material by John Newton.

Yuta Seki is the Senior Pastor of Maple Avenue Baptist Church in Georgetown, ON, and is a Senior Fellow at the Andrew Fuller Center for Baptist Studies.

Ian Shaw is Professor Emeritus at the University of York (UK) and a member of York Evangelical Church.

Baiyu Andrew Song, PhD, FRAS, is a Senior Fellow of the Andrew Fuller Centre for Baptist Studies, an adjunct professor at Carey Theological College, Vancouver, BC, at Redeemer University, Ancaster, ON, and at Wycliffe College, Toronto.

Keith Tillman serves as a Pastor and an Adjunct Professor at Carson-Newman University with an academic and teaching background in leadership, biblical spirituality, and church history.

Garrett M. Walden, ThM (The Southern Baptist Theological Seminary) is a Pastor and farmer in Alabama, where he studies eighteenth-century Baptist history and theology.

Preface

MICHAEL A. G. AZAD HAYKIN

This *Festschrift* for our friend and academic colleague, Dr. Grant Gordon, was originally planned to appear in time for his eightieth birthday, which was in 2021. The pandemic, however, sidelined those plans. Thankfully, the tercentennial of the birth of one of Grant's heroes and mentors, John Newton (1725-1807), provided another opportunity to publish this collection of essays honouring Grant's work as an historian of the long eighteenth century.

All of the contributors to this work know of Grant's fine studies of John Newton, John Ryland, Jr., David George, and the two leading evangelists of the eighteenth century, George Whitefield and John Wesley. Some of us also know him as a close and dear friend. I have personally known Grant for probably close to forty years now, going all of the way back to my early teaching days at Central Baptist Seminary, where Grant had also served at one point.

When I first met Grant, he was on staff at Ontario Theological Seminary (now Tyndale Seminary). I remember clearly one summer around 1990, when I had convinced the Academic Dean of the seminary, Ian Rennie, also an historian, to allow me to offer a course on the Particular Baptists of the eighteenth century. I went to Dr Rennie's office on the first day of the course and he offered to accompany me to the classroom where we were to meet Grant and the students. Well, when we got there, Grant was the sole person in the room, and he informed us that absolutely no one had signed up for the course!

I am not sure if this was the very first time we met, but I am deeply thankful that that disappointing experience—and even a little humbling (never a bad thing!)—did not in any way dampen our developing friendship. There were few men in the Fellowship of Evangelical Baptist Churches in Canada at that time who were interested in church history, and it was a delight for me to meet and then develop what has turned out to be a lifelong friendship with Grant, built around shared historical interests and our dear Saviour.

Now, I am deeply thankful to all of those who turned in essays over four years ago for their patience with regard to the appearance of this final literary product. In the last year, a number of others also agreed to contribute to the project out of their love for Grant's work—especially his *Wise Counsel*, of which one Toronto pastor I know has given away multiple copies. Dear contributors: a huge thank you to each one of you!

After a brief overview of Grant's life and career, written by his son Stephen, we have an essay on John Newton by Marylynn Rouse, the English independent historian and world-renowned expert on all things Newtonian (that is relating to John Newton, not his more famous countryman, Isaac Newton)! The other essays fall into three categories.

First, there are those dealing with the English Particular Baptists, the body of churches to which Newton's close friend, the younger John Ryland, belonged: two essays on Benjamin Beddome, under whom John Ryland's father was converted in a revival in Bourton-on-the-Water, where Beddome was pastoring; one on Robert Robinson, known well to both Newton and the younger Ryland;[1] and then one on the formation of the Baptist Missionary Society and William Carey. Newton once said of Carey: "Such a man as Carey is more to me than bishop or archbishop: he is an apostle." On another occasion, Newton wrote that he did not look for miracles in

---

1   It is from this essay by Bruce Hindmarsh, also an expert on John Newton, that the title for this Festschrift has been derived.

his own day on the order of those done in the Apostolic era, yet, he went on, "if God were to work one in our day, I should not wonder if it were in favour of Dr. Carey."[2]

Then, we have five essays on the Ryland family: John Collett Ryland, a true English eccentric and his two sons John Ryland, Jr., and Herman Witsius Ryland. Given Grant's life-long interest in John Ryland, Jr., these essays are most appropriate for his Festschrift. And finally, there are four essays on aspects of the Evangelical heritage that concerned both Newton and the Rylands: slavery and the slave trade, the relationship of the American Revolution to the emergence of British North America (Canada), the nature of pastoral ministry, and the subject of race.

Let me conclude with a note of thanks to Revd. Jared Skinner and Dr. Jon Cleland for last-minute help, and to Dustin Benge for his expertise in graphic design and book layout.

Dundas, Ontario
May 7, 2025
(the date in 1815 when John Ryland's close friend
Andrew Fuller stepped into heaven).

PS The picture of John Ryland, Jr. on the front cover of this Festschrift is an AI-generated image from ChatGPT and is based upon the portrait of Ryland at Regent's Park College, the University of Oxford.

---

[2] *The Autobiography of William Jay*, eds. George Redford and John Angell James (1854, Edinburgh: The Banner of Truth Trust, 1974), 275; S. Pearce Carey, *William Carey* (London: Hodder and Stoughton, [1923]), 134.

1
Grant A. Gordon: A biographical sketch

STEPHEN GORDON

Grant Alton Gordon was born on April 8, 1941, in Windsor, Ontario, to Willard and Stella Gordon. Earlier in her life, Stella had been in a very bad car accident and was told she would never have children. But by the grace of God, Grant's older brother, Garnet (d. 2004) was born in 1938, followed by Grant, and then a younger sister, Janis (1944-). They grew up living near the outskirts of town on a large yard where the two brothers and their neighbourhood friends spent their summers building forts and towers and playing games.

Grant's mother was Free Methodist/Brethren and his father was Anglican, but because they lived in a somewhat isolated neighbourhood, there were no churches from these denominations nearby. However, a few blocks away was a little Sunday School mission (Hebron Gospel Hall) led by a Mr. Todd, a Brethren layperson. Grant's parents valued Sunday School, so they sent their three kids at an early age to this Sunday School.

When Grant was around eleven, Mr. Todd sold the mission to Lloyd Deline, with whom he worked at Chrysler. Lloyd Deline was a Baptist, so it became Emmanuel Baptist Church. When Grant was twelve, he accepted Christ as his Saviour and was baptized a few years later once the little congregation had built a larger building with a baptistry. By this time, an Anglican church had been built across the road from their home. Grant's dad attended this church and was active in the choir, and his older brother started attending there as well. Grant and his sister stayed at the Baptist church. His mother did not attend church regularly. Both of his parents continued to be supportive of them attending the Baptist church, and would attend special services and events, especially when their children were involved.

While in Grade 12, Grant had a near-drowning experience. From that point on he decided he wanted to make his life count for God. He had heard of Bible colleges, so he thought he would attend one rather than going to university. He even thought about becoming a pastor but remained uncertain about that path. Grant's exposure to some articles and sermons by Dr. J. C. Macaulay in Wheaton, Illinois, led him to consider the London College of Bible and Missions (LCBM; now Tyndale University), especially when Dr. Macaulay became the president of the school. While attending there, Grant discerned God's call to be a pastor.

There were many amusing stories told over the years about Grant's time in Bible college. Once, when he was working in the kitchen washing dishes and became frustrated that the kitchen help kept putting sharp knives in the dishwater, Grant decided to play a practical joke on them. He put ketchup on a bent finger and told one of the helpers, "I told you not to put knives in the sink!" Understandably, she ran out of the kitchen screaming!

Upon graduating from LCBM with a Bachelor of Theology (Honours Pastoral Studies), Grant felt the need for more training before becoming a pastor. He asked his New Testament professor, Dr. Kermit Ecklebarger, for advice. Dr. Ecklebarger recommended a few American schools, including Gordon Divinity School (now Gordon-Conwell Theological Seminary). He chose it because of its excellent reputation, but this choice had another long-lasting impact: it was where he met his future wife.

Margaret Schmidt began attending Gordon College the same week that Grant started at the Seminary on campus. In the first week of school, a staff person called out, "Grant, come meet a fellow Canadian." From that initial meeting, their relationship began to develop. They didn't have a lot of spare time or money, so they got to know each other mostly over the cafeteria table, enjoying longer than normal mealtimes together. As their relationship grew closer, they talked about marriage. Eventually, they chose to marry before graduating because Grant's mother was seriously ill with cancer and hoped to attend their wedding. They were married Easter weekend at Margaret's home church, Knox Presbyterian Church, in Toronto, Ontario, on April 9, 1966. It was there that she had valued the strong biblical preaching of Dr. William Fitch. The newlyweds then returned to Gordon College and Seminary to complete their studies.

Grant and Margaret both convocated in April of 1967. While waiting for a pastoral position, Grant worked as a machinist in Toronto at Leavens Brothers Aircraft, which made parts for De Havilland Canada. After many years of studying and working part-time to graduate without debt, working as a machinist allowed Grant to recuperate from his intensive studies and to spend more time getting to know Margaret's family in Toronto. Margaret, who had been a schoolteacher, returned to teaching.

In October 1967, Grant accepted a call to be pastor of Bowmanville Baptist Church—part of the Fellowship of Evangelical Baptist Churches in Canada. Margaret initially taught at a local school, but later, once their children were born, she became a stay-at-home mom. The young couple trusted God to provide for their financial needs. Grant enjoyed his first pastoral ministry in Bowmanville, but after five years he was ready for a new challenge. His former college professor, Dr. William Foster, and a few other families from Kenmuir Baptist Church in Mississauga asked Grant to pastor their church plant in the new development of Erin Mills in 1972. Therefore, he and Margaret moved their growing family, which now included their oldest daughter Kelly and son Stephen, to Mississauga to pastor the young congregation. When the church grew to the point of needing a building, Grant took on an additional role, that of part-time building supervisor. To help the church save considerable money during their build-

CHAPTER ONE

ing project, he volunteered to oversee members of the congregation who were doing much of the construction work themselves. During this time, Grant and Margaret welcomed their third child, Karyn.

While serving as a pastor in Mississauga, Grant began part-time studies to strengthen his ministry. The Doctor of Ministry program was just beginning to be offered in some seminaries in the US, but many had poor academic standards. Therefore, he chose Princeton Theological Seminary because of its strong academic standards and history of Reformed theology. Grant was also very impressed with their extensive library. In 1981, Grant received his Doctor of Ministry degree from Princeton Theological Seminary.

In 1982, Grant accepted a call to serve as the pastor of a church plant in Ancaster, Ontario, called Heritage Baptist. As this congregation grew, it

also needed a church building. Under Grant's leadership, the church was able to purchase an empty school building on a five-acre lot at the edge of town. Again, Grant was actively involved in the renovation and redevelopment of this property to meet the needs of this young congregation. He also continued part-time studies at Princeton and in 1987 completed his Master of Theology degree with a thesis on John Newton (1725-1807), author of the famous hymn, "Amazing Grace."

The previous year, Dr. Ian Rennie, the Academic Dean of Ontario Theological Seminary (now Tyndale Seminary) in Toronto invited Grant to join the faculty as Director of Field Education to oversee students in their practical assignments. Dr. Rennie knew of Grant because Grant had taught New Testament evening courses at Ontario Bible College (now Tyndale University), on the same campus as the Seminary. Grant had also been an adjunct professor of Christian Ethics (from 1967 to 1973) at Central Baptist Seminary (now Heritage College and Seminary).

While serving at Tyndale and with their children off at university, Grant encouraged Margaret to study for a Master of Divinity degree in Counseling at the school. Further studies led her to become a hospital chaplain, leading to a position as Co-ordinator of Spiritual Care at Southlake Regional Hospital in Newmarket, where she worked for twelve years until her retirement.

Although a Director of Field Education, Grant also taught courses on Baptist History and Polity. It was while he was in these roles that Grant developed a deeper interest in church history. His initial interest in research arose during a course he took at Gordon-Conwell Theological Seminary with Dr. Roger Nicole, who had been very affirming of Grant's research in that course.

Grant's main interests in research have always come out of his desire to unearth facts about historic Christian figures. His first book was the result of a request by Dr. Jarold K. Zeman, of Acadia Divinity College, Nova Scotia, to write a biography of David George (1743–1810), a Black Baptist preacher in Nova Scotia. Dr. Zeman had heard Grant present a paper on David George at a conference and later asked him to expand the paper into a book. Grant said, "Dr. Zeman, you heard me at the conference. That's everything I know!" Nevertheless, Dr. Zeman continued to press Grant, so he consented but asked for three months to see if he could find any new material with which to start a book. Grant unearthed the needed material that launched his first book, published in 1992.

In 1996, Grant's career path changed again, as he returned to work as a church pastor for another 15 years. However, in this phase of his career, he served as an Intentional Interim Pastor in numerous churches (seven churches in five denominations) where he focused on helping congregations resolve internal issues before they called their next pastor. In addition, he provided conflict mediation for various non-profit organizations and gave seminars on this topic in churches, denominational gatherings, and seminaries. These years of helping churches find healing gave him exceptional joy.

Although he was no longer in a formal academic setting, Grant's passion for research never waned. Throughout his professional life, he was drawn towards the person of John Newton. Grant had been blessed by Newton's writings and wanted to learn more about him and his ministry. In a way, Grant viewed Newton as his own pastor throughout his ministry because of his faithful, godly model. Grant's research resulted in three books: *Wise Counsel: John Newton's Letters to John Ryland Jr.* (2009), *A Great Blessing to Me: John Newton Encounters George Whitefield* (2016), and *An Instrument of Divine Grace: John Newton Encounters John Wesley* (2025). A major strength of Grant's books and articles is his extensive original research, especially in locating original manuscripts and letters, many of which have been previously unpublished. For example, for his most recent book, Grant found a missing middle volume diary of John Newton at the Morgan Library and Museum in New York City. Grant's discovery completed a three-volume set of diaries; the middle volume's location had been unknown to researchers since 1868.

Now retired, Grant and Margaret reside in Stouffville, Ontario, where they are active members of Springvale Baptist Church. For ten years they served as part-time staff overseeing the ministry to seniors. Now they volunteer to provide pastoral care to the seniors in the church and care for members of their retirement community. Grant continues to fulfill his passion for researching on and writing about the eighteenth-century evangelical church. He and Margaret love spending time with their family, which now also includes their three children's spouses and seven grandchildren.

Rev. John Newton (1725–1807).

This portrait, 10 cm in diameter, is in "pencil and wash" by William Watkin Waite (1778–1856) of Abingdon who specialized in portraiture, especially miniatures. Some of his work was shown at the Royal Academy The signed inscription on the back reads "Revd John Newton drawn by W. W. W. from memory." Taking Waite's age into account at the probable time of drawing it (c.1800), this is the latest portrait of Newton and shows him a little heavier than he appears in earlier portraits. It is uncertain where Waite saw Newton. It probably was during Waite's internship and early career in London. The fluted column in the background is like the twelve columns that dominate the sanctuary of St. Mary Woolnoth, London, where Newton served 1780–1807. The hand-written notation on the back, "Rev. John Newton drawn by W.W. W. from memory" is his acknowledgement that Newton did not sit for this. A descendant of John Waite who owned this portrait, and many of Waite's originals, informed Grant Gordon in a letter that Waite kept this original hanging on his studio wall.

2

John Newton's letters to Thomas and Sophia Ring

MARYLYNN ROUSE

The longest period of any stage in John Newton's life was spent as rector of St. Mary Woolnoth in London from the close of 1779 until his death in 1807, yet much written about him today features this, if at all, disproportionately. As J. I. Packer has expressed it, Newton was "without peer" in his pastoral ministry.¹ The publication of a collection of his private letters as *Cardiphonia, the Utterance of the Heart*, has edified thousands of Christians over the centuries, but it is probable that in his prolific correspondence many hundreds of his letters remain unpublished.

It has been a great privilege therefore to have been given access to a private collection of Newton's correspondence during his London ministry, and particularly in that it covers the lesser known period of his last decade, with some very personal details. The letters were written to a young socialite couple, married at Gretna Green and living in Reading. When Newton met them, they had just recently been converted under the ministry of William Bromley Cadogan, rector of St. Giles.

1   https://johnnewton.org/Groups/231004/The_John_Newton/new_menus/About_the_Project/Board_of_Reference/Board_of_Reference.aspx

CHAPTER TWO

Dr. Thomas Ring, a medical doctor, and his wife Sophia invited Newton to stay with them. He recorded in his diary on Tues, September 24, 1793:

> In the evening by Mr Ring's desire, we had a meeting in his drawing room of about 40 people … I thank thee, my Lord, for the hope that it was a good time. And, especially that thou hast enabled this young couple to give such a public testimony, that they are decidedly on the side of thy Gospel. How soon canst thou damp the glare of the world, and give those whose hearts thou drawest to thyself, much more and better than they ever conceived of, while living in gaity. [2]

Arriving back in London he wrote to them:

> Please to give my love to your forty friends, and mine, whom I had the pleasure of meeting in the drawing-room. When you first spoke of inviting some friends to meet me, I thought they would be only a few to dinner or tea, and was not in the least aware of the public step you were going to take. I was a little apprehensive for the consequences. But by what I saw and heard before and after, I am persuaded that it was not the effect of a transient warmth, but that you had deliberately counted the cost, and were willing to let it be known far and near, that you had made up your minds, and were determined by the grace of God, that whatever others do, you and your house, so far as your influence can prevail, will serve the Lord. In this view, I greatly rejoiced in the opportunity, and it pleased me highly to see a room consecrated to Him, which I suppose has formerly been filled in a very different manner.[3]

Newton counselled them in a later letter, dated January 24, 1794:

---

[2] Princeton University, John Newton's Diary, John Newton Collection, CO199 (https://catalog.princeton.edu/catalog/9933444933506421).

[3] Letter dated October 1, 1793, at https://johnnewton.org/ringletters.

We are not our own. We are bought with a price. There is but one thing to us, worth living for—that we may live to him, and for him—to show forth his praise, by obedience, by submission, by usefulness to others—in visiting the afflicted, assisting them by our sympathy, counsel, prayers, or purse, as the case requires, in supporting the cause of the Gospel, and forwarding whatever bids fair for the good of society. These aims ought chiefly to engage our time, talents and influence. Oh, what an honour [it] is to be the instruments of the Lord in diffusing his benefits around us! to be the followers of Him who went about *Doing good*![4]

Thomas Ring began a Free Dispensary, and subsequently founded the Royal Berkshire Hospital, where the poor received free treatment. He served on the committees of several Christian organisations. His obituary noted his "unwearied assiduity in the discharge of his professional duties, unblemished integrity, and extensive benevolence, founded on Christian Principle."[5]

The Rings were devasted by the sudden death of Cadogan. "Come, My dear Madam," Newton wrote to Sophia on January 23, 1797,

I think you have wept enough. I now invite and entreat you to wipe away your tears. You have had a great wound, and you cannot but feel it; but it was not the wound of an enemy. I hope you are now aiming to say, "The will of the Lord be done." For this afflictive dispensation did not spring out of the ground, nor happen by chance. It was the appointment of him, whose wisdom and love are infinite. He could easily have prevented it, and undoubtedly would, if it was not his

---

[4] Letter dated January 24, 1794, at https://johnnewton.org/ringletters, emphasis original.

[5] Cited Roger W. Scott, "The Retrospective Address," *The Transactions of the Provincial Medical and Surgical Association* 9 (1841): 243-244 (https://en.wikisource.org/w/index.php?title=File:Transactions_of_the_Provincial_Medical_and_Surgical_Association,_volume_9.djvu&page=249; accessed May 6, 2025).

purpose to overrule it eventually for good.[6]

He advised "a candid patient hearing" of Cadogan's replacement, reminding them of the Scripture, "you have need of patience."

> The united prayers of such a people are not spoken into the air. No—they enter the ears of the Lord of Hosts, the Great Shepherd, who is attentive to every single sheep or lamb wherever scattered. Much less will he neglect the cries and desires of a whole flock, that call upon him night and day, though he seem to bear long with them.[7]

When it became clear that the believers at St. Giles were being consistently deprived of Scriptural teaching, Newton wrote again:

> I think you are all free, as matters stand, to hear the Gospel, how or where you please, or can. Only I would advise you to keep a rallying point, to have some place and times for meeting together, in a body, and as a body, considering yourselves as still bearing the same relation to each other, that you did in Mr Cadogan's time … As to the Sacrament—if the Dissenters will admit you without joining, I think I should in similar circumstances accept the offer, but I should not be hasty, in becoming a church member. I wish you, for a time at least, to be preserved entire as a body, without losing so much as a little finger from among you.[8]

This core of believers from St Giles eventually sought to acquire their own chapel and often consulted Newton on who they might call to be their minister. He regretted that he was not free to come himself, but kept their needs in mind, offering guidance on how to progress:

---

6   Letter dated January 23, 1797, https://johnnewton.org/ringletters.
7   Letter dated January 23, 1797, https://johnnewton.org/ringletters.
8   Letter dated August 5, 1797, https://johnnewton.org/ringletters.

Our Church service is, in the main, excellent. But it is not essential either to our salvation, or our consolation. It may be, and perhaps, at some times, it is overvalued. I hope and pray that the Lord may send you a Pastor entirely according to your own wishes. But above all I pray that he may dwell in your hearts, in your houses, and afford you his gracious and enlivening presence, when you wait upon him, in such opportunities of public worship, as his will and providence may afford you.[9]

The chapel they founded in 1798 is still ministering the Gospel today: St Mary's Castle Street.[10]

Newton visited the Rings several times. In 1801 his adopted daughter Betsy Catlett, niece of his wife, underwent a distressing ordeal—as did Newton, expressed in his annotated *Letters to a Wife*:

Thou hast now tried me, as Thou didst Abraham, in my old age, when my eyes are failing and my strength declines. Thou hast called for my Isaac, who has so long been my chief stay and staff; but it was Thy blessing that made her so. A nervous disorder has at length issued in lunacy and she is now in Bethlehem [Bedlam], where I desire to leave her under Thy care, and chiefly pray for myself, that I may be enabled to wait Thy times and will, without betraying any signs of impatience or despondence unbecoming to my profession and character.[11]

Newton's letters to the Rings reveal more of this challenging time; they also describe Betsy's gradual recovery, his own increasing deterioration in

---

9 Letter dated December 21, 1797, https://johnnewton.org/ringletters.
10 https://www.stmaryscastlestreet.org.uk/welcome.htm.
11 Newton's annotated copy of his *Letters to a Wife* (Cowper & Newton Museum; https://cowperandnewtonmuseum.org.uk/).

health, her care for him, and his comments in his dying days. A fortnight before his death Betsy informed Sophia:

> It is a great mercy that my dear Father suffers but little pain that he can sleep well and eat as much as is requisite though no meat, he takes a good many eggs, broth etc; he likes tea as well or better than anything else; he gets up to dinner every day and seldom lies down afterwards. He sits up till 9 o'clock.[12]

The last hymn on his lips was by Moravian John Cennick, "Thou dear Redeemer, dying Lamb,/I love to hear of Thee."

This unpublished collection of letters provides a fascinating insight into Newton's very personal pastoral counselling and his advice on church planting, together with detailed glimpses into his family life and the final days of this exceptionally influential servant of God. The John Newton Project aims to publish an annotated edition of these precious letters in print. They can be read at https://johnnewton.org/ringletters.

---

12   Letter dated December 5, 1807, https://johnnewton.org/ringletters.

I.
English Evangelical Baptists

William Carey,
based on a sketch by the Arts and Crafts Movement artist C. E. Mallows (1864-1915) in James Culross and John Taylor, *Founders and Pioneers of Modern Missions* (Northampton: Taylor & Son 1899).

3

"Clothed in white raiment": A sermonic reflection by Benjamin Beddome[1]

MICHAEL A.G. AZAD HAYKIN

During the era of the long eighteenth century (i.e., the 1680s to the 1810s) English Particular Baptists had a high view of the ordinances of baptism and the Lord's Supper. Baptism was the "place" where the believer affirmed his or her determination to be a disciple of Christ before the world and was the doorway into the local church, while the Lord's Supper, generally celebrated monthly, was seen as a vital means of spiritual nourishment. Nevertheless, Baptists in this time-period were quite adamant that without the life-giving presence of the Holy Spirit, these ordinances were of no spiritual value. Keeping in step with the Spirit was what was necessary when it came to the nurture of the believer's soul or the sustenance of the inner life of a congregation. Thus John Sutcliff (1752–1814) of Olney, Buckinghamshire, observed that "the outpouring of the divine Spirit … is the grand promise

---

[1] This essay was originally presented at the American Society of Church History, British Nonconformity in the Long Eighteenth Century Working Group Day Conference, at St Mary's University, Twickenham, on June 22, 2023. I am indebted to comments made by Profs John Coffey and Stephen A. Marini that led to the final paragraph.

of the New Testament." The Spirit's "influences," he stressed, "are the soul, the great animating soul of all religion. These withheld, divine ordinances are empty cisterns, and spiritual graces are withering flowers."[2] His older Baptist contemporary, Benjamin Beddome (1718–1795) of Bourton-on-the-Water, Gloucestershire, made the same point from a somewhat different perspective in a sermon on 1 Corinthians 7:19.[3] When people stand before "the awful tribunal of Christ" on the day of judgment, Beddome stated, the great question "will not be … whether our bodies were immersed in water; but whether we had 'washed our robes, and made them white in the blood of the Lamb' [Revelation 7:14]."[4]

Now, the paradoxical nature of this cleansing—red blood making a raiment white—surely indicates that the statement from Revelation 7 must be seen as figurative, though Beddome did not provide any elaboration of this figure of speech at this point in his sermon. Yet, in another sermon that he preached on Revelation 4:4,[5] Beddome did devote a section of the discourse to explicating the significance of the whiteness of the elders' clothing.[6] In what follows, his reflections on the white raiment are explored after a brief sketch of his life and ministry.

Being Benjamin Beddome

Converted in the late summer of 1737 when he was nineteen years of age, Benjamin Beddome trained for pastoral ministry for two years at Bristol

---

2   John Sutcliff, *Jealousy for the Lord of Hosts illustrated* (London: W. Button, 1791), 12.

3   "Circumcision is nothing, and uncircumcision is nothing, but the keeping of the commandments of God." All Bible references will be cited as found in the King James or Authorized Version.

4   Benjamin Beddome, "Practical Religion More Important Than Ceremonies" in *The Sermons of Benjamin Beddome* (1835, Knightstown, IN: Particular Baptist Heritage Books, 2022), 1:260.

5   "And round about the throne were four and twenty seats: and upon the seats I saw four and twenty elders sitting, clothed in white raiment; and they had on their heads crowns of gold."

6   Benjamin Beddome, "Sermon IV" in his *Short Discourses Adapted to Village Worship, or The Devotions of the Family* (London: Samuel Burton; Simpkin and Marshall, 1825), VIII, 34–44.

Baptist Academy and then spent a further year of academic and ministerial preparation in London.[7] He was set apart for pastoral ministry in early 1740 by the London Baptist congregation that gathered at Prescot Street. That same year he was invited to serve as a probationer minister by the Baptist congregation in the Cotswolds village of Bourton-on-the-Water, Gloucestershire. Significant for the shape of his future ministry was a local revival that took place during his ministry at Bourton in the early months of 1741 when some forty individuals were converted. Deeply satisfied with the shape and direction of his ministry, the Bourton Baptists extended a formal invitation to Beddome in July of 1743 to become what the Minute Book of the church called a "teaching elder." Readily acceding to their request, he was ordained on September 23 of that year.

In the 1740s, the Bourton church experienced significant numerical growth. Between 1740 and 1750 the church membership more than doubled and by 1751 it stood at 180. However, during the 1750s and the first half of the 1760s this growth began to slow such that by 1795, the year that Beddome died, the church had 123 on the membership roll. Yet, although fewer were taking the vital step of believer's baptism that led to church membership, Beddome was increasingly known as a fine preacher and his Sunday congregations numbered between 500 to 600 hearers. After his death, nine volumes of his sermons were published that provide our main access to his sermons.[8] Other notable publications included a catechism

---

7   For Beddome's life and ministry, see especially John Rippon: "Rev. Benjamin Beddome, A.M. Bourton-on-the-Water, Gloucestershire," *Baptist Annual Register* 2 (1794–1797): 314–326; Thomas Brooks, *Pictures of the Past: The History of the Baptist Church, Bourton-on-the-Water* (London: Judd & Glass, 1861), *passim*; Derrick Holmes, "The Early Years (1655–1740) of Bourton-on-the-Water Dissenters who later constituted the Baptist Church, with special reference to the Ministry of the Reverend Benjamin Beddome A.M. 1740–1795" (Certificate in Education Dissertation, St Paul's College, Cheltenham, 1969); and Michael A.G. Haykin with Roy M. Paul and Jeongmo Yoo, ed., *Glory to the Three Eternal: Tercentennial Essays on the Life and Writings of Benjamin Beddome (1718–1795)*, Monographs in Baptist History, vol. 13 (Eugene, OR: Pickwick Publications, 2019).

8   *The Sermons of Benjamin Beddome* contains 67 sermons. There is also a series of eight volumes, *Short Discourses Adapted to Village Worship, or The Devotions of the Family*,

CHAPTER THREE

and a book of 800 or so hymns.[9]

"Clothed in white"

Clive Edwards notes that by the eighteenth century, Western culture had long associated white with purity and deity.[10] In part, this comes from the employment of this colour to envisage scenes of heavenly transcendence in the Bible.[11] As Michel Pastoureau observes, this colour has a particularly "dominant place" in the Book of Revelation where it is "the color of victory and justice."[12] Nina Edwards, in her recent history of white clothing, also notes the way that such "clothing is allied to spiritual purity and heaven itself" throughout Revelation.[13] As support, she cites Revelation 3:5a[14] and 19:14.[15] She could also have cited Revelation 4:4, the verse that provided the text for Beddome's sermon.

---

each of which is comprised of twenty sermons. Two volumes of this series first appeared on the press of J.W. Morris in Dunstable in 1807. Later editions and printings of the entire series of eight continued to appear down to at least the early 1830s. A copy of the 1807 printing can be found in the Boston Athenaeum. See https://catalog.bostonathenaeum.org/vwebv/holdingsInfo?searchId=4324&recCount=50&recPointer=0&bibId=535868; accessed May 3, 2025.

9 Benjamin Beddome, *A Scriptural Exposition of the Baptist Catechism by Way of Question and Answer*, 2nd ed. (Bristol: W. Pine, 1776) and *idem*, *Hymns adapted to Public Worship, or Family Devotion* (London, 1818).

10 Clive Edwards, "Artifacts" in *A Cultural History of Color in the Age of the Enlightenment*, ed. Carole P. Biggam and Kirsten Wolf (London: Bloomsbury Academic, 2021), 194. See also the discussion of James Fox, *The World According to Color: A Cultural History* (New York, NY: St. Martin's Press, 2021), 141–166, *passim*.

11 "White" in *Dictionary of Biblical Imagery*, ed. Leland Ryken, James C. Wilhoit, and Tremper Longman III (Downers Grove, IL; Leicester, England: InterVarsity Press, 1998), 944.

12 Michel Pastoureau, *White: The History of a Color*, trans. Jody Gladding (Princeton; Oxford: Princeton University Press, 2023), 66.

13 Nina Edwards, *Pazazz: The Impact and Resonance of White Clothing* (London: Reaktion Books Ltd., 2023), 34.

14 "He that overcometh, the same shall be clothed in white raiment."

15 "And the armies which were in heaven followed him upon white horses, clothed in fine linen, white and clean." Edwards actually cited Revelation 19:14 as Revelation 19:4. All told, there are nine references to white raiment in the Book of Revelation: 3:4-5, and 18; 4:4; 6:11; 7:9 and 13-14; and 19:14. Cf. also Revelation 19:8.

After setting this verse in its literary context, Beddome looked first at the meaning of the term "elder" and what might be entailed by the fact that there were twenty-four of them. Beddome confessed that he was not entirely sure as to why twenty-four were specified. He suggested that it might be the sum of the twelve Old Testament patriarchs, the sons of Jacob, and the twelve New Testament apostles. If so, they represented "the whole body of believers under both dispensations."[16] Beddome appears to have assumed this to be the proper interpretation, for when he addressed the question of the meaning of the elders' white raiment in the next section of the sermon, he began by citing Psalm 45:13–14 and Revelation 19:8—in other words, a verse from both Testaments—about the Bride of Christ, who was "arrayed in fine linen, clean and white: for the fine linen is the righteousness of saints."[17]

Beddome's mini-disquisition upon the meaning of the colour white first maintained that the fine, white linen is the "emblem" of the saints' "personal and spotless purity," in other words, their lives of holy living. Such purity is not to be confused, the Bourton minister argued, with Christ's imputed righteousness, which is the basis of their justification. For support, Beddome referenced Revelation 7:14.[18] Beddome then made three specific arguments as to why these elders in Revelation are clothed in white. First, he noted that priests in the Old Testament wore linen garments (Leviticus 6:10; 16:32), which he assumed—possibly from a passage like Revelation

---

16   Beddome, "Sermon IV" in his *Short Discourses*, VIII, 34–37.
17   Beddome, "Sermon IV" in his *Short Discourses*, VIII, 39.
18   "They … washed their robes, and made them white in the blood of the Lamb." Beddome, "Sermon IV" in his *Short Discourses*, VIII, 39. A quick read through the rest of Beddome's sermons does not yield any other discussion of whiteness. As for his hymns, white appears to have been used only once. In that hymn, Beddome urged Christians to "abstain from every sin" and to "keep your garments white and clean,/ Now that grace has made them so" (*Hymns*, Hymn #504, stanza 1). This hymnic use of white emphasizes the vital necessity of a believer living a holy life. It is noteworthy that Beddome never explicitly used white's opposite, namely, black, for sin. Cf. "White" in *Dictionary of Biblical Imagery*, ed. Ryken, Wilhoit, and Longman III, 944: "In the symbolism of the Bible white is not set against black (the great biblical antithesis is light versus darkness)."

19:14—were white, though linen is not naturally white in colour.[19] These elders are so clothed in white, Beddome reasoned, for during their earthly lifetimes they exercised the priestly ministry of prayer, praise, and intercession for others.[20]

Then, the "white raiment" is also the "emblem of victory and triumph." Beddome supported this interpretative comment first with a reference to the book of Esther, where Mordecai is arrayed in "blue and white … and a garment of fine linen and purple" (Esther 8:15) after his triumph over Haman. There is also Revelation 7:9, which depicts the triumphant saints "clothed with white robes." For Beddome, it is thus appropriate that the twenty-four elders appear in white since they are sharers in "the triumphs of the Captain of their salvation."[21]

"The emblem of unspotted purity"

Third, the white apparel of these elders especially bespeaks "perfect purity and righteousness." Beddome found proof for this semiotic affirmation of white as "the emblem of unspotted purity" in a couple of biblical narratives: Daniel's vision of the Ancient of Days, whose "garment was white as snow" (Daniel 7:9) and the transfiguration of Christ, during which his clothing became as "white as the light" (Matthew 17:2; cf. Mark 9:3).[22] The colour white is thus ideal to describe the saints in heaven. For they are clothed in Christ's perfect righteousness and thus completely absolved from all of their sins. Moreover, in terms of their sanctification, they are now "perfectly holy."[23] A favourite description of heaven by Beddome was that it

---

19   The same notion is found in Benjamin Keach, *Tropologia: A Key to Open Scripture Metaphors* (London: Enoch Prosser, 1682), I, 168: "whiteness" is "a metaphor taken from linen, which when foul is restored to its colour by washing and cleansing it from all spots." The spelling of this quote has been modernized.
20   Beddome, "Sermon IV" in *Short Discourses*, VIII, 40.
21   Beddome, "Sermon IV" in *Short Discourses*, VIII, 40.
22   Beddome, "Sermon IV" in *Short Discourses*, VIII, 40.
23   Beddome, "Sermon IV" in *Short Discourses*, VIII, 41.

is "a place of perfect purity, and nothing that is defiled can enter there."[24] Whiteness thus befits the citizens of heaven.

This third meaning assigned by Beddome to the colour white reflects a long-standing interpretative tradition within Beddome's Particular Baptist community. At the very outset of the long eighteenth century, the Particular Baptist pastor-theologian Benjamin Keach (1640-1704) observed that white is "a most exact symbol of inward purity and cleansing from sin."[25] Similarly, in his commentary on the entire Bible, John Gill, (1697-1771), the doyen of the Particular Baptists, remarked regarding the white clothing of the saints in Sardis (Revelation 3:4-5): it is "expressive of that spiritual joy" which the Sardis believers "shall be partakers of, as well as of their spotless purity and innocence in the other world."[26]

The material witness of whiteness

This Particular Baptist understanding of whiteness in Scripture received visible expression in the rite of baptism, which Beddome and most of his fellow Baptists in the eighteenth century did publicly in ponds, lakes, and rivers. As late as the 1830s, the Bourton Baptists were baptizing believers in rivers, possibly in portions of the River Windrush, which flows through the town.[27] And although we do not have detailed accounts of any of the

---

24 Benjamin Beddome, "Sermon V" in *Short Discourses Adapted to Village Worship, or The Devotions of the Family*, 6th ed. (London: Samuel Burton; Simpkin & Marshall, 1824), III, 42. See also Benjamin Beddome, "Sermon XVI" in *Short Discourses*, III, 138: "Heaven is a holy place."

25 Keach, *Tropologia*, I, 168. Keach supported this interpretation by referencing Psalm 51:7; Isaiah 1:18; and Revelation 7:14.

26 John Gill, *An Exposition of the New Testament* (London, 1748), III, 663.

27 See Brooks, *Pictures of the Past*, 104, which describes a baptism by Thomas Coles (1779–1840), who became the pastor of the Bourton church in 1801. See also the reference to baptisms at Bourton in Brooks, *Pictures of the Past*, 91. In the town of Bourton, the River Windrush is no more than ten or so inches deep, clearly not deep enough for the immersion of an adult.

   On Coles, see B.S. Hall, "Memoir of the Late Rev. Thomas Coles, M.A.," *The Baptist Magazine* 33 (1841): 213–221. Coles sat under Beddome's teaching in the early 1790s and took notes of his sermons from the age of eleven onwards. He became a member of the Bourton congregation shortly before Beddome's death in 1795.

baptisms done by Beddome, we do have two lengthy contemporaneous accounts of the baptism of believers, both recorded by Robert Robinson (1735–1790), the pastor of the Baptist cause in Cambridge. In one of the accounts, which narrated the baptism of forty-eight people at Whittlesford, seven miles due south of Cambridge, in the late 1770s or early 1780s, Robinson stated that each of the men wore "a long white baize gown tied around the waist with a sash." The women likewise were dressed "neat, clean, and plain, and their gowns white linen or dimity."[28] This use of white clothing for the baptizands is clearly tied to such passages in Revelation as the one that formed the subject of Beddome's sermon.

The use of white clothing was also an answer to the accusations that Baptists surreptitiously used the baptismal rite for sexual ends.[29] When the Congregationalist pastor, Henry Mayo (1733–1793), described by one source as "the bully of infant-sprinklers," witnessed a baptism by John Gill in 1766, he lost no time in publishing a pamphlet in which he argued that the Baptist way of administering baptism was "insufferably indecent" and "imprudently immodest" for spectators and really nothing less than a potential violation of the seventh commandment for those baptizing women.[30] Twelve years later, Joseph Jenkins (1743–1819), who served as

---

28   Robert Robinson, *The History of Baptism* (London: Thomas Knott, 1790), 541–543, passim.

29   The Anglican minister Daniel Featley (1582–1645) published a vituperative attack on the Baptists entitled *The Dippers dipt. Or, The Anabaptists duck'd and plunged Over Head and Eares* (1645), in which he argued that Baptists were accustomed to stripping "stark naked, not only when they flocke\ in great multitudes, men and women together, to their Jordans to be dipped; but also upon other occasions, when the season permits" (cited Gordon Kingsley, "Opposition to Early Baptists (1638–1645)," *Baptist History and Heritage*, 4, no.1 [January, 1969]: 29). The earliest Particular Baptist doctrinal standard, *First London Confession* of 1644, the doctrinal standard of the first generation of English Particular Baptists, responded to this false allegation by emphasizing that the baptism of believers was carried out with "convenient garments both upon the administrator and subject, with all modesty" ([William Kiffen, John Spilsbury, and Samuel Richardson,] *First London Confession of Faith* XL margin in William L. Lumpkin, *Baptist Confessions of Faith*, 2nd ed. [Valley Forge, PA: Judson Press, 1969], 167). The wording of both quotes has been modernized.

30   Henry Mayo, *The True Scripture Doctrine, of the Mode and Subjects of Christian Baptism; With some Strictures on Dr. Gill's Sentiments of the Moral Law, and Justification*

the pastor of Baptist causes in Wrexham, Wales, and in London, had to refute the assertions that Baptists conducted baptisms in the nude, that they baptized "women apparelled in a *single* garment," and that they even immersed women in the final stages of pregnancy.[31] The chromatic symbolism of white garments for the baptizands—a colour long associated in the Western mind with purity—was a material response to such charges of indecency and a visible declaration that the Baptist community sought to be one marked by "the purity and righteousness of the saints."[32]

---

from Eternity (London: James Buckland, 1766), 16–17. For the description of Mayo, see Philalethes, "Preface" to his *The Humble Attempt of a Layman Towards a Confutation of Mr. Henry Mayo's Pamphlet, call'd the Scripture-Doctrine of Baptism* (London, 1767), A2. For the response of this anonymous pamphlet to the charge of believer's baptism being indecent, see *Humble Attempt of a Layman*, 59–61.

31 Olin C. Robison, "The Particular Baptists in England 1760–1820" (DPhil thesis, Regent's Park College, Oxford University, 1963), 288. On Jenkins, see R. Philip Roberts, *Continuity and Change: London Calvinistic Baptists and The Evangelical Revival 1760–1820* (Wheaton, IL: Richard Owen Roberts, Publishers, 1989), 115–116.

32 For the words in quotation, I am indebted to Leith Eric Schmidt, " 'A Church-Going People Are a Dress-Loving People': Clothes, Communication, and Religions Culture in Early America," *Church History* 58 (1989): 48–49.

4

Pastoral usefulness: Retrieving wisdom from the letters of Benjamin Beddome[1]

YUTA SEKI

Benjamin Beddome (1718–1795) was the pastor of the Baptist church in Bourton-on-the-Water in south central England.[2] On one occasion,

---

1 This chapter was initially presented as a paper at the annual meeting of the Evangelical Theological Society of Ontario & Quebec, Toronto, Ontario, October 12, 2024, which was an adaptation from a chapter in a doctoral thesis on the pastoral theology of Benjamin Beddome. The paper was published as Yuta Seki, "Pastoral Usefulness: Retrieving Wisdom from the Letters of Benjamin Beddome," *Journal of Andrew Fuller Studies* 10 (forthcoming). Used with permission. The doctoral thesis is Yuta Seki, "'Long May Thy Servant Feed Thy Sheep': Pastoral Ministry in the Life and Thought of Benjamin Beddome," DEdMin thesis, The Southern Baptist Theological Seminary, 2025, and will be published as Yuta Seki, *Long May Thy Servant Feed Thy Sheep: The Pastoral Theology of Benjamin Beddome* (Eugene, OR: Pickwick, forthcoming). Used with permission.

2 For sources on Beddome, Monographs in Baptist History see Anonymous, "Memoir" in Benjamin Beddome, *Sermons Printed from the Manuscripts of the Late Rev. Benjamin Beddome, A. M. of Bourton-on-the-Water, Gloucestershire* (London: William Ball, 1835), ix–xxviii; Thomas Brooks, *Pictures of the Past: The History of the Baptist Church, Bourton-on-the-Water* (London: Judd & Glass, 1861), 21–66; Kenneth Dix, "'Thy Will Be Done': A Study in the Life of Benjamin Beddome," *Bulletin of the Strict Baptist Historical Society* 9 (1972); Roger Hayden, *Continuity and Change: Evangelical Calvinism Among Eighteenth-Century Baptist Ministers Trained at Bristol Academy, 1690–1791* (Chipping Norton, UK: Nigel Lynn, 2006), 80–91, 154–158, 168–172; Michael A. G. Haykin, "Benjamin Beddome (1717–1795)" in *The British Particular Baptists, 1638–1910*, ed. Michael A. G. Haykin and Terry Wolever (Springfield, MO: Particular Baptist

Beddome found himself at a meeting of ministers in the nearby town of Fairford, Gloucestershire. Beddome was scheduled to preach, but when the service began, he forgot what he had intended to say. Since he did not preach from notes, he could not consult them. Instead, he asked the host pastor, Thomas Davis (d. 1784), "Brother Davis, what must I preach from?" Taken aback by Beddome's question, Davis replied, "Ask no foolish questions." The Bourton pastor was relieved and took Titus 3:9 as his text, "Avoid foolish questions" and, according to Beddome's first biographer, John Rippon (1751–1836), he "preached a remarkably methodical, correct, and useful discourse on it."[3] Clearly, Beddome was capable in the pulpit. Rippon remarked about Beddome's preaching: "He fed [his people] with the finest of the wheat. No man in all his connexions wrote more sermons, nor composed them with greater care—and this was true of him to the last

---

Press, 2018), 4:258–273; *Glory to the Three Eternal: Tercentennial Essays on the Life and Writings of Benjamin Beddome (1718–1795)*, ed. Michael A. G. Haykin, Roy M. Paul, and Jeongmo Yoo, Monographs in Baptist History 13 (Eugene, OR: Pickwick, 2019); Derrick Holmes, "The Early Years (1655–1740) of Bourton-on-the-Water Dissenters Who Later Constituted the Baptist Church, with Special Reference to the Ministry of the Reverend Benjamin Beddome A.M. 1740–1795" (Certificate in Education dissertation, St. Paul's College, Cheltenham, 1969); Jason C. Montgomery, "Benjamin Beddome: The Fruitful Life and Evangelical Labor of a Forgotten Village Preacher" (PhD dissertation, Southwestern Baptist Theological Seminary, 2018); Stephen Pickles, *Cotswolds Pastor and Baptist Hymn Writer: The Life and Times of Benjamin Beddome* (Upham, UK: James Bourne Society, 2023); Daniel S. Ramsey, "'The Blessed Spirit': An Analysis of the Pneumatology of Benjamin Beddome as an Early Evangelical" (PhD dissertation, The Southern Baptist Theological Seminary, 2017); John Rippon, "Rev. Benjamin Beddome, A. M. Bourton-on-the-Water, Gloucestershire" in *The Baptist Annual Register, for 1794, 1795, 1796–1797* (London, 1797), 314–326.

Hereafter, Brooks, *Pictures of the Past* will be abbreviated to Brooks, *POTP*.

[3] Rippon, "Rev. Benjamin Beddome," 321. The anecdote and the sermon were published as John Rippon, "Sketch of a Sermon by the Late Rev. B. Beddome" in *Baptist Annual Register for 1798, 1799, 1800, and Part of 1801* (London, 1801), 415–421. The sermon was also published as Benjamin Beddome, "Sermon 10" in *Twenty Short Discourses, Adapted to Village Worship or the Devotions of the Family* (London: W. Simpkin and R. Marshall, 1833), 5:81–89. Haykin recounts these events as an example of how "many of the best preachers of this community [the English Particular Baptists of the long eighteenth century] were, of course, able to preach with little preparation, if the need arose." Michael A. G. Haykin, "'Those Who Plead for Thee': English Particular Baptist Preaching in the Long Eighteenth Century," *Evangelical Quarterly* 94, no. 4 (December 2023): 3–5.

weeks of his life."⁴

The Bourton pastor was respected in the Midland Association and amongst the English Particular Baptists.⁵ He produced *A Scriptural Exposition of the Baptist Catechism*, which was widely used in his denomination and at their training center, the Bristol Baptist Academy.⁶ Through

---

4   Rippon, "Rev. Benjamin Beddome," 320. In his day, Robert Hall Jr. (1764–1831) "was renowned as one of the most eloquent preachers of Great Britain." Michael A. G. Haykin, "Robert Hall, Sr. (1728–1791)" in *The British Particular Baptists, 1638–1910*, ed. Michael A. G. Haykin and Terry Wolever (Springfield, MO: Particular Baptist Press, 2019), 5:55; Cody H. McNutt adds, Hall "was one of the most celebrated figures among the Baptists of the Regency era, yet his fame extended far beyond Baptist circles" ("The Ministry of Robert Hall, Jr.: The Preacher as Theological Exemplar and Cultural Celebrity" [PhD dissertation, The Southern Baptist Theological Seminary, 2012], 2). Hall published a volume of Beddome's hymns in 1818 and said of Beddome in the preface, "As a Preacher, he was universally admired for the piety and unction of his sentiments, the felicity of his arrangement, and the purity, force, and simplicity of his language; all which were recommended by a delivery perfectly natural and graceful." See Robert Hall, "Recommendatory Preface" in Benjamin Bedddome, *Hymns Adapted to Public Worship, or Family Devotion: Now First Published, from the Manuscripts of the Late Rev. B. Beddome, A. M.* (London, 1818), v–vi.

5   Rippon wrote, "How acceptable his labours were to the churches, when he could be prevailed on to visit them, has long been known at Abingdon, Bristol, London, and in the circle of the Midland Association." ("Rev. Benjamin Beddome," 322).

6   For a modern reprint of this catechism, see Benjamin Beddome, *A Scriptural Exposition of the Baptist Catechism* (1776, Birmingham, AL: Solid Ground Christian Books, 2006). Haykin says, "The Bristol Baptist Academy [was] the sole British Baptist seminary for much of the eighteenth century." Michael A. G. Haykin, "'Glory to the Three Eternal': Benjamin Beddome and the Teaching of Trinitarian Theology in the Eighteenth Century," *Southern Baptist Journal of Theology* 10, no. 1 (Spring 2006): 77. For the history and impact of the Bristol Academy, see David W. Bebbington, "The Significance of Bristol Baptist College," *Baptist Quarterly* 53, no. 4 (October 2022): 149–166; John Rippon, *A Brief Essay towards an History of the Baptist Academy at Bristol* (London, 1796); Jeongmo Yoo, "The Bristol Academy and the Education of Ministers in Eighteenth-Century England (1758–1791)" in *Church and School in Early Modern Protestantism: Studies in Honor of Richard A. Muller on the Maturation of a Theological Tradition*, ed. Jordan J. Ballor, David S. Sytsma, and Jason Zuidema, Studies in the History of Christian Traditions 170 (Leiden: Brill, 2013). The institution has been variably titled during its existence. For the first fifty years (1720–1770), the school was referred to as an academy, but with the formation of the Bristol Education Society in 1770, the title "Seminary" was used. By 1812, the school was regularly called Bristol Baptist Academy, and in 1841, the printed annual reports called it Bristol Baptist College. See Roger Hayden, "Bristol Baptist Academy, 1720 to present," *Dissenting Academies Online: Database and Encyclopedia* (Dr Williams's Centre for Dissenting Studies, August 2011).

the posthumous publication of his sermons and hymns, Beddome's legacy continued into the nineteenth century.[7] There are extant 225 sermons and 830 hymns, but this essay will focus on a collection of Beddome's letters.

The letters were exchanged between the Baptist churches of Bourton-on-the-Water and Goodman's Fields in London. The latter was called the Little Prescott Street Church and had recently lost its pastor, Samuel Wilson (1702–1750).[8] The deacons of the church searched for a replacement and requested that Beddome relocate to Goodman's Fields. The London church was familiar with Beddome since, a decade earlier, he had been baptized by this church and joined it as a member.[9] The church now found itself inviting a former member to be their new pastor. As for Beddome, the invitation presented the opportunity to minister at a more significant church and have a wider influence. There were seven letters exchanged between Bourton and London between November 1750 and February 1751; to their analysis, we now turn.[10]

---

7 For a list of the primary sources primary and secondary sources on Beddome, see Yuta Seki, "A Resurgence of Benjamin Beddome Studies: A Bibliographic Essay," *Journal of Andrew Fuller Studies* 8 (Spring 2024): 45–60.

8 For a history of the Little Prescott Street Church from 1730–1768, see Joseph Ivimey, *A History of the English Baptists* (London: B. J. Holdworth, 1823), 3:542–561.

   For sources on Wilson, see Anonymous, "Memoir of the Rev. Samuel Wilson," *The Baptist Magazine* 11 (April 1819): 141–145; John Gill, "Sermon … Occasioned by the Death of the Reverend Mr Samuel Wilson" in *A Collection of Sermons and Tracts* (London: George Keith, 1773); 1:477–498; Joseph Stennett, "A Funeral Sermon, at the Internment of the Reverend Mr. Samuel Wilson, in the Burial-Ground at Bunhill, October 12, 1750" in Samuel Wilson, *Sermons on Various Subjects and Occasions* (London: G. Keith and J. Ward, 1753), 1–14.

9 For the sake of clarity, the reader should be aware that the phrases Little Prescott Street church, Goodman's Fields church, and London church will be used interchangeably.

10 These letters have appeared in several locations: Thomas Brooks, "Ministerial Changes a Hundred Years Ago," *Baptist Magazine* 51 (July 1859): 425–429; Thomas Brooks, "Ministerial Changes a Hundred Years Ago," *Baptist Magazine* 51 (August 1859): 482–487; Brooks, *POTP*, 32–47; Dix, "Thy Will Be Done"; Hayden, *Continuity and Change*, 82–86; Pickles, *Cotswolds Pastor*, 63–70. The version in Brooks, *Pictures of the Past* has the fullest information and is the version cited in this article.

Letters 1 and 2: Goodman's Fields to Bourton

At a meeting of the Little Prescott Street Church on November 11, 1750, five deacons and thirty members signed and sent two letters to Bourton-on-the-Water.[11] In the first letter, the Goodman's Fields Church requested Beddome to relocate to London, considering the recent loss of their pastor.[12] If Beddome would come, they promised to love and respect him as a minister of the gospel.[13] The deacons appealed on the grounds of usefulness by drawing upon the Matthean parable of the talents (Matthew 25:14–30).[14] Given they considered Beddome to have five talents, it was clear they

---

11 Goodman's Fields Church to Benjamin Beddome, November 11, 1750, in Brooks, *POTP*, 33.

12 Goodman's Fields Church to Benjamin Beddome, November 11, 1750, in Brooks, *POTP*, 32–33. To avoid excessive footnotes, the letter will be cited at its first mention. Thereafter, only direct quotes will be cited.

13 The duties of churches were set forth in the ordination sermons of English Particular Baptist pastors in the eighteenth century. At the ordination of George Braithwaite to the pastorate of Devonshire Square, London, on March 28, 1734, Wilson preached to the church regarding their duties. Ivimey, *History of the English Baptists*, 3:355. Wilson exhorted the church to have honorable thoughts of their pastor, converse with him respectfully, speak about him with affection and esteem, pray for their pastor, not receive an accusing report against him, follow their minister as he followed Christ, and provide for him cheerfully and generously. John Gill and Samuel Wilson, *The Mutual Duty of Pastor and People, Represented in Two Discourses Preached at the Ordination of the Reverend George Braithwaite, M. A.* (London: Aaron Ward, 1734), 4–27. Thus, the London church echoed the instructions of their former pastor, saying that they would act properly towards Beddome if he would come and be their pastor.

14 As will be demonstrated, usefulness was a prominent theme in the letters between Bourton and London. Beddome himself agreed that Christians should steward their talents according to their ability. In his sermon, "Motives to Usefulness," Beddome preached that Christians "should not be remiss and negligent, but exert themselves to the utmost in the service, and for the honour of their blessed Redeemer." He added while God generally chose lowly persons to be part of his kingdom, he sometimes plucked those "whose intellectual powers fit him for a large sphere of usefulness. Now, where much is given, much is required: a greater improvement is expected from the man who has five talents, than from him who is possessed of two." Beddome here quoted the same passage as the London deacons did in their letter. He continued, describing the kind of talents he had in mind: "A clear understanding, penetrating judgment, lively imagination, strong memory, and the like, are given to men to profit withal; and the service they perform should certainly be proportioned to their superior abilities." Benjamin Beddome, "Motives to Usefulness" in *Twenty Short Discourses, Adapted to Village Worship or the Devotions of the Family*, 2nd ed. (Dunstable: J. W.

thought much of Beddome's gifting and abilities.

The second letter from Goodman's Fields was addressed to the Bourton church and outlined the reasons why Beddome should remove to London.[15] Though they were reticent to call a pastor from the country, they had seen it done successfully by all three Dissenting denominations in the city. They claimed their request was based solely upon necessity as there was no suitable replacement for Wilson. Given the declining state of the church in the city and the careless profession of many Christians, they needed someone of Beddome's caliber. Amongst Baptists, "learned" ministers were scarce, and so Goodman's Fields felt compelled to seek Beddome's removal to London.[16] The deacons were concerned that if Beddome did not come, the people would disperse and the congregation dissolve, like what had happened to the Joiners' Hall church recently under the care of Clendon Dawkes (d. 1758).[17] The deacons concluded by mentioning the presence

---

Morris, 1807), 1:88–89. Thus, Beddome agreed with the London deacons that Christians and ministers should strive for greater usefulness.

15 Goodman's Fields Church to Bourton Church, November 11, 1750, in Brooks, *POTP*, 33–34.

16 The deacons of the London church lamented the scarcity of qualified ministers in the city, especially when "compared with the other two denominations," a reference to the Congregationalists and Presbyterians. Goodman's Fields Church to Bourton Church, November 11, 1750, in Brooks, *POTP*, 33. It is worth noting that Wilson and Beddome were both referred to as "learned" in this letter. Goodman's Fields Church to Bourton Church, November 11, 1750, in Brooks, *POTP*, 33–34. Beddome had first studied at the Bristol Academy but then moved to study at an Independent Academy in London under John Eames (1686–1744). Brooks, *POTP*, 22–23.

In 1796, Andrew Fuller (1754–1815) noted that the greater part of the Baptist ministers in the Northamptonshire Association did not have an "academical education." Andrew Fuller, "Discipline of the English and Scottish Baptist Churches" in *The Complete Works of the Rev. Andrew Fuller with a Memoir of His Life by Andrew Gunton Fuller*, ed. Joseph Belcher (1845, Harrisonburg, VA: Sprinkle, 1988), 3:481. Nearly a half century earlier, when the Goodman's Fields church was looking for a learned minister, an even smaller percentage of ministers would have been educated.

17 Dawkes had been called there in 1735 and pastored the church for about sixteen years. After his departure, the church declined through death and removals and eventually dissolved in 1761. For these and other details concerning Dawkes, see Ivimey, *History of the English Baptists*, 3:504–6.

of a suitable replacement for Beddome amongst the Bourton membership and described the potential relocation to London as being "to more important services."[18]

Letters 3 and 4: Bourton to Goodman's Fields

The response from Bourton also consisted of two letters, one from the pastor and the other from the church. In his letter, Beddome expressed his condolences to the Goodman's Fields church as they faced the death of their pastor.[19] He acknowledged the decision to be no small matter for either party.[20] He elaborated on the motivations to relocate to London: the Goodman's Fields church was more significant and had more resources; there was also the prospect for greater usefulness in the city.[21] Beddome then listed several reasons for remaining in Bourton: he had been ordained to the church there, and strong bonds of affection existed between him and the people.[22] Thus, a divided Beddome said, "I am in a great strait. I

---

18 Goodman's Fields Church to Bourton Church, November 11, 1750, in Brooks, *POTP*, 34. This final phrase is connected to the concept of usefulness introduced in the previous letter.

19 Benjamin Beddome to Goodman's Fields Church, n.d., in Brooks, *POTP*, 34–36. Beddome called Wilson "an instructor," which could be trace back to the days when Beddome was baptized and called to the ministry while under Wilson's care. Brooks, *POTP*, 23; Ivimey, *History of the English Baptists*, 3:553.

20 For the London church, it concerned their spiritual vitality, and for Beddome, he desired to have a clean conscience over the matter.

21 Beddome listed the advantages of relocating to London: the church in Bourton was lowly and had much debt, whereas the London church was thriving and affluent. In the country, Beddome seldom enjoyed hearing and fellowshipping with other pastors, but London had "the best of preachers" and brother pastors who were united by a common cause and affection. Beddome was baptized and called to the ministry at Goodman's Fields, and the church had sent Beddome to Bourton in the first place; thus, Beddome had a special regard for the London church. Bourton was clearly a place of less influence than London, and he acknowledged the Goodman's Fields perspective that Beddome would be of greater usefulness in the city. Gary Brady says that the Little Prescott Street church was "London's largest Baptist church at the time." Gary Brady, "Being Benjamin Beddome: A Biographical Study" in *Glory to the Three Eternal*, ed. Haykin, Paul, and Yoo, 13.

22 The reasons given for his remaining in Bourton were as follows: first, he was ordained over a people who had treated him with great affection, and many had been

CHAPTER FOUR

cry to God for direction, but what way I shall take, I know not," and entrusted himself to the church who would make the final decision concerning his removal to London or not.[23] Beddome placed the Little Prescott Street Church's arguments before his members and instructed them to take a month to pray and talk about the matter before sending a response to London.

---

converted under his ministry. Second, the church was formerly divided but was now united. Third, Beddome had been fruitful in Bourton, as evidenced by the over one hundred people who had been added to the church since his arrival. Fourth, the church's heart was engaged with its pastor. Fifth, they were committed to making Beddome comfortable. And sixth, Beddome had recently recovered from a life-threatening disease, and he attributed his recovery to the care and prayers of his people.

23 Beddome to Goodman's Fields Church, n.d., in Brooks, *POTP*, 36. Benjamin Francis (1734-1799) found himself in a similar situation twenty-two years later when he was requested to leave his church in Horsley, Gloucestershire, for the Carter Lane church in Southwark, London, to be John Gill's (1697-1771) successor. In a letter to Caleb Evans (1737-1791), Francis expressed the perplexity he felt over the decision—whether to remove or to remain—in a manner akin to Beddome:

> My dear friend, I cannot express the astonishment, the shame, the concern, & perplexity, my mind has been overwhelmed with ever since. The thought of parting with my dear people, & of the unhappy consequences that may follow, dissolves my heart, & almost overpowers my spirits; while on the other hand a pleasing prospect of more extensive & general usefulness presents itself ... I do not expect to be more happy in a people than I am at present: they love me exceedingly, as I also do them; nor have I but one material thing to complain of here, namely my being obliged to be so much from home, without which I cannot support my family ... my poor wife is very lonesome & uncomfortable; I shall not be able so well to manage my children ; I cannot visit my people so much as I would; & I have but little time for reading, study, etc. ... *I am in a great strait*, & my mind is in a state of perpetual suspense. (Benjamin Francis to Caleb Evans, February 22, 1772, in Geoffrey F. Nuttall, "Letters by Benjamin Francis," *Trafodion* [1983]: 7-8 [ellipses original, emphasis added])

For further information and sources on this episode in Francis's life, see Thomas Flint, "A Brief Narrative of the Life and Death of the Rev. Benjamin Francis, A. M." in John Ryland, *The Presence of Christ the Source of Eternal Bliss. A Funeral Discourse ... Occasioned by the Death of the Rev. Benjamin Francis, A. M.* (Bristol, 1800), 42-43 and note *; Michael A. G. Haykin, "Benjamin Francis (1734-1799)" in *The British Particular Baptists, 1638-1910*, ed. Michael A. G. Haykin (Springfield, MO: Particular Baptist Press, 2000), 2:17-18; Nuttall, "Letters by Benjamin Francis," 7-8.

The response from the Bourton church was dated December 16, 1750.[24]

They expressed sympathy for their friends in Goodman's Fields and agreed that "more learned and popular ministers" should be in London since country churches benefited from those in the city.[25] The Bourton church hoped God would raise up a pastor to replace Wilson, though not through "such extremes as to deprive another church of its pastor" as proposed by Goodman's Fields.[26]

The Bourton deacons gave several reasons why Beddome should not relocate to London. The strongest reason was their love and esteem for their pastor. This should have been sufficient to deny London's request; however, the deacons listed several more reasons to buttress their position. They saw their pastor as an answer to prayer—first in his initial arrival in Bourton and second in his recent recovery from sickness[27]—and spoke of his usefulness in the conversion of sinners, increase of membership, and raising of pastors.[28] In light of these reasons, the Bourton church denied London's request for Beddome's removal.

In having read the four letters, one would except the correspondence to have stopped. The city church put forth a strong case for Beddome's

---

24 Bourton Church to Goodman's Fields Church, December 16, 1750, in Brooks, *POTP*, 37–39.
25 Bourton Church to Goodman's Fields Church, December 16, 1750, in Brooks, *POTP*, 37.
26 Bourton Church to Goodman's Fields Church, December 16, 1750, in Brooks, *POTP*, 37.
27 The sickness took place shortly after his marriage to Elizabeth Boswell. Beddome contracted a serious disease that lasted for six weeks and brought him close to the grave. The Bourton pastor recovered, and the whole ordeal endeared the church to their pastor since he saw his restoration as an answer to his people's earnest prayers. Similarly, the fact they nearly lost their pastor strengthened the affection of the people for Beddome. For the information in this paragraph, I am indebted to Rippon, "Rev. Benjamin Beddome," 319.
28 According to Rippon, the men raised up for ministry during Beddome's pastorate were John Collett Ryland, Richard Haynes, John Reynolds Jr., Nathaniel Rawlins, and Alexander Payne. See Rippon, "Rev. Benjamin Beddome," 323 and note *.

removal, but the country church denied the request with equal force.[29] However, like the importunate widow in the Gospel of Luke (Luke 18:1–18), the London church was persistent.[30] After a month and a half, the Goodman's Fields deacons once again appealed for Beddome to come and pastor the Little Prescott Street church.

Letter 5: Goodman's Fields to Bourton
This second appeal was sent on February 3, 1751.[31] The deacons invoked a "maxim" which they judged to be applicable to all areas of life, whether civil or religious. The maxim was: "The service of all is to be preferred to that of the part. No man ever said that the interest of one member is of equal importance with that of society in general."[32] This premise served as the basis for their appeal in the letter. According to Goodman's Fields, the question was whether the prosperity of Baptist churches in general or the Bourton church alone was to be preferred.

The London deacons claimed Beddome would be more useful by removing to the city than remaining in his "retired station" in the rural region of the Cotswolds. Their ambition for Beddome was that he become a celebrated preacher in the city and lend credibility to the Baptist cause, which was often criticized by their fellow Dissenters and those of the Church of England.[33]

The deacons brought up again the necessity of "an able and learned ministry" being preserved in their midst. In their thinking, only Beddome was a suitable replacement for Wilson. Bourton's insistence on retaining

---

29 Holmes, "Early Years," 55.
30 Dix, "Thy Will Be Done."
31 Goodman's Fields Church to Bourton Church, February 3, 1751, in Brooks, *POTP*, 39–42.
32 Goodman's Fields Church to Bourton Church, February 3, 1751, in Brooks, *POTP*, 39.
33 The argument of the Goodman's Fields church was that Beddome would have been more useful in London and had a more influential and fruitful ministry there. Considering their comments, though, causes one to wonder whether a desire for prestige and respectability had tinged the motives of the London church.

their pastor was based on a concern for Bourton and the surrounding areas only, and not the Baptist cause more broadly. The Little Prescott Street deacons could argue this way, of course, because they were in London, and city churches had a more significant impact upon the general interest of the Baptist churches than country churches. Additionally, the impact of city churches on the general cause was proportionate to the quality of its ministers. Consequently, the need of London should have been preferred to that of Bourton. The Little Prescott Street deacons posed a hypothetical scenario. Even if the situation was between the Bourton church and a single church in London—without any consideration of the general interest—Beddome would have been more useful in London than in the obscure village of Bourton.[34] In the proposed hypothetical scenario, London was to be preferred.[35]

Further arguments for the propriety of Beddome's removal were then given. The deacons stated the potential of dispersion was greater in London than in Bourton, since their people had forty congregations that they could attend. Bourton's fears of dispersion or dissolution, however, were unfounded because they had a suitable replacement in John Reynolds Jr. Additionally, a learned and popular ministry belonged, not in the obscure village of Bourton-on-the-Water, but in the city.

In their letter, Bourton had cited their love and esteem for their pastor

---

34 In the recommendatory preface to Beddome's hymns, Hall acknowledged the obscurity of Bourton, which accorded with the perspective of the Goodman's Fields church. However, with the advantage of hindsight (he wrote nearly seventy years after the correspondence and over twenty years after Beddome's death), Hall also saw the suitability of a gifted and learned man such as Beddome to have spent his days in a country village in the Cotswolds. Hall, "Recommendatory Preface," vi.

35 We have the total membership of the Bourton and Goodman's Fields churches from around that time. Brooks said that the Bourton membership was 180 in 1751, and Ivimey estimated that the Goodman's Fields church had 150 members in 1753. Brooks, *POTP*, 50; Ivimey, *History of the English Baptists*, 3:278. The Bourton church had a larger membership than the Goodman's Fields church. Considering this, the argument made by the London Baptists here—that even if the situation involved the Bourton church and a single church in London, without regard for the general interest—holds less weight.

as sufficient grounds to refuse London's request. This objection was quickly dismissed by Goodman's Fields since the Bourton church was not considering the general interest and, by their refusal, constraining Beddome's usefulness in the city.[36] The London deacons acknowledged Beddome had been an answer to the prayers of the Bourton church, but they insisted a man with his gifting and graces was "qualified for extensive service" and thus "was not one of those mercies that you can keep or we can take."[37] In a corrective manner, the Little Prescott Street Church stated that if Beddome discerned he should relocate to London, then Bourton's reluctance could not stop him from accepting the call.[38] The letter concluded with general pleasantries and a plea for a favourable response to their request.

Letter 6: Bourton to Goodman's Fields

There were two letters sent in response from Bourton to Goodman's Fields, both signed February 24, 1751. The first was sent by the deacons of the church.[39] While Bourton sympathized with their brethren at Little Prescott Street, they were bothered by the forwardness of the London church.[40] The Bourton deacons asked a hypothetical question to make their point. If a church larger than Little Prescott Street had lost its pastor through death, and they had requested for Wilson's removal—while he was still alive, of

---

36 The London deacons admitted the success of their plan was probable and not certain. To make their case that Beddome would most probably be more useful in London, they pointed to Beddome's past successes in Bourton. This was a shrewd tactic, since the Bourton deacons had enumerated these very points concerning Beddome's usefulness in Bourton as reasons for his remaining there.

37 Goodman's Fields Church to Bourton Church, February 3, 1751, in Brooks, *POTP*, 41.

38 Perhaps there was speculation on the part of the Goodman's Fields Church that the Bourton church was seeking to retain Beddome even though he was inclined to relocate to London.

39 Bourton Church to Goodman's Fields Church, February 24, 1751, in Brooks, *POTP*, 42–44.

40 They wrote, "We are sorry you should desire, much more endeavor, to deprive another church of its fixed pastor, in order to repair the distressing loss of your worthy minister deceased." Bourton Church to Goodman's Fields Church, February 24, 1751, in Brooks, *POTP*, 42.

course—how kindly would they have looked upon such a request?

The Bourton deacons then responded specifically to the "maxim" put forward by Goodman's Fields. Their response to the maxim was significant since usefulness had been an argument employed by Goodman's Fields from the beginning. According to the Bourton deacons, that a popular and learned minister needed to relocate to the city was not a foregone conclusion. To the contrary, it could be argued that eminent ministers were more needed in the country than in the city. Drawing on the imagery in the book of Revelation, the deacons referred to pastors as stars in Jesus's right hand, and thus it was from him that ministers received their brightness and splendor (cf. Revelation 1:16, 20; 2:1; 3:1). If Jesus had placed stars to shine in darker parts of the world, their light was more necessary in those places than in other regions where he had set up a constellation of ministers.

The Bourton deacons addressed the claim that Beddome's removal would likely lead to further usefulness in the city. In many cases, when a minister had been removed from a station where God had placed him, it was not accompanied by great success. If ministers had been appointed to a place by God and then were made to leave that station, it could not be assumed they would enjoy continued usefulness. From the vantage point of Bourton, "Usefulness consists not barely in preaching to a very great auditory, but in honouring religion by serving God and our generation in that post in which he sets us."[41]

The Bourton deacons desired to be directed by divine providence. With respect to Beddome's removal, however, they did not see God was leading them this way, since he had been an answer to their prayers. The Bourton church was thankful for city churches helping country churches, but those writing this letter also detailed the problem of country churches always needing to give up their best ministers to city churches.[42] As for the claim

---

41   Bourton Church to Goodman's Fields Church, February 24, 1751, in Brooks, *POTP*, 43.

42   The Bourton church admitted the London churches consistently helped country churches. However, if the city churches constantly drew away ministers from the coun-

by Goodman's Fields that there was no suitable replacement, Bourton retorted they had plenty of good candidates to choose from. In the end, the Bourton church resolutely refused London's request for Beddome's removal. They concluded with a prayer that "the Shepherd of Israel would settle a pastor over you to your joy and satisfaction."[43]

Joseph Belcher's *Historical Sketches of Hymns* records an anecdote that well reveals the tension that existed between the Baptist churches in Bourton and Goodman's Fields, given the latter's assertiveness in seeking Beddome to be their new pastor. Belcher said that "after sending call after call in vain," the Little Prescott Street church sent "one of their number to urge the matter with [Beddome]."[44] When the Londoner arrived in Bourton, his horse was entrusted to the care of a member of the Bourton church. The Bourton member brought the horse to Beddome's home where the London Baptist was staying. Unhappy with the Londoner's efforts to draw away his pastor, the Bourton member said, "Robbers of churches are the worst of robbers," and then released the horse to go its "own course" or run free.[45] Presumably, the man found his horse and was able to get back to London!

Letter 7: Beddome to Goodman's Fields
In his letter to Goodman's Fields, Beddome reassured the London church that he had not influenced his church's decision. On the contrary, he spoke on behalf of Goodman's Fields and strongly put forward their arguments. Even then, however, the Bourton church refused to release their pastor, and so Beddome submitted to the church's will. He provided several reasons for

---

    try churches, they were simultaneously helping and harming the churches in the rural areas. Such action on the part of the city churches would lead to friction and division between them and the country churches, since the latter would be deprived of their ministers "whom God has fixed over them, and whom they dearly loved." Bourton Church to Goodman's Fields Church, February 24, 1751, in Brooks, *POTP*, 44.

43 Bourton Church to Goodman's Fields Church, February 24, 1751, in Brooks, *POTP*, 44.

44 Joseph Belcher, *Historical Sketches of Hymns, Their Writers, and Their Influence* (Philadelphia, PA: Lindsay & Blakiston, 1859), 83.

45 Belcher, *Historical Sketches of Hymns*, 83–84.

his decision. First, he felt it was not lawful for a pastor to leave his people "without their consent," unless there was a serious deficiency on their part, such as lack of love for the pastor, stinginess in giving, divisions, or opposition.[46]

Second, Beddome leaned on the witness of church history. He specifically cited John Owen (1616–1683).[47] Owen believed every local church should seek to promote the welfare of the universal church and thus removals were sometimes appropriate. In these scenarios, a multiplicity of factors needed to be considered. For Owen, the prospect for greater usefulness occasioned the discussion of a pastor's removal from one station to another, but it was not automatic grounds for removal. If a pastor were to relocate to another church, it required the consent of the churches involved

---

46   Beddome to Goodman's Fields Church, February 24, 1751, in Brooks, *POTP*, 45. Beddome was outlining the basic duties of a church towards one another and their pastor. These duties were captured in the sermons to the church at ordination services of English Particular Baptist pastors in the eighteenth century. Beddome had just written that he would not remove to London. Thus, when he claimed that a church's failure in these duties legitimized a pastor's removal, the Bourton pastor was indirectly stating that his church had been adequately fulfilling their duties towards him and one another. This whole episode, in fact, had led the church towards deeper unity and paying off a large, long-standing debt.

47   John Owen, *The True Nature of a Gospel Church and Its Government* (London: William Marshall, 1689), 113; see also page 112. Owen was leaning on the rulings of the ancient church: once ordained in one place, a bishop or presbyter could not move to another church. This decree was apparently necessary because church officers were making it a habit to move from places of lesser to greater prominence for personal gain. This practice was denounced at the Council of Nicaea in 325 and the Council of Chalcedon in 451. These councils, which are often associated with the respective creedal statements on Trinitarian theology and Christology, issued canons, or laws, that governed ecclesial practice. Owen referred to Canons 15 and 16 from Nicaea and Canons 5 and 20 from Chalcedon. See Henry R. Percival, "Excursus on the Translation of Bishops" in *The Seven Ecumenical Councils of the Undivided Church*, ed. Henry Percival, A Select Library of the Nicene and Post-Nicene Fathers of the Christian Church, Series 2, vol. 14 (New York: Charles Scribner's Sons, 1900), 32 and 35. For the canons from Chalcedon, see "The XXX Canons of the Holy and Fourth Synods, of Chalcedon" in *The Seven Ecumenical Councils of the Undivided Church*, ed. Percival, A Select Library of the Nicene and Post-Nicene Fathers, 14:271, 282. It should not be missed that in responding to a contemporary ministerial crisis, Beddome leaned on the wisdom of Owen from the seventeenth century who, in turn, was leaning on the rulings of Nicaea and Chalcedon from the fourth and fifth centuries.

and the affirming counsel of other churches and elders of the same denomination.

With respect to Owen's "counsel," the Bourton church had not given their consent to Beddome's removal. Beddome also reported in his letter—and this was the third reason why Beddome chose to remain in Bourton—he had consulted friends, fellow pastors, and others who gave the near unanimous advice to remain in Bourton unless the church gave their consent for his removal. The fourth reason was the rarity of success to follow the removal of a pastor. Here Beddome cited Matthew Henry (1662–1714) as an example when the latter had left Chester for Hackney in London in 1712.[48]

Beddome then sought to point out a hole in the argument of the London church. If their premise was true—that greater usefulness was sufficient reason for the removal of a pastor—then it would be impossible for smaller and less significant churches to retain their pastors.[49] For Beddome, who ministered in the obscure village of Bourton-on-the-Water, usefulness in another station was one factor to be considered at the prospect of removal and not the deciding element in every case.

John Gill (1697–1771), pastor of the Carter Lane Church in Southwark, London, had preached the funeral sermon for Wilson.[50] Beddome said Gill had "entirely left out the prospect of greater usefulness, among the motives

---

48 Rather than resulting in greater usefulness, Henry was not overly successful at Hackney, though he labored diligently to the end of his life. As for Chester, Beddome had heard reports that the communicants under Henry were greater than the hearers under his successor, a Mr. Gardiner. For Henry's move from Chester to Hackney, see Allan Harman, "Matthew Henry's Move to Hackney in 1712," *Reformed Theological Review* 80, no. 2 (August 2021): 155–173.

49 This would also have justified the removal of a pastor in every situation since greater usefulness was nearly always cited as a cause for removal.

50 Gill, "Reverend Mr Samuel Wilson" in his *Sermons and Tracts*, 1:477–498. Beddome evidently had access to this sermon as he referred to it in his letter. For biographical sketches of Gill, see Robert W. Oliver, "John Gill (1697–1771): His Life and Ministry," in *The Life and Thought of John Gill (1697–1771): A Tercentennial Appreciation*, ed. Michael A. G. Haykin, Studies in the History of Christian Thought (Leiden: E. J. Brill, 1997), 7–50; John Rippon, *A Brief Memoir of the Life and Writings of the Late Rev. John Gill, D.D.* (1838, Harrisonburg, VA: Gano Books, 1992).

which he looks upon as sufficient to authorize the removal of a pastor from one place to another."⁵¹ Of the reasons listed by Gill for the lawful removal of a pastor, the last was a lack of affection between the pastor and the people since that would undermine the effectiveness of the ministry of the Word and ordinances. According to Gill, when there was a strong bond of love between a pastor and his people, it caused the preaching and the administration of the ordinances to be more effective. Therefore, if there was a strong bond between a pastor and people, it was an argument for him to remain in his current station. This thinking accorded with the argument of Bourton and Beddome in their letters.

At this point, Beddome's decision was made: he needed to remain in Bourton. Had he removed to London, it would have been miserable both for the London church and its new pastor, since Beddome would have been acting contrary to conscience. He hoped he had conducted himself uprightly and clarified if his church had consented to his removal, he would have accepted London's call. Such a departure, though, would have required sacrifice on his part since he deeply loved his people. Since the church refused his removal, however, Beddome concluded, "The will of the Lord be done" (cf. Acts 21:14).⁵² The beloved pastor of the Bourton church was resolved that he would not violently tear himself away from his people.

---

51 Beddome to Goodman's Fields Church, February 24, 1751, in Brooks, *POTP*, 46. Earlier, Beddome stated that a pastor should not leave his people without their consent except in situations where there was a lack on the church's end. Gill expounded and elaborated on the same concept in his funeral sermon and provided a more expansive list of what could have constituted a lack on the part of the church. According to Gill, a pastor may lawfully remove from one church to another if heresies in the church could not be rooted out, immorality was prevalent, discipline was neglected, people refused to submit to Christ's laws, the church could not and would not adequately provide for the pastor and thereby invited the reproach of the world, or "disaffection between him and the people rises so high, on one account or another, that peace and fellowship cannot be maintained, nor the ends of the ministration of the word, and administration of ordinances be answered." Gill, "Reverend Mr Samuel Wilson" in his *Sermons and Tracts*, 1:484. There was, as Beddome pointed out, no mention of the prospect of greater usefulness being grounds for the removal of a pastor.

52 Beddome to Goodman's Fields Church, February 24, 1751, in Brooks, *POTP*, 46.

Instead, he would have rather served God in a lower and less significant station where God had placed him than "intrude" into a higher and more significant station where God had not directed him.[53]

He concluded the letter by remarking how the whole ordeal—though it came to nothing as far as London was concerned—had moved the Bourton church towards greater unity and encouraged them to pay off a large and longstanding debt of nearly one hundred pounds.[54] The Bourton pastor urged his friends at Goodman's Fields to wait upon God and, in due time, he would provide for the Little Prescott Street Church in ways far better than they could have designed for themselves.[55] He exhorted his brethren

---

53 Beddome to Goodman's Fields Church, February 24, 1751, in Brooks, *POTP*, 46–47. The way the Bourton church sought to discern God's guidance over the matter was different from the approach of Goodman's Fields. Beddome began by asking, "To what station has God called me?" Having determined that (through several factors, not excluding the question of usefulness), the Bourton pastor resolved to be faithful in that place. Goodman's Fields, however, began by asking, "Where will this man be most useful?" with useful being defined as ministering in the most prominent churches and having the largest influence on the greatest number of people from that station. Thus, usefulness, understood in this way, was the supreme consideration above all others. Beddome should have removed to London, according to Goodman's Fields, because he would have been most useful there as a pastor. For Goodman's Fields, the other factors that Bourton cited to argue for the retention of their pastor—the love of the church for their pastor, the reading of Providence that Beddome was God's gift to the Bourton church, the necessity of country churches to have continuing pastors, the danger that Beddome's removal would pose to the country church, and the unanimous decision of the Bourton church to refuse London's request—were all subordinate to the sole consideration of usefulness. To Beddome, this seemed too simplistic an approach.

54 The debt had been incurred through three building projects—the construction of the parsonage in 1741, the expansion of the chapel in 1748, and the strengthening of it in 1750. London's request for the removal of Pastor Beddome and the ensuing deliberations in the church stirred them to pay off these debts. Brooks, *POTP*, 47–48.

55 Even if the worst should happen—which was unlikely—and the Goodman's Fields church were to disperse and significantly decline in numbers, God was able to raise them up as he had done previously. When Wilson came to the church about 25 or 26 years prior, the church was "in a low and declining state," according to Ivimey. See Ivimey, *History of the English Baptists*, 3:307. During Wilson's pastorate, the church revived with many people having been converted and edified. In his funeral sermon for Wilson, Gill reflected, "The low estate in which you were, when he came to this place, and the numbers of which you now consist, and the flourishing condition in which you now are, abundantly show the success of his ministration among you." Gill, "Reverend Mr Samuel Wilson" in his *Sermons and Tracts*, 1:496. In their heartache at

in London with the words of Psalm 37:5, "Commit, then, your way unto the Lord; trust also in him, and he will bring it to pass."[56] He signed the letter, "Your affectionate and brother in gospel bonds, B. Beddome."[57] Beddome belonged to God as his servant and, in his mind, he was gifted and called by Christ to serve in whatever station his master had placed him. How relieved must the Bourton membership must have been when their pastor read this letter of refusal to London's request at the church meeting on the Lord's Day, February 24, 1751.[58]

Retrieving wisdom

"Retrieval" is a helpful term to describe the practice of learning from the past. A single lesson will be drawn from this correspondence between the Baptist churches of Bourton-on-the-Water and Goodman's Fields for contemporary Christians and pastors. The lesson was captured by Beddome's biographers, so even in the process of retrieval, I am leaning on earlier writers.

The correspondence demonstrates the propriety of a gifted and learned pastor remaining in the station to which God has called him, even if there is opportunity to remove to a more significant place. That a man of Beddome's caliber ministered for over five decades in the obscure village of Bourton-on-the-Water was not lost on his early biographers. Beddome's memorialist said, "the retirement of Bourton would furnish but few incidents for history."[59] There is irony, of course, in the writing of this essay which seeks to retrieve wisdom from letters that were penned in the remote, obscure village of Bourton-on-the-Water. Later in the memoir, the

---

the loss of their pastor and the anxiety over his replacement, the Goodman's Fields Church had forgotten their own history.

56   Beddome to Goodman's Fields Church, February 24, 1751, in Brooks, *POTP*, 47.
57   Beddome to Goodman's Fields Church, February 24, 1751, in Brooks, *POTP*, 47.
58   Brooks wrote, "At the same time the pastor read his answer to the said letter, for which being also in the negative, the church expressed their thankfulness." Brooks, *POTP*, 42.
59   Anonymous, "Memoir," xxi.

memorialist spoke of Beddome's usefulness in Bourton, pointing to the increase in membership from roughly 70 to 180, from the time he arrived there in 1740 to 1751, and that six men had been called to the ministry during Beddome's pastorate.[60] In a sketch written seventy years after Beddome's death, G. Hester wrote that in Bourton, "he lived a retired, studious, pious, and useful life."[61] Hester's terse statement rebutted any notion that a Christian minister could only be useful in the most prominent and influential places.

Robert Hall Jr. (1764–1831) who captured the peculiar-yet-beautiful picture of an educated and gifted minister who spent his life ministering in a rural village in the Cotswolds thus:

> Though he spent the principal part of a long life in a village retirement, he was eminent for his colloquial powers, in which he displayed the urbanity of the gentleman, and the erudition of the scholar, combined with amore copious vein of attic salt than any person it has been my lot to know. As a preacher, he was universally admired for the piety and unction of his sentiments, the felicity of his arrangement, and the purity, force, and simplicity of his language; all which were recommended by a delivery perfectly natural and graceful.[62]

These early biographers spoke with one voice that there were lessons to be learnt from this letter exchange between Bourton and Goodman's Fields. The letters penned by the Bourton church and Beddome provided a visible pastoral theology, that is, *pastoralia* in action. Beddome's example provided future pastors with counsel if they found themselves in circumstances akin to Beddome's, namely, needing to consider a pastoral move. More broadly, Beddome's decision to remain in Bourton demonstrated to

---

60 Anonymous, "Memoir," xxvi.
61 G. Hester, "Baptist Worthies—Benjamin Beddome," *The Baptist Magazine* 57 (January 1865): 443.
62 Hall, "Recommendatory Preface," vi.

posterity the beauty and legitimacy of a pastor remaining in a station to which God had called him, even if it was a less glamorous and influential place. In other words, bigger was not always better.[63]

---

63   The thinking that bigger is better in pastoral ministry is well-captured by Zach Eswine's testimony regarding his approach to ministry when he was twenty-six and finishing seminary: "It was becoming quite clear to me that if I was to prove successful in ministry, I needed to do something great, and I needed to define something great in terms of how large, famous, and fast I could accomplish it." Zach Eswine, *The Imperfect Pastor: Discovering Joy in Our Limitations through a Daily Apprenticeship with Jesus* (Wheaton IL: Crossway, 2015), 21. The twentieth-century apologist Francis Schaeffer spoke of the temptation facing those engaged in ministry: "All of us—pastors, teachers, professional religious workers and nonprofessionals included—are tempted to say, 'I will take the larger place because it will give me more influence for Jesus Christ.'" Schaeffer continued, "But according to the Scripture this is backwards: we should consciously take the lowest place unless the Lord Himself extrudes us into a greater one. … This is the way of the Christian: he should choose the lesser place until God extrudes him into a position of more responsibility and authority." Francis A. Schaeffer, *No Little People* (1974, Wheaton, IL: Crossway, 2021), 34–35. For the quotation from Schaeffer, I am indebted to Eswine, *Imperfect Pastor*, 146.

5

Was he prone to wander? Robert Robinson (1735-1790)[1]

BRUCE HINDMARSH

More than thirty years ago, early in my doctoral research on the eighteenth-century evangelical clergyman John Newton (1725-1807), I was advised by the late John Walsh of Jesus College, Oxford, to keep an eye out as I trawled through archives to "see if there was a Friday on my island." The allusion was to another great eighteenth-century figure, Daniel Defoe, and his famous novel, *Robinson Crusoe* (1719). Marooned on a deserted island, the eponymous protagonist Crusoe had to use all his own ingenuity and resourcefulness to survive and make his way all alone—until, that is, one day he comes upon a footprint in the sand. It is an electric moment when he realizes that he is not actually alone. The footprint belonged to the man Friday. So, the question was whether I was all alone on my island of research, poring over manuscripts related to John Newton, or was someone else leaving footprints on my island?

Grant Gordon was the man Friday, it turns out, leaving footprints on my island. Then, and for the past thirty years, he has been mapping parts of the island that I didn't know about and doing so with great care and

---

[1] A version of this article was published online, "Was He Too Prone to Wander? Robert Robinson (1735–1790)," *Desiring God*, June 16, 2019; https://www.desiringgod.org/articles/was-he-too-prone-to-wander.

attention. I remember learning that there was an autograph manuscript diary in John Newton's hand that had gone missing from the main archive quite early. The nineteenth-century biographer Josiah Bull thanked a certain "Mrs. Janson" for the use of "the missing volume of the diary." I spent an inordinate amount of time trying to chase it down. In the end, I couldn't find it. I wrote in the preface to my published dissertation, "Extensive researches by the present writer have failed to locate this missing diary or to identify Mrs. Janson with certainty." I can still remember those "extensive researches," including going through subscription lists in nineteenth-century evangelical magazines at the British Library to look for the name "Janson." The British Library used to return your call slip to your desk if there was a problem fetching the books requested. On the back of the slip, there were boxes that could be ticked to indicate the reason the books were not available for delivery. A slip came back for me with the box ticked to indicate that the magazines could not be delivered because "they were destroyed by bombs in the second world war." That was definitely a dead end. I thought "Janson" should be a distinctive enough name for me to find a lead somewhere, surely, but when I then looked up a directory of names and saw a cross-reference, "See Johnson," I decided to give up.

But not Grant. All this was to him like a red rag to a bull. He found the diary and made good use of it too. And he has made other like discoveries since. I admire any archival historian with these sort of bloodhound, sleuthing instincts.

Yet there has been something deeper than shared historical interests for Grant and me, I think, for we have both found the writings of eighteenth-century evangelicals of much more than historical interest. These writings have proved to be a deep spiritual well to drink from. It is with this in mind that I offer the article below in honour of Grant. Taking Robert Robinson as its subject, it touches on eighteenth-century evangelicalism, John Newton, George Whitefield, and hymnody—all subjects of enduring interest, I know, for Grant.

"Prone to wander, Lord, I feel it, prone to leave the God I love"
Robert Robinson wrote these words as a young man in his twenties, a few years after his conversion. They appeared in 1758 in one of the stanzas of his now classic hymn, "Come, thou fount of ev'ry blessing." The hymn is a great testimony to the grace of God that had saved him, notwithstanding a heart that was "prone to wander."

However, by the time of his death at fifty-four years of age, some wondered if Robinson had indeed wandered, at least theologically. He died just after spending time with Joseph Priestley, one of the most infamous political and theological radicals of the late eighteenth century. Priestley and his fellow Unitarians (who denied the deity of Christ) were quick to claim Robinson as one of their own. Priestley even claimed that Robinson "attacked Orthodoxy more pointedly and sarcastically than I had ever done in my life."[2]

So how far had Robert Robinson wandered?

Robinson was born in a small market town near Norwich in southeast England in 1735.[3] He was born the same year that the great evangelist George Whitefield was converted in his college rooms at Oxford, and while a local revival was stirring Jonathan Edwards's parish in New England and

---

[2] H. C. Robinson, "Robinsoniana," *The Christian Reformer, or, Unitarian Magazine and Review*, NS, 1 (1845): 90.

[3] Sources for Robinson's biography, drawn upon for this article, include George Dyer, *Memoirs of the Life and Writings of Robert Robinson* (London: G.G. and J. Robinson, 1796); *Miscellaneous Works of Robert Robinson ... to Which Are Prefixed Brief Memoirs of His Life and Writings*, 4 vols. (Harlow: B. Flower, 1807); *Select Works of the Rev. Robert Robinson, of Cambridge,* ed. with a memoir by William Robertson (London: J. Heaton & Son, 1861); Robinson, "Robinsoniana," 89–92, 347–352; A. B. Grosart, "Robinson, Robert" in *A Dictionary of Hymnology*, ed. John Julian (London: John Murray, 1892), 969–970; Graham Werden Hughes, *With Freedom Fired: The Story of Robert Robinson, Cambridge Nonconformist* (London: Carey Kingsgate Press, 1955); L. G. (Leonard George) Champion, "Robert Robinson: A Pastor in Cambridge," *The Baptist Quarterly* 31, no. 5 (January 1986): 241–46; Christopher Smith, "Robertson, Robert," in *The Canterbury Dictionary of Hymnology*, ed. J. R. Watson and Emma Hornby (Norwich: Canterbury Press, 2013; https://hymnology.hymnsam.co.uk/); Alexander Gordon, revised by Catherine Nunn, "Robinson, Robert (1726/7–1791), Dissenting Minister" (Oxford University Press, September 2004), https://doi.org/10.1093/ref:odnb/23869.

spreading up and down the Connecticut River Valley. But it would be another seventeen years before Robinson would hear Whitefield preach and be himself drawn into the orbit of the revival movement.

In fact, his home was "devoid of piety," and his parents' marriage was described as a disaster. By the time young Robert was just entering his teens, his dissolute father was being sued for debts. His father abandoned the family and died soon afterward. Although his mother's family had wealth, lands, and houses, Robert's grandfather resented the marriage and as a cruel gesture left his daughter only half a guinea (about $100 in today's terms). Indeed, the estate went almost entirely to his mistress, and his will completely ignored his grandson. Robert's mother could see that her son had some intellectual capacity though, and to keep him in school she took in borders and plied the needle as a seamstress. The master of the local grammar school took some pity on the family, and he taught Robert gratis for a period. Soon enough, though, it was all too much, and by the time Robert was thirteen, his formal education had to be given up.

A friend of the family had a brother in London who was a barber, and so the decision was made to send Robert to the city to be bound as an apprentice in that trade. This meant he would become the charge and responsibility of his master for seven years, until his apprenticeship was complete. He would spend his teen years away from home in the big city. One historian talks about "the guilty apprentice syndrome," meaning that there were many such young men who left the morally reinforcing social structures of the countryside and got into trouble when immersed in the anonymity and temptations of a city like London.[4] When such young men happened upon the evangelical preaching that was spreading throughout the metropolis, their consciences were easily wounded, and they knew in their hearts they needed the gospel message being proclaimed.

This is exactly what happened to Robinson. On Sunday, May 24, 1752,

---

4   The phrase "guilty apprentice syndrome" was explained this way to me by the late Dr. John Walsh of Jesus College, Oxford, the eminent historian of eighteenth-century Methodism.

he was one of a gang of young people who went and got a fortune-teller drunk on cheap gin, then visited Whitefield's Tabernacle at Moorfields "to mock the preacher and pity his hearers," but instead Robinson was haunted by a sermon preached by Whitefield on "The Wrath to Come." He remembered that "day and night he was greatly troubled by the sermon." Three years later this culminated in his conversion. We know this from a cryptic notation he made in Latin on a blank leaf in one of his books. It said that on Tuesday, December 10, 1755, he "found full and free forgiveness through the precious blood of Jesus Christ." No wonder he would soon write in his famous hymn that "Jesus sought me when a stranger/Wandering from the fold of God;/He, to rescue me from danger,/Bought me with his precious blood."

About the time he was completing his apprenticeship he began to have thoughts about entering the ministry, and he used to practice preaching sermons to himself for up to an hour at a time. He stayed in London, working in his trade for a couple of more years, and then in 1758 he returned home to his uncle's farm in Suffolk, near where he grew up. He was now twenty-two years of age, and he began in earnest to copy Whitefield and the other Methodists, preaching without notes and gathering a society in the village. He was soon invited to preach at James Wheatley's Tabernacle in Norwich. According to one record, it was in a hymnbook published by Wheatley that Robinson's famous hymn was first published.[5]

Wheatley was a notorious figure. Although he was just leaving the scene in Norwich about this time, he had certainly left his mark locally. He had been in league with John Wesley but was expelled from Wesley's company of lay preachers in 1751 for well-documented scandals with at least seven women. (He was later also charged with adultery at Norwich.) Yet he

---

5   *Church Book; St Andrew Street Baptist Church, Cambridge, 1720–1832*, English Baptist Records 2 (Baptist Historical Society, 1991). Cf. John Julian, "Come, Thou Fount of every blessing" in *A Dictionary of Hymnology*, ed. John Julian (London: John Murray, 1892), 252; and J. R. Watson, "Come, thou fount of every blessing," *The Canterbury Dictionary of Hymnology*, Canterbury Press, http://www.hymnology.co.uk/c/come,-thou-fount-of-every-blessing; accessed March 18, 2025

was a remarkably popular preacher, a firebrand who gathered some two thousand at the Tabernacle in Norwich. When he first showed up in town and began preaching, appalling riots followed with violence in the street. Robinson arrived just after this tumultuous season, as the Tabernacle was being supplied by Whitefield's people from London.

Robinson's connections to Norwich probably marked him for life, especially by demonstrating for him what lively preaching could do to influence a whole region. This was soon what he would do sixty miles to the southeast in and around Cambridge. Though his period in the Norwich area was short, it was significant. It was here that he met and married Ellen Payne, with whom he would have twelve children. Here too his convictions led him to dissent from the Established Church, with whom the Methodists were still closely connected, and to set up an Independent Calvinistic Church in town. Then he went on to receive adult baptism. He would be Baptist ever after.

It was in fact the famous Baptist writer Anne Dutton who informed the deacons in the Stoneyard congregation of Particular Baptists at Cambridge that "there was a youth at Norwich who had been preaching among Methodists but had lately been baptised and wanted to settle in a Baptist congregation." He began preaching for the Cambridge Baptists, but only in a kind of probationary role. He felt unworthy, given his irreligious upbringing, his lack of education, and his youth. But after two years, he was ordained as their permanent pastor. The beginnings were inauspicious, starting with thirty-four people huddled in a "damp, dark, cold, ruinous, contemptible hovel" in a town that despised Dissenters. And in his first six months he was paid only about £3.12 (say, $750 in today's terms). Still, he remained faithful to his calling, and in time a new church meeting house was erected, and within fifteen years there were perhaps two hundred families in the church, with morning congregations of six hundred and evening gatherings of eight hundred. He reached a thousand more through his itinerant preaching in surrounding villages during the week. At a time when the percentage of Dissenters was falling in most of the counties around Cambridge, Robinson's influence pushed things in the other direction in Cambridgeshire. By one calculation, more than eight per cent of the population in the region were Dissenters. In time, these Dissenters would have an important influence politically in the county and the country as a whole.[6]

Robinson was unquestionably a beloved and effective pastor and preacher for three decades in Cambridge. This was his principal ministry. We do not know a lot about his continued use of hymns, but there is a note in the Church Book that will seem familiar to anyone today who has met with conflict over styles of music in worship. "Heady people ... found fault with certain tunes," says the church record. These were the so called "sprightly tunes" introduced in the evening lectures put on by Robinson on Sundays to reach a wider "town and gown" audience. He wanted to vary the style of the services and to make them different in tone. But evidently some church members did not like his "seeker friendly" methods.

In the mid-1770s, Robinson was increasingly drawn into print and public activism to defend religious and civil liberties.[7] Dissenters were keenly aware that the laws of the land still imposed disabilities on them. Robinson was driven to study church history and defend the cause of Nonconformists. For him, the Reformation was principally about freedom of conscience rather than confessional doctrines. He came to dislike the binding of anyone's conscience by a statement of faith. In the political sphere, his championing of liberty meant he was an early and active voice for parliamentary reform (and was mentioned by name in the House of Commons by Edmund Burke). He was also an early voice against slavery

---

6   See further *Church Book; St Andrew Street Baptist Church, Cambridge*; James E. Bradley, "Religion and reform at the polls: nonconformity in Cambridge politics, 1774–1784," *Journal of British Studies* 23, no.2 (1984): 55–78.

7   See, e.g., Robert Robinson, *Arcana: Or the Principles of the Late Petitioners to Parliament for Relief in the Matter of Subscription: In VIII. Letters to a Friend* (Cambridge: Fletcher & Hodson, 1774). See also Karen Smith, "The Liberty to Not Be a Christian: Robert Robinson (1735-90) of Cambridge and Freedom of Conscience" in *Distinctively Baptist: Essays on Baptist History*, ed. Marc A. Jolley and John D. Pierce (Macon, GA: Mercer University Press, 2005), 151–170.

and the slave trade, preaching against it in 1786 and petitioning against it in 1788. He argued clearly that slavery was incompatible with Christianity. He similarly welcomed the American and French Revolutions. In fact, he was visited by General Read, Washington's second-in-command, and other high-ranking officials, who offered him passage to America and land, if he would drop everything and come.

Robinson was a man open to other viewpoints and tolerant to a fault. Yes, perhaps, to a fault. He was friendly with political and theological radicals, including Unitarians and others with low views of Christ's divinity (Socinians). There was a small Socinian group in his congregation in Cambridge, and he refused to take sides against them when division opened up in the church over the question. Like many others before and since, Robinson wanted to appeal only to the Bible and not to any statements of faith or creeds. But there is always a danger that this way of thinking can lead to an unhealthy elevation of private judgment. If we think we can recover the true Bible message on our own, without any dependence on theological statements derived from Scripture and received by the wider church, we are "prone to wander."

How far Robinson in fact wandered by the end of his life is a question still debated. If he hadn't gone to Birmingham and preached in Priestley's church just days before his death, he might have been remembered differently. A year before he died, he reaffirmed what he had written earlier, that the Socinians were mistaken brethren, and in one of his last letters he affirmed he was neither a Socinian nor an Arian. Six years after Robinson died, the Anglican evangelical John Newton wrote to Robinson's (Unitarian) biographer. Newton said he hoped his own spiritual history would terminate where Robinson's began. He worried that Robinson in his later years was more inclined to help people doubt than believe. And he thought he descried Robinson travelling the same road as Joseph Priestley, not far behind on the path from skepticism to Unitarianism.[8]

---

8   Timothy Whelan, "Six Letters of Robert Robinson from Dr Williams's Library," *Baptist Quarterly* 39, no. 7 (July 2002): 347–359, https://doi.org/10.1179/bqu.2002.39.7.004.

It is hard to know for sure. But Newton was right about the early years of Robinson's ministry. There is abundant evidence from the 1750s and 1760s to show that Robinson was then a robust evangelical Calvinist with a piety that was sometimes compared to Jonathan Edwards.

We should also remember with some sympathy that he was, late in life, a broken man. By 1790, the year he died, he was physically and mentally ill. His sermons were often incomprehensible, and some described him as "insane." He suffered the death of his seventeen-year-old daughter Julie in 1787 and never recovered from the grief. He was burdened with his scholarship and faced a financial crisis that could have sent him to debtors' prison. And, of course, his friends had turned against him for his liberalism.

Thinking of his suffering at this distance, the final verse of his great hymn takes on more poignancy for its anticipation of seeing Jesus face to face. The verse isn't sung much anymore, but we may take it as Robinson's hope in the face of death:

On that day when freed from sinning
  I shall see thy lovely face,
Clothèd then in blood-washed linen
  How I'll sing thy boundless grace;
Come, my Lord, no longer tarry,
  Take my ransomed soul away,
Send thine angel-hosts to carry
  Me to realms of endless day![9]

---

9 This verse is cited in J. R. Watson, "Come, thou fount of every blessing," *The Canterbury Dictionary of Hymnology,* Canterbury Press, accessed March 18, 2025, http://www.hymnology.co.uk/c/come,-thou-fount-of-every-blessing, as one of the original verses in *A Collection of Hymns for the Use of the Church of Christ: Meeting in Angel-Alley, Whitechappel, Margaret-Street, near Oxford-Market, and Other Churches in Fellowship with Them : To Which Is Prefix'd, The New-Testament Church, or, A Short View of Christianity According to the Scriptures* (London, 1759).

6

From theology to praxis: Theological renewal in eighteenth-century Particular Baptist life and the formation of the Baptist Missionary Society

PETER J. MORDEN

Introduction

The young William Carey (1761-1834) is famously said to have stood up in a Ministers' meeting and proposed Jesus' "great commission" as a subject for discussion. "Is not Jesus' call to go to the nations binding on all generations?" Carey asked. According to the anecdote, an older Minister, John Collett Ryland (1723-1792), rose to his feet and gave the future pioneer missionary a stern rebuke: "Sit down young man, you're an enthusiast! If God wants to convert the nations he will do so without your help and mine." Carey's proposal that they debated the contemporary relevance of Jesus' words in Matthew 28:19-20 was firmly rejected.

Historical research sometimes spoils a good story. The evidence indicates this incident did not happen in quite the way it is usually related.

Nevertheless, even if the story has been progressively reworked and embroidered by later generations for dramatic effect, in my judgement something reasonably like it probably did take place.[1] Certainly, Collett Ryland's words reflect an attitude that was widespread in English Particular Baptist life at the time. Moreover, the story vividly illustrates a broader point: *theology matters*. Carey and his critic were both eighteenth-century Calvinistic or Particular Baptists, so-called because they believed in particular rather than general redemption.[2] Yet Collett Ryland held to an understanding of God's sovereignty which greatly minimised the place of human responsibility. This theology had the effect of cutting off evangelistic mission at its roots. The argument ran as follows: it is God who converts and he will accomplish his work "without your help and mine." Carey took a different view of the relationship between God's sovereignty and human agency, doing so as a result of extensive biblical reflection, wider reading, and discussion with friends. He wholeheartedly affirmed the sovereignty of God in salvation but also believed God used human "means" to accomplish his saving purposes. Consequently, he was sure that Christians had been given the task of sharing the gospel as widely as possible, urging men and women to trust in Christ. The clash between the two men was not rooted in dif-

---

1   The incident on which the anecdote is based is recorded by John Webster Morris in his "tombstone" biography of Andrew Fuller, originally published in 1816 (*Memoirs of the Life and Death of the Rev. Andrew Fuller*, 2nd ed. [London: Wightman and Cramp, 1826], 100-101). Collett Ryland's son, John Ryland Jr., denied his father could have said such a thing, describing the story as an "ill-natured anecdote" (*The Work of Faith, the Labour of Love, and the Patience of Hope Illustrated in the Life and Death of the Rev. Andrew Fuller*, 2nd ed. [London: Button and Son, 1818], 112). Even so, Morris continued to defend what he had written. Given he was at the meeting in question, it seems reasonable to give credence to his account, especially as he stated in print that he believed Carey himself would corroborate his version of events. However, Carey's and Collett Ryland's words as Morris recorded them are somewhat different from those usually quoted today. It is the "popular" version of the story that I have essentially reproduced. The incident, according to Morris, took place in 1786.

2   For more on Particular Baptist life in this period, see Peter J. Morden, "Continuity and Change: Particular Baptists in the 'Long Eighteenth Century (1689-1815)," in *Challenge and Change: English Baptist Life in the Eighteenth Century*, ed. Stephen Copson and Peter J. Morden (Didcot: The Baptist Historical Society, 2017), 1-29.

ferences of personality or temperament. Rather, their different theological perspectives led directly to their sharp disagreement.

Collett Ryland, as he appears in the story, was an advocate of the theology known as high Calvinism. By contrast, Carey espoused an evangelical, invitational Calvinism. This chapter seeks to show how high Calvinism in eighteenth-century Particular Baptist life largely gave way to evangelical thinking. This shift in theology led in turn to a shift in practice, as Particular Baptists increasingly gave themselves to expansive mission. The story of Carey's own life and ministry illustrates how this dynamic worked. He put his theological convictions into practice by becoming one of the founders of Baptist Missionary Society in 1792, sailing to India the following year under the auspices of the Mission.[3] A renewed evangelical theology led directly to pioneering gospel ministry.

This theme— theological renewal for mission—is, I believe, an appropriate one to explore in a Festschrift for Grant Gordon. This is because Dr. Gordon has focused much of his research and writing on the theology and praxis of eighteenth-century evangelical Calvinism as it was exemplified by prominent figures in the movement such as the Anglican John Newton (1725-1807) and the Baptist John Ryland Jr (1753-1825), Collett Ryland's son. Newton had known the father and developed a deep friendship with the son carried on mainly through correspondence. This friendship is wonderfully illuminated by Dr. Gordon in *Wise Counsel*, a carefully edited collection of the Anglican clergyman's letters to his younger Baptist friend.[4] Newton was a vital influence on Ryland Jr., weaning him away from the high Calvinism that was part of his Particular Baptist milieu and pointing him to an Evangelicalism that was both thoroughly Calvinistic and unequivocally missional. Thus, Grant Gordon's work has already explored—

---

3   The original full title was "The Particular Baptist Society for Propagating the Gospel Among the Heathen." The authoritative history is Brian Stanley, *The History of the Baptist Missionary Society, 1792-1992* (Edinburgh: T. & T. Clark, 1992). The title was soon abbreviated to the Baptist Missionary Society (BMS).

4   *Wise Counsel: John Newton's Letters to John Ryland Jr.*, ed. Grant Gordon (Edinburgh: Banner of Truth, 2009).

with great profit—the theological and missiological shifts examined in this essay.

Theological renewal

An understanding of high Calvinism is important if we are going to trace the trajectory of theological renewal. It has already been stated that high Calvinists exalted the sovereignty of God in ways which greatly underplayed the importance of human response. In particular, it was no one's "duty" to repent and believe the gospel, since total depravity rendered such a response impossible. Building on these shaky theological foundations, high Calvinists refused to "offer" the gospel freely to all. Andrew Fuller (1754-1815) attended Soham Baptist Church in Cambridgeshire as a youth. He recalled that his pastor at that time, John Eve (d. 1782), "had little or nothing to say to the unconverted." Eve and other like-minded ministers would not preach to a group of unbelievers "inviting them to apply to Christ for salvation."[5] Such invitations to trust in Christ were, high Calvinists claimed, a nonsense since faith was not a duty and the "elect" would come to believe anyway in God's good time. Furthermore, applied evangelistic preaching was dangerous because it encouraged false professions of faith which could sully the purity of the church. Maintenance rather than mission was the order of the day. There were some churches, especially in the west of England, which stood against high Calvinism. However, the evidence suggests its influence in Particular Baptist life in England for much of the eighteenth-century was both broad and deep.[6]

Yet from the 1770s onwards the Particular Baptists underwent what Michael Haykin has described as a "profound rejuvenation and transformation."[7] This rejuvenation accelerated towards the end of the eighteenth

---

5   Ryland Jr., *Fuller*, 11, 31-32. For a recent study of Fuller, see Peter J. Morden, *The Life and Thought of Andrew Fuller (1754-1815)* (Milton Keynes: Paternoster, 2015).

6   For more detail, see Morden, *Fuller*, 19-28.

7   Michael A.G. Haykin, "The Baptist Identity: A View from the Eighteenth Century," *Evangelical Quarterly*, 67.2 (1995): 150.

century and continued strongly into the nineteenth. In addition to the establishment of the BMS, there was significant church growth at home. Many existing churches grew, often enlarging their meeting houses to accommodate increased numbers, and extensive church planting took place.[8] A complex cluster of factors fed and shaped this revivification, but even so theological renewal was central to what happened. The aforementioned Andrew Fuller was at the heart of this recasting of Particular Baptist theology. In 1785 he published his seminal treatise, *The Gospel of Christ Worthy of All Acceptation* which set out his views in detail.[9] Fuller grounded his work in some of the theological and philosophical reasonings of the New England Congregationalist Jonathan Edwards (1703-1758). In his *Freedom of the Will*, Edwards had distinguished between "natural" and "moral" inability and argued that although people were incapable of responding to the gospel without the regenerating grace of God, they were still morally culpable if they failed to do so.[10] Fuller's debt to the New England theologian was considerable but he did not simply repeat Edwards's arguments. Rather he engaged with them critically and contextualised them to serve his own purposes, insisting it was the duty of all to believe and therefore the duty of Christians—especially pastors—to engage in evangelistic ministry.[11] Important as this line of reasoning was, Fuller was a thoroughgoing Biblicist and it was the Bible itself that was his foundational text. He had

---

8   On the growth of Particular Baptists in England, see Morden, "Continuity and Change," 1-29, especially, 23-26.

9   Andrew Fuller, *The Gospel of Christ Worthy of All Acceptation*, 1st ed. (Northampton: Thomas Dicey, 1785). The 2nd ed. is printed in Andrew Fuller, *The Complete Works of the Rev. Andrew Fuller, with a Memoir of his Life by the Rev. Andrew Gunton Fuller*, ed. Andrew Gunton Fuller, rev. ed. Joseph Belcher; 3 vols, 3rd ed. (1845, Harrisonburg, VA: Sprinkle Publications, 1988), II:328-416.

10 Jonathan Edwards, *Freedom of the Will* in The Works of Jonathan Edwards, vol. 1, ed. Paul Ramsey (1754, New Haven, CT: Yale University Press, 1985), especially 135-440. Edwards was an important influence on all the leading BMS figures.

11 Edwards's purpose in writing had been to challenge Arminian concepts of human freedom. For a discussion of the ways Fuller draws from Edwards, see Chris Chun, *The Legacy of Jonathan Edwards in the Theology of Andrew Fuller* (Leiden: Brill, 2012). See pages 10-65 for material directly relevant to the *Gospel Worthy*.

become convinced that, whilst the Scriptures taught doctrines such as election and predestination, they also showed Christ and his apostles urging all their hearers to trust in Jesus, including those who would never come to believe. Ministers and others, he urged, must follow their example.[12] So, high Calvinism was rejected in favour of an evangelical Calvinism which was expansive and missional.

Although Fuller provided the authoritative statement of Edwardsean evangelical Calvinism in an English Particular Baptist context, he was certainly not the first in eighteenth-century Particular Baptist life to articulate such an evangelical theology, nor was he the first to advocate it in print. Robert Hall Sr (1728-1791) was another who wrote against the high Calvinists, with his *Help to Zion's Travellers* actually published four years before the *Gospel Worthy*. It was Hall Sr.'s work that was especially influential in Carey's own theological development.[13] As the young man wrestled with the issues and prayed them through, he found Hall's biblical arguments compelling and the source of much joy. "I do not remember ever to have read a book with such raptures," he said, and years later he was to inform Fuller that "its doctrines are the choice of my heart to this day."[14] In addition to Hall's treatise, spiritual friendship with evangelicals such as Fuller, Ryland Jr and the like-minded John Sutcliff (1752–1814) shaped his theology. This evangelical Calvinism provided the seed bed out of which the BMS would spring.

Applied theology: Carey's Enquiry

Carey took this theology and applied it directly to the subject of world mission. His pamphlet, *An Enquiry into the Obligations of Christians to use*

---

12 Fuller, *Gospel Worthy*, 1st ed., especially 40, 162-63, 166.
13 Robert Hall Sr, *Help to Zion's Travellers* [1781]. *The Complete Works of the Late Robert Hall*, ed. John W. Morris (London: W. Simpkin and R. Marshall, 1828), 47-199, contains the 2nd ed.
14 Eustace Carey, *Memoir of William Carey* (London: Jackson and Walford, 1836), 15-16. Carey probably read *Help to Zion's Travellers* in 1782-1783.

Means for the Conversion of the Heathens, was published on May 12, 1792.[15] It is clear from the *Enquiry* that, for Carey as for Hall and Fuller, the sovereignty of God in salvation was not in dispute. Yet, as Carey expressed it in the title of his treatise, Christians were "obligated" to use "means" (he especially had in mind preaching and the distribution of the Scriptures) to take the gospel to those who had never heard it. The great commission (Matthew 28:19-20) was vital to him and formed a central plank in his argument. He admitted there were many who believed the commission "was sufficiently put in execution" in the days of the apostles. And, of course, he was aware of those who said that if God intended "the salvation of the heathen" he would accomplish this "some way or other" without human agency.[16] Carey rejected such thinking. As he posed the question he had wanted to discuss at the minister's meeting—Is the commission still God's command?—he answered it strongly in the affirmative. The "commission is a sufficient call," he insisted, "to venture all, and, like the primitive Christians, go everywhere preaching the gospel."[17]

He argued his case with precision and passion. At one point he observed that, if the command to go and make disciples of all nations was not binding in his own day then surely, to be consistent, the command to baptize was not binding either since they are both part of the same commission. No Particular Baptist would argue that believers should not be baptized, but you could not have it both ways. As far as Carey was concerned, both directions were still in force. Why did more Christians not respond to the call to evangelise, and why were more not willing to put this call into practice overseas?[18]

As he pressed home his argument in the *Enquiry* he repeatedly con-

---

15 *An Enquiry into the Obligations of Christians to use Means for the Conversion of the Heathens* (Leicester: Ann Ireland, 1792). It has also been published in facsimile (London: Kingsgate Press, 1961).
16 Carey, *An Enquiry into the Obligations of Christians*, 8.
17 Carey, *An Enquiry into the Obligations of Christians*, 73.
18 Carey, *An Enquiry into the Obligations of Christians*, 6-13. Cf. 77, 73.

nected theology and practice, insisting that one must lead to the other. He wanted to move beyond words to actions and impress on his readers the wide-ranging implications of their evangelical theology. The proposal that a Society should be formed to enable cross-cultural mission was explicitly articulated. Possible objections were acknowledged and swept aside.[19] Carey concluded his pamphlet thus:

> We are exhorted *to lay up treasure in heaven, where neither moth nor rust doth corrupt, nor thieves break through and steal* … It is true all the reward is of mere grace, but it is nevertheless encouraging; what a treasure, what an[sic.] harvest must await such characters as *Paul*, and *Elliot*, and *Brainerd*, and others, who have given themselves wholly to the work of the Lord. What a heaven will it be to see the many myriads of poor heathens, of Britons amongst the rest, who by their labours have been brought to the knowledge of God. Surely a crown of rejoicing like this is worth aspiring to. Surely it is worthwhile to lay ourselves out with all our might, in promoting the cause, and Kingdom of Christ.[20]

Carey here refers to John Eliot (1604-1690) and David Brainerd (1718-1747), two men who had already engaged in cross-cultural mission to Native Americans.[21] Their examples were important to him. Yet it was the life and ministry of apostle Paul and the words of Jesus himself that were central. Carey believed that high Calvinism was less than biblical not least because it did not lead to the missional impulses that are exemplified

---

19 Carey, *An Enquiry into the Obligations of Christians*, e.g., 83-85.
20 Carey, *An Enquiry into the Obligations of Christians*, 86-87. Matthew 6:20. Capitalisation has been modernized (the names of Paul, Eliot and Brainerd); the italics are original. Carey spelt Eliot's name two l's.
21 Of these two, Brainerd was the most important for both Carey and Fuller. His influence was mediated to them through Jonathan Edwards's famous *Life of Brainerd*. For the text, see *The Life of David Brainerd* in The Works of Jonathan Edwards, vol. 7, ed. Norman Pettit (1749, New Haven, CT: Yale University Press, 1985).

in the character of a man like Paul. The author of the *Enquiry* had imbibed evangelical theology in such a way that he was determined to give his life "wholly to the work of the Lord" and lead the missional life this theology inspired.

The BMS formed

Carey went on to preach from Isaiah 54:2-3 at a meeting held at Friar Lane, Nottingham, on Wednesday, May 30, 1792. The central points of this message have often been written as "Expect great things from God; Attempt great things for God," although the evidence suggests the shorter title, "Expect great things; Attempt great things" is strictly accurate.[22] "Great things" could be expected of a sovereign God who had promised to pour out his blessing and grow his Kingdom. Confident of this, his servants could "attempt great things," for they themselves were the means—the human agents—by which God would accomplish his sure purposes. With Carey's prompting, it was Fuller who submitted the resolution, "that a plan be prepared … for forming a 'Baptist society for propagating the Gospel among the Heathen.'"[23] The founding meeting took place on October 2 in the home of Martha Wallis (d. 1812), a leading member of the church Fuller pastored in Kettering, Northamptonshire. As well as Carey and Fuller, Ryland Jr. and Sutcliff were also present.[24] The evangelical theology and missional spirituality of this small group of English Particular Baptist ministers were now being worked out in practical action. Their efforts would have global ramifications.

---

22   Cf. Andrew Fuller, Letter to John Fawcett, August 30, 1793, Typescript Andrew Fuller Letters, transcribed by Joyce A. Booth, superintended by Ernest A. Payne, Angus Library, Regent's Park College, Oxford, in which Fuller recorded Carey's headings as: "1. Let us *expect* great things; II. Let us *attempt* great things." Italics original.

23   *The Baptist Annual Register*, ed. John Rippon (London: Dilly, Button and Thomas, 1793), 1:375, 419.

24   *Periodical Accounts Relative to the Baptist Missionary Society*, 5 vols (London: Baptist Missionary Society, 1794–1816), I:3-4; Stanley, *History of the Baptist Missionary Society*, 15.

CHAPTER SIX

The BMS in India

John Thomas (1757–1801) and Carey himself were the Society's first missionaries. They set sail with their families on the Danish East Indiaman the Kron Princessa Maria on June 13, 1793, arriving in India on November 7, 1793.[25] In the years immediately following, Carey faced a series of setbacks which could easily have led to the failure of the Mission.[26] Loneliness was a major issue. Thomas was unreliable and partly because of this they quickly encountered financial hardship. William Carey's wife, Dorothy (née Plackett) (d. 1807) had been extremely reluctant to go to India and increasingly experienced problems with her mental health.[27] An extract from Carey's journal for April 19, 1794, included in the BMS *Periodical Accounts* gives a flavour of what the Mission was facing. The obstacles were so great and so many he thought his "hopes would utterly die away" if it were not for the sovereign, sustaining grace of God.[28] There were no conversions for seven years. Between 1794-1799 he worked at indigo planting in Mudnabati as he sought to mitigate extreme financial hardship. Thanks in part to strenuous fundraising efforts at home, Carey and his family—by now operating largely independently of Thomas—were joined by a number of co-workers. Some of these died soon after disembarking. For example, William Grant, who arrived in 1799, died from cholera and dysentery less than a month after stepping ashore in India. But two men who had travelled with him, Joshua Marshman (1768-1837) and William Ward (1764-1823), survived

---

25 Francis A. Cox, *History of the Baptist Missionary Society. From 1792 to 1842*, 2 vols (London: T. Ward and G. & J. Dyer, 1842), I:2, 24. Carey lacks a modern, critical biography. The best study is probably still Timothy George, *Faithful Witness: The Life and Mission of William Carey* (Leicester: IVP, 1991). Thomas was a medical doctor who had already worked in India already before serving there with the BMS. For detail, see Charles B. Lewis, *The Life of John Thomas* (London: MacMillan, 1873).

26 For information in this and the following paragraph, see Stephen Neill, *A History of Christian Missions* (Harmondsworth: Penguin, 1964), 262-264; E. Daniel Potts, *British Baptist Missionaries in India, 1793-1837* (Cambridge: Cambridge University Press, 1967), 172; Stanley, *History of the Baptist Missionary Society*, 36-39; 70.

27 The story of her life in India and her death in 1807 is one of the tragedies of the Mission.

28 *Periodical Accounts*, I:175.

the dangerous early months and would become extremely significant for the developing work.[29]

Between 1799 and 1800 the missionaries established a new base in Serampore (Srirampur), about fifteen miles north of Calcutta (Kolkata) on the Hugli River. Carey, Marshman and Ward worked closely together and became known as "the Serampore Trio." Carey and Marshman engaged in extensive Bible translation work, and Ward, a printer and journalist, was instrumental in establishing a press at Serampore so that the Scriptures and other Christian literature could be printed and distributed. The first Hindu convert was Krishna Pal (d. 1822), a carpenter who embraced the Christian faith and was baptised in 1800, with more conversions and baptisms following. Carey's evangelistic vision was beginning to bear fruit.

When reports of the first Indian converts reached Kettering, Fuller was elated. He wrote directly to Krishna Pal, Sister Joymonee, and others on behalf of the home committee:

> In you we see the first fruits of Hindustan, the travail of our Redeemer's soul, and a rich reward for our imperfect labours. You know, beloved, that the love of Christ is of a constraining nature. It was this, and only this, that constrained us to mediate the means of your conversion. It was this that constrained our brethren that are with you to leave their country and all their worldly prospects, and to encounter perils, hardships and reproaches. If you stand fast in the Lord and are saved this is their and our reward.[30]

Fuller was aware that the group's "labours" had been "imperfect." Yet, he

---

[29] For an appreciative nineteenth-century account of Ward, see Samuel Stennett, *Memoirs of the Life of the Rev. William Ward* (London: J. Haddon: 1825). For Marshman, see John Clark Marshman, *The Story of Carey, Marshman and Ward, The Serampore Missionaries*, vol. 1 (London: Alexander Strahan, 1864).

[30] Andrew Fuller, Letter to Brother Krishna, Sister Joymonee … August 19, 1801, Letters to Carey, Marshman and Ward, Angus Library, Regent's Park College, Oxford. Fuller was alluding to 2 Corinthians 5:14, "For the love of Christ constraineth us" (KJV). Cf. also 1 Corinthians 15:1-2.

said, the love of Christ had constrained them to make great efforts to share the gospel cross-culturally. The venture had involved considerable sacrifice, yet the conversions of those they did not hesitate to call "brethren" had been their great reward.[31]

The Serampore Form of Agreement

On October 6, 1805, the twelfth anniversary of the formation of the BMS at Kettering, the trio and six other missionaries who by then were at Serampore signed a "Form of Agreement" (henceforth SFA) following a day's meetings which commenced at 6.00 a.m. with corporate prayer. Carey had been in Bengal for the full eleven years of the Mission's life and, together with Ward and Marshman, at Serampore for five. The SFA crystalised the principles which had already guided them and mapped out how they planned to proceed, especially important as they hoped to fan out and establish mission stations away from Serampore.[32] Ward drafted the document but it expressed the mind of the trio.[33] The principles, as summarised by S. Pearce Carey, are as follows:

1. To set an infinite value on men's souls.
2. To acquaint ourselves with the snares which hold the minds of the people.
3. To abstain from whatever deepens India's prejudice against the Gospel.
4. To watch over every chance of doing the people good.
5. To preach "Christ crucified" as the grand means of conversions.
6. To esteem and treat Indians always as our equals.

---

31 For Fuller, "brethren" is here inclusive of both male and female believers.
32 For the full text, together with some commentary on it [anon. but probably by Ernest A. Payne] see "The Serampore Form of Agreement," *Baptist Quarterly*, 12.5 (1947): 125-138. The SFA was printed in *Periodical Accounts*, III:198-211 and is also reproduced in full in other places, e.g., William Yates, *Memoirs of Mr John Chamberlain* (Calcutta and London: Baptist Mission Press/Wightman & Cramp, 1926), 190-201.
33 For Ward's authorship, see J. C. Marshman, *Carey, Marshman and Ward*, I: 229.

7. To guard and build up "the host that may be gathered."
8. To cultivate their spiritual gifts, ever pressing upon them their missionary obligation, since Indians only can win India for Christ.
9. To labour unceasingly in Biblical translation.
10. To be instant in the nurture of personal religion.
11. To give ourselves without reserve to the cause, "not counting even the clothes we wear our own."[34]

These principles are enlightened and far-sighted, deeply embedded in biblical theology, and full of nuanced reflection on context. They are worthy of study by missiologists today and it is encouraging that a major international project to examine the different dimensions of the SFA is, at the time of writing, getting underway.[35] The SFA as a whole distils the essence of the missionary effort Carey and his colleagues—both in India and back in England—were so deeply committed to. There is not space here to analyse the whole Agreement. Instead, the focus is on the heart of the SFA, which is the commitment to evangelistic mission. Once again, we see how theology shapes practice.

The full text of the SFA articulates the missionaries' core convictions concerning humanity, God and the gospel. They were convinced God had created all men and women in his image. They had fallen away in sin and rebellion, yet God had shown his continuing love by sending his Son, Jesus, who died and rose again for them. In the message of "Christ crucified" there was salvation for everyone who believed. In line with their previous convictions and with Particular Baptist theology, they continued to affirm God's sovereignty in salvation; indeed, this was something they insisted on. As they had made clear in the preamble to the Agreement, they were firmly

---

34 Samuel Pearce Carey, *Memoir of William Carey*, 8th ed. (1923, London: Hodder and Stoughton, 1934), 262.
35 Led by Samuel Masters, Principal of the Seminario Bíblico William Carey in Córdoba, Argentina.

persuaded that "only those who are ordained to eternal life" would believe, for "God alone" can add to the church "such as shall be saved." Paul might plant and Apollos might water but all would be in vain if God did not give the increase.[36] Salvation was God's work.

Yet, as the references to Paul and Apollos indicate, they were similarly clear that God used "means"—especially biblical, Christ-honouring, crucicentric preaching—to accomplish his saving purposes. As Fuller had put it in his letter to the first BMS converts, the missionaries were the means of "mediating" their conversion. It was not that they evangelised in spite of a commitment to God's sovereignty in salvation; rather, their Calvinistic convictions were a spur to gospel work. It was their great privilege to be used by God as his "instruments" in his great plan of human redemption and they believed he would work graciously and powerfully through them.[37] Carey's optimistic post-millennial eschatology informs the SFA here alongside the commitment to God's sovereignty. This eschatology was shared by Marshman and Ward and by other leading Particular Baptist figures such as Fuller. Fired by the hope that a great dawn for gospel work was at hand, they expected God to do "great things" through them. Consequently, they were emboldened to "attempt great things" even as they experienced a vast array of difficulties.

Overall, it should be clear that evangelistic mission to the glory of God was at the heart of BMS work in India. This fundamental commitment had inspired their work from the beginning and in the SFA the trio reaffirmed their desire "to give themselves without reserve to the cause." As they expressed themselves in clause six, "We can never make sacrifices too great when the eternal salvation of souls is the object."[38]

The missionaries were not only passionately committed to their work but also thoughtful and informed about how to carry it on. The SFA reveals

---

36   SFA, Preamble, 129; 1 Corinthians 3:6. All the following quotations from the SFA are from the text as reproduced by the *Baptist Quarterly*.
37   SFA, Clause X, 137.
38   SFA, Clause VI, 132.

much about their evangelistic *modus operandi*. It was vital, they believed, that their gospel ministry proceeded only on the basis of peaceful persuasion. Aware of the history of Roman Catholic Jesuit mission, they insisted that any use of force to bring about "conversions" was anathema.[39] A further strand to their evangelistic strategy was encapsulated in clause eight of the SFA, summarised by Pearce Carey thus: "To cultivate [the Indian converts] spiritual gifts, ever pressing upon them their missionary obligation,—since Indians only can win India for Christ." It was only by "means" of Indian evangelists that the gospel would spread far beyond their Serampore base. Various reasons were brought forward in the SFA to support what was a central contention of the trio. Europeans were too few; sending and supporting them in sufficient numbers was too expensive; there was a real possibility they would succumb to the "intense heat" of the climate and to disease; there were language and cultural barriers which made the task of outreach difficult for Europeans. Anyway, the task was simply too large. On one level, the use of Indian evangelists was a practical necessity driven by their overarching goal to spread the gospel in Bengal and beyond. But the telling use of one of their favourite words—"means"—surely indicates their belief that such a strategy was part of God's plan. The gifts of Indian believers were to be identified, nurtured—the word "cherish" was used—and then released. Investment in indigenous preachers was the missionaries' "absolute duty" and they aimed to send out as many as possible to engage in gospel work.[40] Here was a big vision: the trio did not merely want to add new converts but multiply missional disciples. In this way the English Particular Baptists would play their part in offering Christ throughout the Indian subcontinent and set a pattern for missional work throughout the globe.

Carey and his colleagues also affirmed a commitment to forms of mission that were not directly evangelistic.[41] This included the provision of

---

39   SFA, Clause VI, 132.
40   SFA, Clause VIII, 134.
41   SFA, Clause IX, 137.

"free schools" for Indian children. Joshua and Hannah Marshman (1767–1847) were vital to this dimension of the work. Hannah was a true pioneer, serving the Mission with distinction for nearly forty-eight years, despite the indifferent health which necessitated her one and only return to England in 1820–1821. The couple began in 1800 by opening two fee-paying boarding schools. These quickly grew in reputation and increasingly contributed to the Mission's finances.[42] But they also established schools for the very poorest, with education provided free of charge.[43] Girls as well as boys attended, with Hannah taking the lead role in female education. In 1824, there were 160 Indian girls attending six schools under Hannah Marshman's direction, a ministry she developed whilst continuing to have a large share in the running of the missionary household. However, it should be noted, that in the minds of the missionaries these schools still provided a vital context in which evangelism could take place. There was no pressure to convert but opportunities were regularly given to respond to the Christian message. Further, the education offered would, they believed, lead to a greater receptivity to the gospel in time. Their approach was an integrated one, yet the overarching priority remained evangelism, a priority shaped and sustained by their core theological convictions. Because they had imbibed these convictions so deeply, they were determined to put them into practice.

Conclusion

The Introduction to this essay contains the simple yet profound statement: theology matters. The story of English Particular Baptist life in the "long eighteenth century," especially the formation and subsequent progress of the BMS, illustrates this principle. High Calvinism deadened missional

---

42   J. C. Marshman, *Carey Marshman, and Ward*, I:131.
43   S. P. Carey, *William Carey*, 195-196. For more detail, see M. A. Laird, "The Contribution of the Serampore Missionaries to Education in Bengal, 1793-1837," *Bulletin of the School of Oriental and African Studies* 31.1 (1968): 92-112, especially 94. Unfortunately, Laird does not bring out Hannah Marshman's crucial role.

impulses, producing the sort of negative attitudes and lack of action displayed by the John Collett Ryland of the opening anecdote. By contrast, the theology advocated by evangelical Particular Baptists—still Calvinistic but insisting that a true understanding of divine sovereignty actually undergirds the importance of human action—bred such missional practitioners as William Carey, Joshua and Hannah Marshman and a host of others. A contemporary reflection on this story suggests itself: if we are not engaging in evangelistic mission as the early Christians did, perhaps we should emulate Particular Baptists such as Fuller and Carey and re-examine our theology.

II.
The Rylands

Rev.ᴰ John Ryland M.A.
Late of Northampton,
Departed this Life July 24, 1792, Aged 69 Years.

John Collett Ryland (1723–1792)

7
"Spiritual friendship is the union of souls": The ecclesiology of John Collett Ryland

GARRETT M. WALDEN

John Collett Ryland (1723–1792) was a Particular Baptist pastor-theologian in England. He is most remembered as the senior statesman who rebuked young William Carey at a ministers' fraternal in 1785, when Carey proposed the idea that the church bears a responsibility to take the gospel message to foreign lands. Allegedly, Ryland met Carey with a gruff rebuke: "Sit down, young man; when God pleases to convert the heathen He will do it without your aid or mine."[1] This anecdote is typically retold to highlight Carey's courage in the face of the prevailing hyper-Calvinism in Particular Baptist churches at the time. In my assessment, Ryland's reputation as a hyper-Calvinist is unfortunate and mistaken, but sadly, that single negative interaction with Carey has become his legacy.

In reality, Ryland had a fiery personality, and the term that appears most

---

1 See the discussion of this supposed rebuke in Michael A. G. Haykin, *The Missionary Fellowship of William Carey* (Orlando, FL: Reformation Trust, 2018), 38–42.

often in describing him is "eccentric."[2] Anecdotes abound of Ryland making the most blunt, surprising, and often humorous statements. For example, he once admonished a church for its poor congregational singing by telling them that an angel was likely to descend from heaven and "wring their necks off!"[3] Here was a man prone to the dramatic, which suited him well in his role as a schoolmaster, but opened him up to frequent misunderstandings and personal indiscretions in his pastoral ministry.

Ryland served as pastor of the Particular Baptist churches in Warwick (1750–1759) and Northampton (1760–1785), before concluding his minis-

---

[2] For instance, see John Webster Morris's note that Ryland Sr. was an "excellent and eccentric man" in J. W. Morris, *Memoirs of the Life and Writings of the Rev. Andrew Fuller, Late Pastor of the Baptist Church at Kettering, and Secretary to the Baptist Missionary Society. New Edition, Corrected and Enlarged* (London: Wightman and Cramp, 1826), 102. Also, William Field in 1815 noted that Ryland "was possessed of considerable abilities, but a strong and ardent imagination was not controlled by equal soundness, or strength of judgment; and a great degree of what is called *eccentricity* marked not only the manner of his public services, but even his conduct in private life," in William Field, *An Historical and Descriptive Account of the Town and Castle of Warwick* (Warwick: H. Sharpe, 1815), 140. See also Michael A.G. Haykin, "'Hazarding All for God at a Clap': the Spirituality of Baptism Among British Calvinistic Baptists" *Baptist Quarterly* 38.4 (2016): 189, where he describes Ryland as "that eccentric Baptist largely remembered today for his dampening rebuke of William Carey's zeal for overseas missions." Or once more, one of Ryland's descendants, Ryland Adkins, wrote in an 1897 introduction that Ryland Sr. was

> ardent, with a marked individuality, and with all that vehement temperament preferring eccentricity to platitude, which would have been congenial to the two previous centuries or to ours, but which was in sharp collision with the prevalent tendency of his own…He finds himself hostile to the mode of his day…he is very likely to intensify his antagonism to his contemporaries, and hugging his cloak of antique virtue about him, to become an obscurantist, detesting not only the new opinion and the new temper, but even polite learning and general culture, as being alienated from his dearest religious ideas. It is John Ryland's great claim to distinction that he did the exact opposite of this, and showed untiring zeal for culture as well as for religion.

> See W. Ryland Bent Adkin's introduction to James Culross, *The Three Rylands: A Hundred Years of Various Christian Service* (London: Elliot Stock, 1897), 6.

[3] William Newman, *Rylandiana: Reminiscences Relating to the Rev. John Ryland, A. M. of Northampton. Father of the Late Rev. Dr. Ryland, of Bristol* (London: George Wightman, 1835), 9.

try in Enfield, a suburb of London (1786–1792).[4] In speculating about the reasons why Ryland left his pastorate in Northampton, Philip Naylor suggests that perhaps one of his weaknesses was "a defective churchmanship."[5] Naylor offers no reason for this assertion, and I believe the comment is misguided. Therefore, my thesis is that, far from being a "defective churchman," Ryland maintained a profound ecclesiology by grounding it in the idea of "spiritual friendship," and I believe this image should be recovered for modern ecclesiology because of the unique way it emphasizes the relational aspect of the church's life and structure. I will demonstrate this by analyzing Ryland's ecclesiology through the lens of the 1777 circular letter he wrote for the Northamptonshire Baptist Association.[6] I will show how

---

4   It is unclear if Ryland was indeed the pastor at Zion Chapel near the end of his life. He certainly was a regular preacher there. There are a few records that indicate that he was formally the pastor till just before his death. For instance, the church that now stands where Zion Chapel was recounts in its own history that Ryland was its minister in 1788 ("A history of Christ Church" [http://www.ccurc.org.uk/history; accessed November 6, 2021]). There was no Baptist church in Enfield till 1867, so it is reasonable to believe that Ryland joined the Congregationalists at Zion Chapel in his final years. See A. P. Baggs, Diane K. Bolton, Eileen P. Scarff, and G. C. Tyack, "Enfield: Protestant nonconformity" in *A History of the County of Middlesex: Volume 5, Hendon, Kingsbury, Great Stanmore, Little Stanmore, Edmonton Enfield, Monken Hadley, South Mimms, Tottenham*, ed. T. F. T. Baker and R. B. Pugh (London: Victoria County History, 1976), 250–253 (*British History Online* [http://www.british-history.ac.uk/vch/middx/vol5/pp250-253; accessed November 6, 2021]).

5   Peter Naylor, "'Sit down, young man': John Collett Ryland's alleged rebuke to William Carey," *Strict Baptist Historical Society Bulletin* 25 (1998): 18. I am grateful to David Woodruff and Graham Ward of the Strict Baptist Historical Society for providing me this source digitally.

6   John Collett Ryland, *The Beauty of Social Religion: Or, the Nature and Glory of a Gospel Church Represented in a Circular Letter from the Baptist Ministers and Messengers, Assembled at Oakham, in Rutlandshire, May 20, 21, 1777* (Northampton: T. Dicey, 1777). For several years prior to 1777, the circular letters of the Northamptonshire Association were used as an opportunity to instruct church leaders and their congregations in sound doctrine. The letters were printed and distributed widely, and in a time of rising literacy in the country, there was little barrier to accessibility. Each of these churches affirmed the Second London Baptist Confession of Faith, and Ryland notes from the outset that he is pleased with the leaders of the association concerning their confessional adherence: "We believe there is no apparent apostasy in our ministers and people from the glorious principles we profess." But concerning the general knowledge of doctrine among the membership, he is less approving: "[The] catechizing of children

the theme of spiritual friendship is what unifies the seven-fold ecclesiological framework by which he structures the letter.

The Church as a society of spiritual friends

Ryland was a respected, leading voice on the Baptist scene in England, and despite his personal eccentricities, he was well connected and had an irenic, catholic spirit. He valued relationships (however inconsistently) with "outsiders" like George Whitefield, Philip Doddridge, and James Hervey.[7] Therefore, it is not out of character that Ryland constructs his ecclesiology under the overarching theme of friendship:

> Spiritual friendship is a pleasing attraction of the heart towards the beautiful and good qualities which we esteem, and the amiable image of God we admire in true Christians—which produces a mutual inclination between two or more persons to promote each other's holiness and happiness. … Spiritual friendship is the union of souls by means of vital holiness, which is the common cement or bond of their mutual and ardent affection.[8]

Where did this connection between ecclesiology and "spiritual friendship" originate for Ryland? In the letter, he commends Daniel Turner's 1758 book, *A Compendium of Social Religion*, which lays out clearly, though in different form and style, many similar principles to Ryland's work.[9] It is in

---

is most sadly neglected, both in private families and in public congregations: and with respect to our printed confession of faith, we judge, that not one in an hundred of all our church members have ever so much as seen it." (Ryland, *The Beauty of Social Religion*, 7) The circular letters were an attempt at remedying this neglect.

[7] In a letter dated April 21, 1753, Hervey writes of Ryland, "Your heart is made for friendship. Though mine is much less warm and tender, it has, I assure you, a very warm and tender regard for Mr. Ryland." See John Ryland, *The Character of the Rev. James Hervey, M. A., Late Rector of Weston Favel, in Northamptonshire, Considered* (London: W. Justins and R. Thompson, 1790), 12.

[8] Ryland, *The Beauty of Social Religion*, 2–3.

[9] Daniel Turner (1710–1798) was the Baptist pastor and a hymn-writer in Abingdon. It

Turner's work that I have found the only other similar reference among Baptists connecting the ideas of ecclesiology and friendship.[10] Turner writes:

> Our frequent meeting one another, and worshiping together in so solemn and enduring an ordinance, as the Lord's Supper, upon such mutually condescending and generous principles, as we should do in the case supposed; must certainly have (besides the general advantages) a particular and powerful tendency, to subdue our mutual prejudices—remove the occasions of our jealousies and animosities—keep in awe the angry and contentious passions—harmonize our spirits—inspire us with the most ardent and sincere *friendship*,—and thus enable us to carry out *our social unity* to the greatest heights of perfection it is capable of, this side of heaven: which would not only fully justify our pretensions, to the most peaceable and benevolent system of religion in the world, but also more clearly evince the divine original of the *church*, and render her appearance far more illustrious and venerable than ever, since the apostolic times.[11]

Interestingly, this is not the first time Ryland and Turner leaned on one another in working out ecclesiological issues. The two became allies

---

should be noted that Turner's book saw a second printing in 1778, a year after Ryland's circular letter was published. One wonders if Turner revised and reproduced his work based on Ryland's letter. See Daniel Turner, *A Compendium of Social Religion, or the Nature and Constitution of the Christian Churches, with the Respective Qualifications and Duties of their Officers and Members Represented in short Propositions, confirm'd by Scripture, and Illustrated with Occasional Notes* (London: John Ward, 1758).

10 Interestingly, the Nonconformist minister, Henry Hurst, uses the phrase "spiritual friendship" with reference to the church once in his 1678 work, *The Revival of Grace*. In his explanation of the Lord's Supper, Hurst writes, "It doth therefore bear the name of Communion; and Christ hath prepared this spiritual Feast to keep up spiritual friendship. Christ would have but one Table for Believers, that Believers might have but one heart for each other." (Henry Hurst, *The Revival of Religion* [London: Thomas Parkhurst, 1678], 104–105). I am indebted to Lon Graham for pointing me to this reference via personal correspondence.

11 Turner, *A Compendium of Social Religion*, 138–139, emphasis mine.

in 1772 during "the communion controversy," when Turner revised and republished a work of Ryland's defending mixed communion.[12] More will be said of this issue below.

Ryland's letter follows the contours of the ecclesiology of the *Second London Confession*, even mentioning the Confession and the *Baptist Catechism*, i.e. what is known as *Keach's Catechism*, explicitly. But the "friendship" lens through which he looks portrays the church in more warmly relational terms, rather than as a dry or formal adherence to a governing document. Admittedly, some parts take the tenor of professorial doctrinal instruction; however, interspersed throughout the didactic prose are almost-sermonic insertions and an exposition of 1 Corinthians 13, on the role of love in the church. In what follows, I will show that if Ryland suffered from a "defective churchmanship," it was not on account of his stated doctrine. I will do this by re-presenting the substance of his letter, highlighting how it is governed by the theme of friendship. Ryland's letter proceeds in seven parts entitled: (1) the nature of a gospel church in its matter, constitution, and form; (2) the dignity and privileges of a gospel church; (3) the faith and order of a gospel church; (4) the officers of a gospel church; (5) the worship and ordinances of a gospel church; (6) the spirit and conduct of a gospel church; and (7) the glorious ends and uses of a gospel church.

"The Nature of a Gospel Church in Its Matter, Constitution, and Form"

At the head of his exposition of the doctrine of the church, Ryland defines the church of Jesus Christ as

> a peculiar society of gracious souls, who are called out of a state of sin and misery by the almighty Spirit of God, associated by their own

---

12 As will be reiterated below, Lon Graham has persuasively argued that Ryland was the principal author of a tract entitled *A Modest Plea for Free Communion* (1772). It seems that Ryland wrote the tract, and then Daniel Turner edited it, personalized it to his situation of conflict, and then published it pseudonymously under the name Candidus. See Lon Graham, "John Collett Ryland, Daniel Turner, and A Modest Plea," *Baptist Quarterly* 52:1 (2021): 34–42.

free consent to maintain the doctrines of grace—to perform gospel worship, and celebrate gospel ordinances, with the exercise of holy discipline to the glory of the divine perfections, and to promote their own usefulness and happiness in time and eternity.[13]

Based on this definition, and through the capacious image of "spiritual friendship," Ryland sets out the matter, constitution, and form of the church.

The matter of the church. Ryland states that the church ought to be made up of "real believers in the Lord Jesus Christ"—regenerate Christians who have truly repented of sin.[14] These believers possess a "new and divine nature" through the regenerating work of the Holy Spirit, along with a faith which "receives Christ alone, without retaining any of their lusts and idols, or mixing their own detestable rags with the divine satisfaction and righteousness of Christ."[15] They share deep convictions about sin and righteousness as the Holy Spirit enlightens their eyes to apprehend God and themselves truly, reforms their wills so that they pursue holy ends, and reshapes their "affections towards God and heavenly things," that they might "feel a new taste for all that is good and beautiful in heaven and earth."[16] The church's faith is Christ-centered and receives "a full Christ" in his three-fold office: "full of wisdom as a prophet, full of divine and infinite worthiness as a priest, and full of power and grace as an almighty king."[17] These Christians are devoted disciples, and "they receive Christ regardless of all threatening consequences; they take him at all hazards, they deliberately count the cost and are determined to conquer their enemies, or die in the conflict."[18] Put simply, Christians are the "matter," or the materials, of

---

13   Ryland, *The Beauty of Social Religion*, 3.
14   Ryland, *The Beauty of Social Religion*, 3.
15   Ryland, *The Beauty of Social Religion*, 3.
16   Ryland, *The Beauty of Social Religion*, 4.
17   Ryland, *The Beauty of Social Religion*, 3.
18   Ryland, *The Beauty of Social Religion*, 4.

a gospel church.

The constitution of the church. According to Ryland, the Holy Spirit assembles, or constitutes, the materials of a gospel church after the pattern of "the heavenly original."[19] This "heavenly original" is the divine nature, image, and law, which are unalterable. Therefore, the church is the work of God, whose design may not be violated, because the "sacred society" of the church participates in the divine nature, resembles the divine image, and receives the divine law.[20] What God has constituted, "it is not possible for men or devils to destroy … as long as the world shall endure." Since Jesus Christ is Lord and protector of his church, "every attempt to alter or to injure this divine constitution is not only unjust but daringly wicked." Citing 1 Corinthians 3:17 ("If any man shall attempt to defile the temple of God, him shall God destroy; for the temple of God is holy, which temple ye are," KJV for the most part), Ryland concludes by pronouncing a woe upon those who might "defile the Church with capital errors, or attempt to suppress or destroy it with the spirit of persecution."[21]

The form of the church. If the materials are Christians and the constitution is the work of the Holy Spirit, then the form of a gospel church is the voluntary nature of the society. Ryland elaborates that the church's form

> consists in the free and mutual consent of believing persons to walk together before God. A Church is a voluntary society: no man is naturally born into a Gospel Church; no man can be forced into it; but every true Christian must be a volunteer: he is made willing in the day of the victorious power of the Spirit of God, and then they give themselves to the Lord, and to one another, by the will of God.[22]

Ryland references 2 Corinthians 8:5 to indicate that Christians commit

---

19 Ryland, *The Beauty of Social Religion*, 4.
20 Ryland, *The Beauty of Social Religion*, 4.
21 Ryland, *The Beauty of Social Religion*, 4.
22 Ryland, *The Beauty of Social Religion*, 4.

themselves, spiritually and voluntarily, to the church. There is no compulsion, even from God, because "Jesus, our glorious general, disdains to impress men by a mere force into his armies: he infuses freely a divine life into our souls, and then we freely give ourselves to God."[23] His view comports well with Reformational articulations of the freedom of the will, since it is the infusion of grace into the believer which reforms the will so the subject may give himself freely to God, and by extension, to the church of God.[24]

As they pertain to the theme of friendship, the church's matter, constitution, and form provide a common foundation for spiritual relationship. They make the church a society distinct from all other associations. It is "very much distinguished from the merely civil and political societies of the world, by the spiritual nature of their constitution … And such a spiritual society is avowedly separated from, and opposed to, the power and kingdom of Satan in this world."[25] These fundamental peculiarities—a new nature and a voluntary consent to "walk together"— are wrought by the Spirit as "the common cement or bond of their mutual and ardent affection" as spiritual friends.

"The Dignity and Privileges of a Gospel Church"

Ryland defines "dignity" as "such a state of mind as to be above the dominion of sin, the spirit of the world and the tyranny of the devil: it consists in a connexion with the eternal God through Christ, and a sense of his approbation and delight in us to make us happy."[26] In other words, Christian dignity is rooted in God's delight in his people in Christ, along with his determination to make them truly happy. "Privilege," on the other hand, is "a peculiar exemption from censures, dangers, and penalties; with a just right

---

23 Ryland, *The Beauty of Social Religion*, 4.
24 Timothy George, *Theology of the Reformers*, rev. ed. (Nashville, TN: B&H Academic, 2013), 77.
25 Ryland, *The Beauty of Social Religion*, 3.
26 Ryland, *The Beauty of Social Religion*, 4.

to rich goods, honors and pleasures from God in Christ."²⁷ That is, Christian privilege is the freedom from impending judgment and full rights to the spiritual blessings secured in Christ for God's elect. Because the church possesses such dignity and the riches of these privileges in Christ, the church is uniquely blessed. To highlight this blessedness, Ryland shows the trinitarian shape of the dignity and privilege of the church—a shape that follows the classic taxis of divine activity from the Father, through the Son, by the Spirit.

From the Father. The church's dignity and privileges "arise from our connexion with God the Father."²⁸ The Father is the ultimate source of every spiritual blessing in the church. Because of the Father's delight and pleasure, the church is spiritually adopted, which places him as "the root of our spiritual and divine existence, and his voice in his promises is clear, tender, and condescending: he speaks to us with all the ardor and compassion of a Father and a God."²⁹

Through the Son. These blessings of dignity and privilege are mediated to the church through the Son and arise "from our vital union with the Lord Jesus ... [which] includes all that is rich, great, and honourable to eternity."³⁰ Since Christology was Ryland's most beloved doctrine,³¹ it is no surprise to find that he slows his treatise at this point for a devotional meditation on the relationship between Christ and the church:

---

27 Ryland, *The Beauty of Social Religion*, 4.
28 Ryland, *The Beauty of Social Religion*, 5.
29 Ryland, *The Beauty of Social Religion*, 5.
30 Ryland, *The Beauty of Social Religion*, 5.
31 As early as 1744, in a diary entry for July 18, while a student in Bristol, Ryland expressed his desire to write his own treatment of the doctrine of Christ: "I wish I may Live to Compose and Preach over and afterwards publish and Excellent Compleat Body of Christology—with a Curious Hymn to each part or branch." This he did in 1782 in *Contemplations on the Divinity of Christ, Evinced from His Names Jehovah, God, and Sovereign Lord; His Attributes and Actions; the Beauties of Creation, Providence, and Redemption; and the Acts of Worship Paid to Him in Scripture* (Northampton: Thomas Dicey and Co., 1782). For his diary entry see "A Student's Programme in 1744," *Baptist Quarterly* 2:6 (1925): 251.

Hence flows relief to the mind under every trouble, hence arises strong consolation to the soul by the inward preference of a heart cheering good, which will out balance all the pressures of pain and evil which we feel or fear. Christ is our glorious head and faithful guardian: we are members of his body, of his flesh, and of his bones. He is our legal head, or head in law—our federal head, or head in covenant—our political head, as a king over his subjects—our representative head, as he sustained the persons of all his people before God in eternity—he is our vital head to give us life, and moral and conjugal head to impart his love—he is our surety to pay our debts, bear our sins, endure our punishment, and give us a right to acceptance with God in eternal life… Christ is our divine tutor, or prophet, to reveal the whole will of God for our salvation: we are his disciples, to be instructed by him in time and to all eternity: he will for ever lead us to new fountains of truth, knowledge, and happiness.[32]

Here we find a rich and experiential reflection on the dignity and privileges of the believer's union with Christ, along with a strong, confessional federalism emphasizing Christ's headship in his three-fold office.[33]

Ryland concludes his section on the Son's relation to the church by portraying Christ as "our most valiant general, or commander in chief." The church carries the banner of Christ, wields the weapons provided by Christ, exercises a "military discipline" taught by Christ, marches to fight alongside Christ, prays in accordance with the will of Christ, conquers devils, storms strongholds, and routs the foes of Christ, "and with him we triumph, and shout Victory forever."[34] This militant language is particular to the church in the age between Christ's first and second advents, and

---

32   Ryland, *The Beauty of Social Religion*, 5.
33   To compare Ryland's words with the *Second London Baptist Confession of Faith* 8 concerning the mediation of Christ in his three-fold office, see William L. Lumpkin, *Baptist Confessions of Faith*, ed. Bill J. Leonard, rev. ed. (Valley Forge, PA: Judson Press, 2011), 251–252.
34   Ryland, *The Beauty of Social Religion*, 5.

it communicates the dignity of victory in battle and the privileges of the spoils of war.

By the Spirit. Ryland makes only one explicit comment on the Holy Spirit at this point: "Christ has a legal right and power to send the Holy Spirit to lead us into all truth."[35] In other words, the Spirit is sent by the Son to lead the church into the enjoyment of the dignity and privileges secured by the Son. Even though he is brief in his words about the Spirit directly, he develops this ministry of the Spirit further by commenting on the unity Christians enjoy with one another in the church, with the angels, and with the natural world.

Ryland reminds the reader that the church universal, in heaven and on earth, enjoys the dignity and privileges of the gospel. Christians are "spiritual freemen" of the heavenly city, educated "in the most liberal and divine knowledge."[36] Because of the extraordinary dignity and privilege of heavenly citizenship and knowledge, "We are allured into the most honourable and divine connexions with the best companions and relations, and rise into the most sublime converse with all the best and brightest beings in heaven and earth."[37] The church is the spiritual friendship of "the best and brightest beings in heaven and earth," made such by their common Savior and knit together by his Spirit.

Curiously, Ryland notes that our dignity "arises also from our union with the angels of God."[38] These angelic beings rejoice in the Christian's conversion, watch over and guard the church, "to guard and guide, to for-

---

35   Ryland, *The Beauty of Social Religion*, 5.
36   Ryland, *The Beauty of Social Religion*, 6.
37   Ryland, *The Beauty of Social Religion*, 6.
38   Ryland, *The Beauty of Social Religion*, 6. As far as I can tell, the "union" with angels he has in view is *not* a federal union like the Christian has with Christ. He seems to be using "union" in a broader sense to mean that the Christian's story is connected to the angelic story. As ministers sent by God for the well-being of the saints, angels and Christians are united in their pursuit of joy in God: "Angels triumph in our souls; they look on us as the excellent of the earth, as fit to receive good, and as fit to do them good."

tify and animate the people of God."[39] Similarly, the church's dignity and privileges arise from "the natural and moral world," because "our souls are the end for which the visible world, with the starry heavens, were created."[40] All of creation, "from an angel to a reptile, and from the blazing sun to a clod of earth," is devoted to the service of the people of God. In this way, "the souls of true believers are the ornament and glory of the universe."[41] Since "the soul is an image of the spiritual nature, the immutable essence, the immortal life, the infinite understanding, the almighty power, the rich goodness, and unspotted holiness of God," then, "a believer in Christ is the greatest and worthiest character in life."[42] So Ryland concludes:

> O, Christians! you can never think too humbly of yourselves, as you are related to your first head Adam, the root of sin, misery, and ruin. You can never think too highly of your souls, as they stand in a vital relation to your second head, the Lord Jesus Christ, the source of holiness, happiness, strength, beauty, and invincible perseverance in grace.[43]

Thus, for Ryland the dignity and privileges of the church, in its Trinitarian shape, should be every Christian's frequent meditation, the foundation of the constant study of divine things, and the motivation for pursuing true friendship with those who share in these common blessings of grace.

"The Faith and Order of a Gospel Church"

Those who have been effectually called by God are "really blessed with true faith; which is not a mere cold assent to the truth, in the understanding, but a cordial consent of the will, and an hearty approbation of the whole of

---

39   Ryland, *The Beauty of Social Religion*, 6.
40   Ryland, *The Beauty of Social Religion*, 6.
41   Ryland, *The Beauty of Social Religion*, 6.
42   Ryland, *The Beauty of Social Religion*, 6.
43   Ryland, *The Beauty of Social Religion*, 6.

revealed truth."⁴⁴ What is the substance of this revealed truth? Ryland's answer: "our confession of faith, and our Catechism," by which he means the *Second London Baptist Confession* and the *Baptist Catechism*, respectively. Ryland's point is that the *Confession* and *Catechism* are "published to the world," and so the Northamptonshire Baptists should be unashamed of the faith they profess. He continues, "from these glorious principles we hope you will never depart," by which he means that there is no need to revise or diverge from the system that has been faithfully handed down and received.⁴⁵ Concerning confessional adherence, Ryland celebrates the state of the ministers in Northampton, writing, "At present, blessed be God we believe there is no apparent apostasy in our ministers and people from the glorious principles we profess."⁴⁶ However, he acknowledges that, while the churches as a whole were in step with the confession, many families and church members remained ignorant of the confession and catechism in private: "with respect to our printed confession of faith, we judge, that not one in an hundred of all our church members have ever so much as seen it."⁴⁷ He acknowledges that the pastors in the association should do a more thorough job commending both the confession and the catechism, noting that new editions were at the printer.⁴⁸

When discussing the order of the church, Ryland explicitly labels their polity as congregational, "or what is usually stiled [sic] independent."⁴⁹ He then clarifies what is meant by independent in two ways. First, by negation: "We do not judge ourselves independent of civil government, as we are

---

44 Ryland, *The Beauty of Social Religion*, 7.

45 Ryland, *The Beauty of Social Religion*, 7.

46 Ryland, *The Beauty of Social Religion*, 7. Interestingly, this statement of Ryland is misquoted in George M. Ella, *John Gill and the Cause of God and Truth* (Durham, UK: Go Publications, 1995), 20. Ella adds a phrase at the end which includes, "Much of the credit for this unswerving allegiance to the doctrine of Scripture under God must be attributed to John Gill, known affectionately as Dr Voluminous." It is probable, however, that this nickname for Gill originated with Ryland.

47 Ryland, *The Beauty of Social Religion*, 7.

48 Ryland, *The Beauty of Social Religion*, 7.

49 Ryland, *The Beauty of Social Religion*, 7.

members of society ... nor do we mean an independence on the providence and grace of God—here we profess ourselves dependent every moment to eternity."[50] Then, positively:

> By the word *independent*, we mean, that the Lord Jesus Christ, the sole fountain of all spiritual rights and power, has given us allowance and command to associate together to incorporate ourselves into regular societies, to carry on all the parts of public worship and discipline, to choose our pastors and deacons, to receive in new members, to admonish and reprove those that violate his laws, and to exclude from us all that prove incorrigible and impenitent: in a word, that we have a right and power to do every thing that shall be for the glory of Christ and our own happiness, without being necessarily obliged to call in the aid of other pastors and churches, or of being subject, in matters of faith and worship to any pretended spiritual power on earth whatsoever.[51]

Ryland thus summarizes the heart of Baptist independency, in a circular letter of their voluntary inter-ecclesial association no less! Just as true friendship cannot be under compulsion but is "a pleasing attraction of the heart" and "a mutual inclination between two or more persons to promote each other's holiness and happiness," so Ryland affirms the voluntary nature of the church's order.

"The Officers of a Gospel Church"
Ryland identifies God himself as the supplier of the officers of the church, given "for the edification, strength, beauty, and happiness of the church ... to promote the general welfare of that society to which they belong." However, even though God gives these leaders, they are "chosen and set apart,

---

50   Ryland, *The Beauty of Social Religion*, 7.
51   Ryland, *The Beauty of Social Religion*, 7.

with solemn prayer, by the vote of the church."[52] Therefore, in Ryland's view, church officers are identified by both God and the local congregation.

There are "two classes or orders of officers": elders and deacons. Elders are "appointed and ordained" to perform three primary functions: (1) to faithfully bear witness to "the whole system of truth in the law and gospel"; (2) to lead the congregation in worship, including the administration of the public ordinances; and (3) to lead the church in business matters, calling for and counting votes, and executing "every part of the peoples' determinations."[53] Deacons "have the honour to be ordained of God our saviour, to represent his compassionate heart to the poor of the church; and also to represent and express the affections and bowels of the church to their dear pastors, that they may be supplied with a competence of temporal good, and rendered easy and happy in their studies and labours."[54] Therefore, the work of the diaconate is both to oversee the benevolence ministry of the church, and to assist the pastor with the necessary means to carry out his responsibilities.

Then, not as a separate office, but as an elaboration on the work of an elder, he elaborates on the character requirements and titles of the Christian preacher, "to the end that you may discern the respect that is due to them, and give them that attention which their work and their great Lord demand."[55] He notes that in Scripture, preachers are called laborers, servants, watchmen, overseers, workmen, husbandmen, shepherds, householders, builders, stewards, soldiers, elders, oxen, eagles, lions, cherubs, seraphs, lights, stars, fathers, nurses, saviors, justifiers, ambassadors, earthen vessels, and angels.[56] After mentioning each of these images with their scriptural proof texts, he concludes that faithful pastors should receive "cordial esteem … ardent affection … encouragement, attention, succour, and sup-

---

52   Ryland, *The Beauty of Social Religion*, 7–8.
53   Ryland, *The Beauty of Social Religion*, 8.
54   Ryland, *The Beauty of Social Religion*, 8.
55   Ryland, *The Beauty of Social Religion*, 8.
56   Ryland, *The Beauty of Social Religion*, 8–9.

port," from church members.[57]

"The Worship and Ordinances of a Gospel Church"

For Ryland and his Northamptonshire brethren, their spiritual friendship entailed "the union of souls by means of vital holiness," and nothing demonstrates "the common cement or bond of their mutual and ardent affection" like their shared convictions about biblical worship. He defines worship as

> a deep and powerful sense of the infinite perfections and glories of God, expressed in the most ardent and pathetic manner, with the highest veneration and love for the divine nature and subsistences, agreeable to the revealed idea of God, and in an exact correspondence to our connexions with God, and obligations to him as redeemed souls; called by his Spirit, and made heirs of eternal salvation through Christ's blood and intercession.[58]

With this general definition of worship set down, he surveys its elements, focusing on singing and the ordinances.

First, when Ryland mentions singing as an element of worship, he refers *only* to "sing[ing] his praises in the psalms of the inspired scriptures."[59] The omission of the singing of hymns is noteworthy because of the intense history of the hymn-singing controversy in Particular Baptist life in the not-so-distant past. Ryland commends hymns elsewhere, and many of his close friends, including his own son, composed hymns to be sung in corporate worship.[60] Why would he not include hymn-singing in the letter?

---

57   Ryland, *The Beauty of Social Religion*, 9.
58   Ryland, *The Beauty of Social Religion*, 9.
59   Ryland, *The Beauty of Social Religion*, 9.
60   The younger John Ryland is reported to have written 799 hymns, even receiving writing advice from his long-time family friend, John Newton. For a sketch of the hymnody of Ryland Jr., see Christopher Crocker, "The Life and Legacy of John Ryland Jr. (1753–1825): A Man of Considerable Usefulness—An Historical Biography" (PhD

CHAPTER SEVEN

Even though the hymn-singing controversy had subsided by the 1760s, perhaps Ryland stuck to the non-controversial affirmation of the singing of psalms, a subject which no one disputed, and allowed his readers to decide for themselves whether there is biblical permission to sing extra-biblical human compositions like hymns.[61] An associational circular letter was for Ryland an occasion to unite around shared and foundational beliefs, not to rehearse challenging history or to take positions on intramural squabbles. Accompanying the singing of scriptural psalms are prayers of adoration, confession, supplication, and thanksgiving— "thus we ought to worship God in reading his word, hearing his faithful ministers preach and explain his law and gospel."[62]

Second, and consistent with the *Confession* and with most Baptists before him, Ryland affirms "two positive institutions of the New Testament, called baptism and the Lord's supper, which demand your best attention and affection."[63] In a fascinating footnote, Ryland paraphrases with approval a remark from Daniel Waterland that

> the true doctrine of the Trinity, and the atonement of Christ, have been kept up in the Christian church, by the institutions of Baptism and the Lord's Supper, more than by any other means whatsoever; and, humanly speaking, these glorious truths, which are essential to salvation, would have been lost long ago, if the two positive institutions had been totally neglected and disused amongst professors of Christianity.[64]

---

dissertation, University of Bristol, 2018), 372–376. Also, see Lon Graham "'All Who Love Our Blessed Redeemer': The Catholicity of John Ryland Jr." (PhD dissertation, Vrije Universiteit Amsterdam, 2021), 30–32. Evidence that the Rylands' College Lane Church in Northampton engaged in congregational singing dates back to at least 1715–1716, according to Naylor, *Calvinism, Communion, and the Baptists*, 51.

61   See Crocker, "The Life and Legacy of John Ryland Jr.," 373, where he refers to 1760–1800 as the "golden age" of Baptist hymnody.
62   Ryland, *The Beauty of Social Religion*, 9.
63   Ryland, *The Beauty of Social Religion*, 9.
64   Ryland, *The Beauty of Social Religion*, 10. Daniel Waterland (1683-1740) was an

In other words, the doctrines of the Trinity and atonement survived despite centuries of Roman Catholic distortion because of the continued practice of the ordinances. Because of this, baptism and the Lord's Supper "appear to be of unspeakable importance to the glory of God and the very being of the true church of Christ on earth."[65] Therefore, baptism should be considered an act of worship performed "but once in the life of a Christian—but once to eternity." He notes that baptism is "a great privilege and honour" when it is involves "a right subject, and in a right manner," which surely meant a professing believer as the subject and full immersion as the manner.[66]

Finally, Ryland comments hardly at all on the Lord's Supper (just two sentences), but he refers readers to a book he had published earlier on the subject.[67] Here, he simply calls the Supper a "precious ordinance of divine

---

Anglican theologian, Cambridge academic, and controversialist, particularly on the topics of the Trinity and the Eucharist. I am unable to locate the specific reference of Ryland's paraphrase, but it seems likely to have come from one of these two sources: Daniel Waterland, *A Review of the Doctrine of the Eucharist, as Laid Down in Scripture and Antiquity*, 2nd ed. (London: Innys and Manby, 1737), 600, or his "Christ's Divinity Proved from the Form of Baptism: The Eighth Sermon Preached April 6, 1720" in *The Works of the Rev. Daniel Waterland D. D.*, ed. William Van Mildert, vol. 2, 2nd ed. (Oxford: Oxford University Press, 1843), 187.

65 Ryland, *The Beauty of Social Religion*, 9.

66 Ryland, *The Beauty of Social Religion*, 9. The last thing Ryland mentions about baptism is a book by Samuel Wilson entitled, *Scripture Manual on the Ordinance of Baptism*, reproduced by "our zealous and public-spirited friends at Bristol," Ryland's alma mater. Originally published in 1750, it was in its ninth edition when John Rippon edited and reproduced it in 1785, and it was later revised and recirculated by Abraham Booth in 1797. Ryland here commends the acquisition of this "excellent essay as a proper enlargement on this subject." See Samuel Wilson, *A Scripture-Manual: or, A Plain Representation of the Ordinance of Baptism* (London: William Button, 1797).

Ryland also footnotes a recommendation of John Fellows' essay, *Six Views of Believers Baptism*, which had just seen its fourth edition earlier in 1777, appended to Fellows' work, *Hymns on Believers Baptism. To which is Prefixed, An Introduction, containing Six Views of that Holy Ordinance* (London: G. Keith, 1777).

67 See John Ryland, *Contemplations Suited to the Lord's Supper, for the Service of Serious Christians When They Commemorate the Death of Christ: Extracted from the Judicious Dr. Witsius's Admirable Treatise on the Covenants of God with Man* (Northampton: Thomas Dicey, 1770).

worship, which draws into it the whole of faith and practice," and "that most glorious and reviving institution."[68] It may have been strategic for Ryland to omit elaboration on the Lord's Supper since he was one of the principal interlocutors in the communion controversy at the time. He was an avid defender of the minority position of open communion, which holds that believer's baptism by immersion should not be a criterion for admission to the Lord's Supper. Lon Graham has persuasively argued that Ryland was the primary author of the tract *A Modest Plea for Free Communion* in 1772.[69] It seems that Ryland wrote the initial tract, and then Daniel Turner edited it, personalized it to his situation of conflict, and then published it pseudonymously under the name *Candidus* with a slightly modified title. Here, however, like his brevity about hymn-singing, Ryland seems to have steered a middle course so his letter to the churches of Northamptonshire would not be encumbered by an intramural polemical issue. For a "plunging, roaring mountain cataract" like Ryland, his restraint at this point stands as an instance of maturity and self-awareness.[70] It demonstrates that his warmly relational theology of the church affected his practice, at least in this presentation.

"The Spirit and Conduct of a Gospel Church"

Ryland insists that "the spirit and temper" of the spiritual friendship that marks the church should be noticeably different from that of "the world, the devil, and popery," and it should be "as near an approach to the disposition and moral perfections of God and to the spirit and temper of the lovely Lord Jesus, and his primitive Christians, as we can attain."[71] In particular, he has in mind that the church, even in a "state of imperfect sanctification," should be marked by love. In the church, "the whole law is summed in one

---

68 Ryland, *The Beauty of Social Religion*, 10.
69 Graham. "John Collett Ryland, Daniel Turner, and A Modest Plea," 34–42.
70 This epithet is from Thomas Wright, *Augustus M. Toplady and Contemporary Hymn-Writers* (London: Farncombe and Sons, 1911), 76.
71 Ryland, *The Beauty of Social Religion*, 10.

word, *Love*; and the whole temper of a true believer is summed up in one word, *Love*."[72] How might one conceive of this love? Ryland defines it thus:

> True Christian love is a single thought, or simple perception, that our fellow-Christian is an excellent and worthy object, good in himself, fit to do us good, and fit to receive good; with a delight in the sight of him, as he bears the image of Christ, and is designed to live with us in the presence of God to eternity.[73]

Notice how similar his definition of *love* is to his definition of *friendship*:

> Spiritual friendship is a pleasing attraction of the heart towards the beautiful and good qualities which we esteem, and the amiable image of God we admire in true Christians—which produces a mutual inclination between two or more persons to promote each other's holiness and happiness. ... Spiritual friendship is the union of souls by means of vital holiness, which is the common cement or bond of their mutual and ardent affection.[74]

Both are perceptions and attractions of the heart to another person, ultimately ordered toward the good of the other. Both are grounded in the image of God (assuming the "image of God" in his definition of friendship is synonymous with the "image of Christ" in his definition of love). Both love and friendship unite souls in the pursuit of holiness and happiness, which reaches a consummation in "the presence of God" in eternity. In other words, Christian love is both the fountain and *telos* of spiritual friendship. Spiritual friendship is the relational matrix of Christian love. And both are essential to "the spirit and temper" of the church.

Of this love, Ryland says that "we are no farther Christians than we

---

72 Ryland, *The Beauty of Social Religion*, 10.
73 Ryland, *The Beauty of Social Religion*, 10.
74 Ryland, *The Beauty of Social Religion*, 3.

evidence this beautiful disposition of soul in our whole life and conversation." He then sets out on "a compendious view of the true Christian temper, as consisting in love," and he does so by expounding 1 Corinthians 13:4–8.[75] In this exposition of 1 Corinthians 13, Ryland's point is to emphasize the one-anotherness of the ecclesial community. In keeping with his metaphor of friendship, these qualities that constitute a blessed personal friendship also make for a blessed community of love. I shall highlight just a few themes from Ryland's treatise which emphasize "the beauty of social religion."

Love inclines one to overlook undesirable qualities in another. He writes that love "scorns resentment at little things."[76] Love is not "highly and bitterly provoked, so as to fall into fits of violent anger on every imaginary or real wrong done to us."[77] Or from another angle,

> Love is not forward to reason out or dig up mischief concerning other men: it takes no pleasure in raking into characters, in order to expose them or prying into the secrets of private families, in order to blast their reputation. Love is not violent to impute evil to other men, and rashly and cruelly to charge evil to another man's account, and to think the worst of every man we dislike.[78]

In Ryland's own life, he experienced this grace of spiritual friendship as he frequently exposed himself to scandal and misunderstanding through his unusual verbal outbursts and financial indiscretions in the world of publishing. In the last decade of his life, his most generous friend and overlooker of faults was probably his own son and co-pastor, John Ryland Jr. At several points, with his father on the brink of financial ruin and public shame, Ryland Jr. wrote to John Newton for counsel as to how to protect

---

75 Ryland, *The Beauty of Social Religion*, 10.
76 Ryland, *The Beauty of Social Religion*, 10.
77 Ryland, *The Beauty of Social Religion*, 11.
78 Ryland, *The Beauty of Social Religion*, 11.

his father's reputation and provide for his financial needs.[79] Once, after some especially embarrassing and public remarks by his father, Ryland Jr. again sought the wisdom of Newton about whether he should publicly oppose his father's antics. In each of these situations, Newton encouraged the young man to be patient and remain silent, and to be prepared to leverage his own reputation and material resources to care for his aging and undisciplined father.[80]

Without a doubt, the grace of Ryland Jr. is an example of friendship and love which Ryland Sr. here commends as the proper spirit and temper of the church:

> True Christian love has a veil to throw over all unallowed [sic] blemishes, and to hide, in a sweet-tempered manner, all lamented imperfections in a Christian brother; and this is a most useful and happy temper in a church of Christ, and will produce most glorious advantages to preachers and people. Such a temper will prevent the hurt and shame of our brother's character, and prevent the sad disgrace of

---

[79] John Newton met Ryland Sr. in 1765, and Ryland Jr. became co-pastor alongside his father in August of 1781. Both Rylands maintained a friendship with Newton. For an example of Newton's wise and loving counsel to Ryland Jr., see "Letter Thirty-Five," dated April 7, 1786, after Ryland Sr. had resigned his pastorate in Northampton and moved to Enfield. Newton writes:

> You love your father, and so do I. Amidst all the inconsistencies and improprieties of his conduct, I have always seen or thought I have seen, something truly excellent and sterling in his character. His faults I chiefly impute to constitution, and therefore [I] am more disposed to pity than to censure many things in him which I cannot approve. Seldom have I been in his company without observing something to pity, and much to admire. I can form but a faint judgment of what you, as a good son, must feel for such a father, from the fuller knowledge you have of the whole of his case in the complex.

In Grant Gordon, ed., *Wise Counsel: John Newton's Letters to John Ryland Jr.* (Carlisle, PA: Banner of Truth Trust, 2009), 175–176.

[80] Newton writes, "You had better quit the town, or even the kingdom, than write against your father ... He acts according to the impetus of his spirits, is hurried away, and I believe he cannot help it ... I would no more write against such a man, though he is not *my* father, than I would employ my right hand to wound my left." (John Newton, Letter to John Ryland Jr., January 31, 1792, in Gordon, *Wise Counsel*, 255–256).

religion in the world.[81]

When Ryland Sr. penned these words, Ryland Jr. was not yet co-pastoring with him in Northampton. Surely, the elder could not have anticipated how he would need his own son to hold true to these principles of love and spiritual friendship for his own sake. In the sermon preached at Ryland Sr.'s funeral, John Rippon, one of his closest friends, preached, expressing a similar sentiment:

> Here I think it right to observe that the natural warmth of his temper sometimes hurried him into indiscretions, which were the fruitful sources of after sorrow to him; and far be it from any of us to attempt to justify what he himself so heartily criminated; yet I presumed to say,
>
> Defects through nature's best productions run,
> Our friend had spots, and spots are in the sun.
>
> And defects, in such a man as he was, must be seen. It has been remarked by one of the Puritans, I think, "that a small speck in scarlet is more visible than a great stain in russet." ...If the Sun is eclipsed one day, it attracts more attention than the shining of it for *forty years*.[82]

It seems that many of Ryland's friends also recognized this feature of loving, spiritual friendship which overlooks undesirable qualities in the other and seeks to cover over faults.

Love prefers the good of others to one's own. Christian love "feels no

---

81 Ryland, *The Beauty of Social Religion*, 11. Ryland must have meant "unhallowed blemishes."
82 John Rippon, *The Gentle Dismission of Saints from Earth to Heaven: A Sermon, Occasioned by the Decease of the Rev. John Ryland, Senior, A.M.* (London, 1792), 47–48.

pain or ill-will at another man's excellence, nor does it covet any good with an ambitious affectation of superiority."[83] One marked by love "does not act rashly, with a proud ostentation of our own gifts, talents, and imaginary or real advantages; it scorns to boast of any excellence which we possess."[84] Love "will not haughtily invade another man's province or office, or scornfully trample on his person, honour, and usefulness."[85] So in the church, the preference for the good of others presents an accountability such that "true love expects good from every believer in the same church, or in the same family … Thus love inspires a cheering and vigorous hope through all ranks and classes of true Christians."[86] This preference for the good of another person leads neatly to a final theme of his exposition.

Love is generous toward others. Love communicates "wise advice, kind affections, and temporal blessings."[87] Love shares truth and encouragement with another.[88] It abounds in "ardent prayer for each other in all cases and distresses." Ryland highlights how this unique act of love forges spiritual friendships where those who pray for each other "take part in each other's

---

83 Ryland, *The Beauty of Social Religion*, 10.
84 Ryland, *The Beauty of Social Religion*, 10.
85 Ryland, *The Beauty of Social Religion*, 11.
86 Ryland, *The Beauty of Social Religion*, 12.
87 Ryland, *The Beauty of Social Religion*, 10.
88 Ryland, *The Beauty of Social Religion*, 12. Ryland mentions Samuel Wright's *Treatise on Justice and Love* to emphasize that love rejoices in the truth. Samuel Wright (1683–1746) was a Presbyterian nonconformist minister and participant in the Salters' Hall conferences. See Alexander Gordon, "Wright, Samuel" in *Dictionary of National Biography* (New York: The Macmillan Company, London: Smith, Elder & Co., 1900), 63:127. Ryland cites his reference to Wright's "admirable *Treatise on Justice and Love*, 8 vo. 1730." However, I believe Ryland is paraphrasing from Wright's 1732 work, *Charity in all its Branches: or, a Collection of the Rules of Scripture that Teach Men to Love Mercy* (London: Richard Hett, 1732), 43–44: "the joy and satisfaction which Charity is here said to have, ariseth from the power and success of the Gospel, manifested in the lives of those that are molded by it … Charity will not suppress the satisfaction it takes in another; nor will it withhold any encouragements, which the discovery of its own joy would give, to useful and beneficial actions or endeavours." Ryland mentions Wright's work under the section themed "Love rejoiceth in the truth," which is precisely where the above quotation appears in Wright's exposition of 1 Corinthians 13.

prosperity and joy."[89] Because of this outward orientation, "self-pleasing, self-will, self-applause, and self-interest alone, are no guides to generous love, nor have they power to rule and tyrannize over a benevolent and gracious heart."[90] Thus, for Ryland, love in the ecclesial community expresses itself in the context of friendships that are "active and generous in the free diffusions of good, i.e. of temporal blessings, and of spiritual sentiments, and inward experience, to warm and animate each other's hearts."[91]

Social religion like this is indeed beautiful. And ultimately, such love propels the church toward zealous gospel ministry:

> If this omnipotent and everlasting love reigned in your hearts, how vast, how mighty would be your zeal for the glorious gospel: how would you relish and prize, and propagate divine revelation: how lion-like would be your strife for the doctrines of pure grace: and how valiant and bold would you be for the purity, extent, and eternity of the moral law, as it is the copy of the shining purity of the perfections of God ... your hearts would expand as wide as the whole church on earth, and rise with a noble glow of refined affection to the church of God in heaven![92]

The proper spirit and temper of a gospel church is inclusive and heart-expanding, seeking to draw others into the bonds of friendship and truth. Where such love abounds, there is no conflict between zeal in evangelistic effort and care in doctrinal precision.

This summary of his exposition of 1 Corinthians 13 supports his theme of spiritual friendship, which is formalized by the bonds of Christian love in the community of church members with all their rights and duties one to another. Therefore, Ryland writes: "Sincere believers, who are endued

---

89   Ryland, *The Beauty of Social Religion*, 13.
90   Ryland, *The Beauty of Social Religion*, 11.
91   Ryland, *The Beauty of Social Religion*, 13.
92   Ryland, *The Beauty of Social Religion*, 14.

with such a spirit of evangelical love, will feel a delight in the practice of all relative duties to each other. They will see and feel, that love is the supreme and immutable law of God, which powerfully attracts and unites all gracious souls to Christ, and to each other."[93] This law of love is the intersection of friendship and covenanted church membership, because love is to characterize the spirit and conduct of the church, making it a peculiar society of "ardent fellow-feeling with each other":

> 'Tis love, unfeigned and fervent, 'tis love only that makes church fellowship sweet and profitable; for without love a church is not a palace, but a prison; not a paradise of pleasure, but a dungeon of darkness, without one ray of consolation or usefulness. A church is a barren desert, a howling wilderness, full of savage and hateful creatures, if love, unfeigned and ardent, be absent there.[94]

"The Glorious Ends and Uses of a Gospel Church"

Ryland identifies four purposes for the existence of the church: (1) "to represent God's true character in the world"; (2) to "stop the mouths of the wicked and condemn the finally impenitent at the last day"; (3) "to allure awakened and inquiring souls to Christ"; and (4) "to promote each other's present and eternal happiness."[95] He briefly develops each of these points, which will be noted below.

The church represents God to the world. The church takes an active part in demonstrating the communicable attributes of God—Ryland specifies God's goodness, wisdom, and power. The rest of creation does this passive-

---

93 Ryland, *The Beauty of Social Religion*, 13.
94 Ryland, *The Beauty of Social Religion*, 13. With this statement, Ryland points the reader to John Gill: "See John Gill on a Gospel Church. Body of Practical Div. Vol. III." I believe he is referring to "Chapter IX. Of the Grace of Love" in John Gill, *A Complete Body of Doctrinal and Practical Divinity* (London: Mathews and Leigh, 1839; reprint, Paris, AR: The Baptist Standard Bearer, 1984), 762–773.
95 Ryland, *The Beauty of Social Religion*, 14–15.

ly.[96] The unregenerate have the capacity to represent God, but they have no desire to do so, and so they, in fact, represent the Devil and his works in the world. Therefore, it is left to Christians willingly and faithfully to bear witness to God the Creator by embodying wisdom, goodness, kindness, holiness, justice, sincerity, faithfulness, and truthfulness. In doing so, the church enjoys the "infinite honour … to be the living images of God to the world; to exhibit a beautiful image of God our Redeemer, to men, to angels, to devils! to shew to all the worlds of rational minds the beautiful character of God."[97] As noted above, this ecclesial imaging of God is a feature of Ryland's vision of spiritual friendship. Since the church is in the image of God, it demonstrates to the world these beautiful and good qualities of God.

The church stops the mouths of the wicked. In representing God, the church will stop the mouths of the wicked on the last day by bearing witness to God's just judgement. Until Christ returns, the church will be the recipient of accusations and opposition from the unbelieving world, but a church demonstrating the moral perfections of God will be vindicated by the Lord on the final day of judgment.

The church allures the lost. Since the day of judgment is coming, the third purpose of the church is "to allure awakened and inquiring souls to Christ, to be happy in his great and precious salvation," since, "nothing has a greater tendency to allure, to encourage, to animate the hopes of convinced sinners, than the holy, cheerful, godlike tempers and conversation of the members of a gospel church."[98] In other words, the Spirit-empowered and transformed lives of Christians living in intimate communities of spiritual friendship has a magnetic attraction to God's elect who are yet

---

96   Ryland, *The Beauty of Social Religion*, 14.

97   Ryland, *The Beauty of Social Religion*, 14.

98   To this point, Ryland says, "Next to the salvation of our own souls, what can be imagined more dear, more excellent, more desirable, than to be the instruments of the salvation of our fellow-sinners?" (Ryland, *The Beauty of Social Religion*, 15.) Surely, this is an important piece of evidence that he was *not* the frigid hyper-Calvinist he is often made out to be.

unsaved. By the church's fellowship, "we comfort their hearts with an assurance, that the master we serve is good and great, generous and kind, mild and gentle, easy to be intreated, full of mercy and good fruits, without partiality, severity, or hypocrisy."[99] The allure of Christian fellowship is ultimately the goodness of Jesus Christ displayed in their godly "tempers and conversations." Ryland concludes this point by calling on all Christians "to rouse up all [their] powers to this great and good work!" as a demonstration of their ambition for God's glory, justice, and compassion.[100]

The church promotes one another's present and eternal happiness. Here again, Ryland is using the same language that he employed in defining spiritual friendship. In light of the Fall and its effects, the church is the singular place where a social element is demonstrated in the way God intended, even if imperfectly and only as a foretaste. To further develop the point, Ryland leans heavily on the one-anotherness of man's created nature, and he writes:

> Man was originally made a sociable being. Grace gives us a capacity and a strong inclination to the best company in the world; and in religious society we attain the highest ends of our existence. We watch over each other for good—we communicate new thoughts to each other—we mingle souls in prayer at the throne of grace—we warn and reprove the negligent and disorderly—we stimulate and provoke to higher improvements in the intellectual, social, and divine life—we comfort each other in affliction and sorrow—we attend on the dying beds of our departing friends, and commit them to the bosom and the blessing of the dear redeemer—we ascend, by faith, with their separate spirits, and long to follow them into the blissful and transforming presence of God![101]

---

99   Ryland, *The Beauty of Social Religion*, 15.
100 Ryland, *The Beauty of Social Religion*, 15.
101 Ryland, *The Beauty of Social Religion*, 15.

Here Ryland sees the church as a society of friendship through which "we attain the highest ends of our existence," and in approving, delighting in, and "long[ing] to possess all the utmost advantages of such a state," the Christian evidences his friendship with God.[102] Only in such a society of friendship are the hardships of life endured and the most cherished spiritual ends attained.

Conclusion

Through the governing theme of spiritual friendship, Ryland affirms a thoroughly Baptist ecclesiology, from a believer's church to believer's baptism by immersion to congregational polity. In this circular letter, *The Beauty of Social Religion*, he is rigid where rigidity is necessary, but he allows for flexibility where the issues are debatable. While some of the circular letters of the Northamptonshire Association were primarily instructional or polemical, this one was intended to be catholic—unifying his readers around shared convictions. An evidence of that intention is seen in the "Minutes" appended to the end of the letter: "At four we met to examine the contents of the circular letter, the design of which was approved—some alterations for the better were made, and it was agreed that the letter should be printed."[103] Apparently, Ryland's original wording was in need of alteration at points, though precisely at what points it is now impossible to discern. But Ryland approved and considered them to be friendly amendments. Then, it is noted that he concluded the meeting in prayer and was elected to be the preacher at the next year's meeting.

A key part of the irenic and catholic spirit of the letter is the theme of friendship. Ryland seems to be conscious of how this unifying theme has a universal resonance in the heart:

> On this view of the beauty of social religion, or the true nature and

---

102 Ryland, *The Beauty of Social Religion*, 15.
103 Ryland, *The Beauty of Social Religion*, 16.

glory of a gospel church, who, that has any spiritual sense, will not approve of it, highly delight in it, and long to possess all the utmost advantages of such a state of divine friendship? and who, that has any sense of gospel honour in such societies, will not strive to strengthen, comfort, and adorn it?[104]

If Christians have a mutual love for Christ and his church, and the notion of friendship has a universal appeal, then all Christians should unite to preserve "the nature and glory of a gospel church."

In one of the few modern references to Ryland's letter, Christopher Ellis writes, "Not only is this a vision of the faithful living of the teaching of the New Testament, but, as such, it embodies a vision of a covenant community in which discipline is an action of love and fellowship a foretaste of heaven; a vision in which men and women begin to live as they were created to live and, by grace, are still called to live, in the *koinonia* of the Holy Spirit."[105] So, far from having a "defective churchmanship," John Collett Ryland was an exemplary theologian of the church among the eighteenth-century Baptists. Even as an imperfect practitioner, he was one who gave the entirety of his adult life to the church—forty-two years as a pastor. This "excellent and eccentric man"[106] was possessed by a sense of "gospel honour" and exercised every effort "to strengthen, comfort, and adorn [the church]."[107] Sinner though he was, he was ever giving and ever in need of spiritual friendship, and of his many public and private faults, "defective churchmanship" and a deficient ecclesiology were not among them.

---

104 Ryland, *The Beauty of Social Religion*, 15.

105 See Christopher J. Ellis "The Beauty of Social Religion: Local Baptist Life in the Eighteenth Century" in *Challenge and Change: English Baptist Life in the Eighteenth Century*, ed. Stephen L. Copson and Peter J. Morden (Didcot: Baptist Historical Society, 2017), 99. Though Ellis borrows Ryland's title, Ellis's work includes almost nothing about the material content of Ryland's letter, save one choice quotation at the conclusion of his chapter.

106 Morris, *Memoirs of the Life and Writings of the Rev. Andrew Fuller*, 102.

107 Ryland, *The Beauty of Social Religion*, 15.

8

"Sing on, Blest Pilgrim!": The hymns of John Ryland, Jr. (1753–1825)

RYAN GRIFFITH

John Ryland Jr. (1753–1823) is widely known for his contributions to evangelical Baptist life as a theologian, pastor, missions-mobilizer, and educator. Less well known, however, are Ryland's noteworthy contributions to the hymnody of the period.[1] Over the fifty years of ministry in Northampton and Bristol, Ryland heralded the importance of singing in corporate worship—modeling it in his pastoral ministry, encouraging it among evangelical churches, and contributing to its practice by composing over one hundred hymns. Published in numerous periodicals and hymn compilations, Ryland's verse reflects his wide interests and broad education—touching on Scripture, natural science, experimental Christianity,

---

1   My interest in Ryland's hymnody was sparked by Grant Gordon's excellent work on and Ryland's formative relationship with John Newton. See Grant Gordon, ed., *Wise Counsel: John Newton's Letters to John Ryland, Jr.* (Edinburgh: Banner of Truth Trust, 2009). The title of this essay comes from Ryland's reflection on Hosea 2:15: "Sing on, blest pilgrim! All the way/Thou hast good cause to sing/and God shall keep the night and day/And safe to Zion bring." Daniel Sedgwick, ed., *Hymns and Verses on Sacred Subjects by the Late Rev. John Ryland, D.D.* (London: Daniel Sedgwick, 1862), 23.

and even classical literature. While few of his compositions have stood the test of time, the devotional piety, evangelistic zeal, and practical concern for congregational instruction evident in his hymns were influential in the churches he served and among the students he taught as the principal of the Bristol Baptist College (1793–1825). This essay examines Ryland's unique contribution in two parts. Part one sketches Ryland's intellectual and spiritual formation and briefly situates him in the larger context of Baptist hymnody. Part two analyzes the authorship, publication, and content of his hymns, paying attention to their focus on the affections, the celebration of doctrine, and the edification and mission of the church.

Furnishing praise: Ryland's intellectual and spiritual formation

John Ryland, Jr. was born on January 29, 1753, to John and Elizabeth in the small country town of Warwick, nestled against the river Avon in Warwickshire. His father, John Collett Ryland, was pastor of the Baptist church and schoolmaster of the boys' boarding school he founded soon after his arrival in 1745.[2] Little is known about Elizabeth. The younger Ryland mentions that her custom was to teach him Bible stories using the tiled fireplace in the parlor.[3] John's father, however, would have substantial impact on the spiritual and intellectual development of his son.

After the loss of his mother in 1729 when he was only five years old, the elder Ryland had "surrendered himself to the follies of youth." Only when a revival swept through Bourton-on-the-Water in 1741, did Ryland come under the influence of spiritual awakening. Under the preaching of a young Benjamin Beddome (1718–1795), Ryland was brought to repentance and faith. On October 2 of that year, he was baptized and received

---

2   Grant Gordon, "John Ryland, Jr. (1753–1825)," in *The British Particular Baptists, 1638–1910*, ed. Michael A. G. Haykin, vol. 2 (Springfield, MO: Particular Baptist Press, 2000), 77.

3   John Ryland, *Pastoral Memorials Selected from the Manuscripts of the Late Rev. John Ryland D.D. of Bristol with a Memoir of the Author in Two Volumes*, ed. Jonathan Edwards Ryland, vol. 2 (London: B.J. Holdsworth, 1828), 4.

into the membership of the Baptist church in Bourton.[4] Soon afterward, he resolved to dedicate his life to gospel ministry.

At the encouragement of Beddome, John Collett Ryland studied at Bristol Academy from 1744–1745, at that time the center of the evangelical revival. During his time in Bristol, Ryland encountered Charles Wesley (1707–1788), James Hervey (1714–1758), and George Whitefield (1714–1770)—rising figures in the evangelical movement. Here Ryland was also significantly influenced by the writings of Particular Baptist theologians John Gill (1697–1771) and John Brine (1703–1765). Unlike others of his day, evangelical piety and high Calvinist soteriology managed to reside peacefully in his understanding. Perhaps this is why biographers have characterized Ryland as a man born for another age, "ardent, with marked individuality, and with all that vehement temperament preferring eccentricity to platitude which would have been congenial to the two previous centuries or to ours, but which was in sharp collision with the prevalent tendency of his own."[5] As a "very strong personality, with a brilliant, creative mind" and a preference for the theology, politics, and culture of his Puritan forebears, Ryland could have succumbed to antagonism and obscurantism.[6] Adkins writes that it "is John Ryland's great claim to distinction that he did the exact opposite of this, and showed untiring zeal for culture as well as for religion."[7] More even than his firm Calvinist convictions, Ryland's brilliance, eccentricity, zeal, vision for broad education in the humanities, and ecumenical friendships played a profound role in shaping the spirituality and mental opulence of his son.[8]

---

4   Michael A. G. Haykin, *One Heart and One Soul: John Sutcliff of Olney, His Friends and His Times* (Darlington, UK: Evangelical Press, 1994), 70.

5   James Culross, *The Three Rylands: A Hundred Years of Various Christian Service* (London: Elliot Stock, 1897), 4.

6   Gordon, "John Ryland, Jr. (1753–1825)," 77.

7   Culross, *The Three Rylands*, 5.

8   Despite his love for biblical languages, theology, and the great works of Christian (and pagan) antiquity, it does not appear that John Collett Ryland authored any hymns. While he was close friends with popular hymn writers like Benjamin Beddome and John Newton and even wrote a preface for Maria De Fleury's *Divine Poems and Essays*

CHAPTER EIGHT

In 1759, Ryland assumed the pastorate of College Lane and moved his young family to Northampton where he ministered for the next three decades. His preaching ministry at College Lane (1759–1786) was fruitful—the church was twice expanded in order to accommodate the growth in membership.[9] Undoubtedly one of his greatest strengths, however, was his cultivation of catholic friendships. Ryland maintained close personal relationships with Whitefield, as well as Anglican pastors John Newton (1725–1807) and Augustus Toplady (1740–1778).[10] Congregationalist William Jay (1769–1853), who knew Ryland in his later years in Northampton, commented that Ryland

> was intimate with Mr. Whitefield and Mr. Rowland Hill and much attached to many other preachers less systematically orthodox than himself; and labored as opportunity offered, with them. He was, indeed, a lover of all good men and, while many talked of candour, he exercised it. Though he was a firm Baptist, he was no friend to bigotry or exclusiveness.[11]

Growing up in this rich environment, John Ryland, Jr. was formatively shaped by his father's strong commitment to Reformed doctrine, his God-centered zeal for learning across multiple disciplines, and exposure to

---

on Various Subjects (which included several of her hymns). Neither Rippon, Sedgwick, or Gadsby mention hymns authored by the elder Ryland. See Maria De Fleury, *Divine Poems and Essays, on Various Subjects in Three Parts* (London: T. Wilkins, 1791); John Rippon and Isaac Watts, *A Selection of Hymns from the Best Authors: Including a Great Number of Originals Intended to e an Appendix to Dr. Watt's Psalms and Hymns* (Boston, MA: S.T. Usick, 1801); William Gadsby, J. Hart, and J. C. Philpot, *A Selection of Hymns for Public Worship* (Conrad, MT: Trinagle Press, 1998); Sedgwick, *Hymns and Verses of Sacred Subjects*.

9 Haykin, *One Heart and One Soul*, 72.
10 According to John Ryland, Jr., Whitefield came to see his father in September of 1767 during one of his last preaching tours in Britain. See "Extracts from the Diary of the Late Rev. Dr Ryland," *American Baptist Magazine* 12, no. 5 (May 1832): 134.
11 William Jay, *The Autobiography of William Jay* (New York: R. Carter & Brothers, 1855), 293. See Haykin, *One Heart and One Soul*, 73.

his father's congenial friendships with evangelical Calvinists. The younger Ryland's unusual giftedness became evident early in his youth.[12] Not long after taking up residence at College Lane, John Collett Ryland wrote:

> John is now eleven years and seven months old. He has read Genesis in Hebrew five times through; he read through the Greek Testament before nine years old; he can read Horace and Virgil; he has read through *Telemachus* in French; he has read Pope's *Homer* in eleven volumes, Dryden's *Virgil* in three volumes, Rollins' *Ancient History* in ten volumes; and he knows the pagan mythology surprisingly.[13]

This description reflects the elder Ryland's "ardent passion for educating his pupils in a broad range of subjects" and is undoubtedly what caused Grant Gordon to label Ryland Jr. a "child prodigy."[14] Ryland's broad educational formation would be one of the many assets valued by Bristol Academy when they called him as president in 1791. During his tenure, Ryland taught Hebrew, Greek, Latin, theology, church history, rhetoric and logic.[15] Robert Hall, Jr. (1764–1839) noted that Ryland was a "scholar from his infancy" and, in addition to his remarkable attainment in Hebrew, "had a general acquaintance with the principles of science" and a "passion for natural science."[16] Hall wrote that Ryland was "extremely addicted to study

---

12   According to his son (Jonathan Edwards Ryland), Ryland took an early interest in Hebrew and was able to read Psalm 23 at the age of four. See Ryland, *Pastoral Memorials*, 2:9.
13   Quoted in A. C. Underwood, *A History of the English Baptists* (London: Kingsgate, 1956), 168.
14   Gordon, "John Ryland, Jr. (1753–1825)," 77. Robert Hall mentions that Ryland read a chapter of the Hebrew Bible (Genesis) to James Hervey when he was only four years old. See Robert Hall, *The Works of Robert Hall, A.M.*, ed. Olinthus Gregory, 12th ed., vol. 1 (London: H. G. Bohn, 1855), 390. These volumes of Hall's works will be abbreviated as *WRH*.
15   Gordon, "John Ryland, Jr. (1753–1825)," 85.
16   Hall, *WRH*, 1:404.

and meditation" and that "his reading was various and extensive."[17] But, despite his great learning, Ryland was known as a remarkably humble man; "his mental opulence was much greater than his modesty would permit him to reveal; his disposition to conceal his attainments being nearly as strong as that of some men to display them."[18] Humility was, in fact, "the most remarkable feature of his character ... he might most truly be said, in the language of scripture, to be *clothed* with it."[19]

While the younger Ryland frequently heard the gospel as a child, it was not until 1765, when he was 12 years old, that he began to feel a concern about his spiritual condition. Prompted by his friends' interest in spiritual matters, Ryland searched his own heart. In the account of his conversion, Ryland writes that he could not "suppose but I had head knowledge of these things but now I trust I knew it indeed and I endeavored to pray for mercy."[20] But there was no quick resolution; a recurring theme of his narrative is the absence of assurance of salvation despite much exposure to the Word. His agonies over his eternal state continued for the better part of the next three years, Ryland only beginning to find relief through consistent application of gospel promises in 1769. It seems that his struggles, while not unparalleled with other young men, were particularly intertwined with a high Calvinist understanding of eternal justification. If his election or reprobation was eternally fixed, all his own efforts were vain.[21]

Ryland nevertheless pushed past this period. He banded together with a

---

17 Hall, *WRH*, 1:404.
18 Hall, *WRH*, 1:404.
19 Hall, *WRH*, 1:393.
20 See "The Experience of John Ryland, Jr. as wrote by himself in a letter to Thomas R. T.; Dated February 23, 1770" in H. Wheeler Robinson, "The Experience of John Ryland," *The Baptist Quarterly* 4, no. 1 (January 1928): 18.
21 In a versed catechism that Ryland composed in 1769 (see below, n.26) he answers the question "is union a consequence of faith"?: "No this was in election done/God put and chose us in his son/Cause we're united, faith he gives/That in communion we may live." Quoted in D. Bruce Hindmarsh, *John Newton and the English Evangelical Tradition: Between the Conversions of Wesley and Wilberforce* (Oxford: Oxford University Press, 1996), 148.

group of other boys serious about spirituality and soon became the group's leader. His appetite for learning was evidenced in the publication of several poetical works in the succeeding years.[22] Over the course of 1768 or 1769, Ryland also read through a number of volumes in his father's theological library, including the works of John Gill and John Brine. In May of 1770, he preached at College Lane for the first time during the Thursday service. He was received with such a degree of approbation that he was asked to preach eleven additional times that year. When his father fell ill in January of 1771, Ryland was asked to preach for a Sunday service and, by the end of the following summer, the congregation had affirmed his call to ministry. Ryland was eighteen.[23] He would serve alongside his father until his ordination in 1781, when he succeeded him as pastor of College Lane.

Ryland inherited more than a strong commitment to Reformed doctrine and an appetite for expansive learning. Owing to his father's remarkable network of relationships, Ryland gained an early ally who would be instrumental in his maturation as an evangelical leader. In January of 1768, John Newton had invited Ryland Jr. to visit him in London. Despite being thirty years his senior, Newton struck up an intentional friendship with the younger Ryland. Beginning in 1771, Newton and Ryland began exchanging letters, a practice that continued until Newton's death nearly four decades later.[24] While Ryland's poetic efforts emerged before his first contact with

---

22 Ryland apparently published two anonymous works, certainly at the prompting of his zealous but proud father, *An Oration by a School-boy Twelve Years of Age, Composed for the Juvenile Philosophical Society* (1765) and *The Plagues of Egypt, by a School-boy Thirteen Years of Age* (1765). Three years later he published a twenty-three-page *Compendious View of the Principal Truths of the Glorious Gospel of Christ for the Use of Youth, The Divine Inspiration and Authority of the Holy Scriptures Asserted and Approved: A Poem* and *Perseverance: A Poem* (1769), as well as an appendix to one of his father's works. See Timothy Whelan, "John Ryland at School: Two Societies in Northhampton Boarding Schools," *The Baptist Quarterly* 40, no. 2 (April 2003): 110.

23 Gordon, *Wise Counsel*, 8–9.

24 Despite Newton's contribution to evangelical hymnody and his indefatigable support of the abolitionist cause, perhaps his most lasting impact was through his remarkable ministry of letter-writing—to John Ryland and countless other evangelical leaders and laypersons during his lengthy ministry. Grant Gordon has collected the 83 extant letters from Newton to Ryland in *Wise Counsel*. Newton also serves as a foil for Ryland's

Newton, their correspondence underscores their shared interest in hymnody.[25] When Newton published the *Olney Hymns*, he sent Ryland an early copy.[26] Frequently in his correspondence with the younger man, Newton infers Ryland's agreement regarding the power and utility of hymns to communicate meaningful truth.[27] While evidence for direct influence is modest, Newton's remarkable influence in Ryland's life suggests that in this area, too, Ryland learned much from his older friend.

Thus, John Ryland's unique spiritual and intellectual development and the catholic friendships inherited from his father, powerfully shaped him as a pastor, educator, friend, and poet. His life was marked by remarkable piety, keen powers of observation, a command of history and literature, and a practiced ability to communicate—features that would equip him to be one of the more influential pastors of the eighteenth century. Among his numerous legacies was his hymnody. Here, too, Ryland was heir to a great tradition.

Benjamin Keach (1640–1704) had been the first among Particular Baptists to introduce hymn singing into services on the Lord's Day.[28] He began by inserting a hymn after the celebration of the Lord's Supper and,

---

experience with his father. In his spiritual autobiography mentioned above, Ryland Jr. hints that the elder Ryland could be insensitive. At a moment of spiritual crisis, Ryland's father misreads his son's tenderness and sends him home from school (Robinson, "The Experience of John Ryland."). Robert Hall notes in his funeral sermon that Ryland was subjected to "an injudicious mode of treatment in early life" and witnessed in his father "an excess of vehemence, a careless intrepidity of temper" that affected him for the rest of his life (Hall, *WRH*, 1:401). Gordon observes that later Ryland "often turned to Newton, rather than his own father, for paternal advice (Gordon, "John Ryland, Jr. (1753–1825)," 81.

25 Only Newton's letters to Ryland have survived.
26 Gordon, *Wise Counsel*, 127, 131.
27 Gordon, *Wise Counsel*, 138.
28 Early English Presbyterians and Congregationalists were convinced that only Psalms should be sung in corporate worship. Haykin notes that Calvinistic Baptists prior to Keach believed that worship should not be songless and that hymns should be used in addition to Psalms (Michael A. G. Haykin, *Kiffin, Knollys and Keach: Rediscovering English Baptist Heritage* [Leeds: Reformation Today, 1996], 91).

over time, extended the practice to allow a hymn every Sunday.[29] Keach eventually produced a substantial hymnbook for congregational use and continued to encourage hymn-singing despite the increased persecution of Dissenters from the state church under the Test Acts of 1673 and 1678.[30] Others, like Isaac Marlow, publicly attacked the practice as a distraction from the simplicity of Puritan worship, especially in the way that hymns might introduce the formalism that dissenting churches had long fought to escape.[31] Keach's response in *The Breach Repair'd in God's Worship* (1691) effectively demonstrated that, rather than being a cause for formalism, the singing of hymns was actually a means to spiritual renewal.[32] Open debate on the issue ultimately had the effect of encouraging more Baptist churches to adopt the practice.[33]

Hymnody especially flourished among Baptists because of the way it brought biblical reality and personal experience to expression in public worship. Particular Baptists saw the composition and singing of hymns as obedience to Paul's command to the church in Ephesus (Ephesians 5:19). Employing hymns in public worship rehearsed biblical doctrine, reminded congregants of God's wisdom and goodness, and gave expression to their heartfelt experience of the Christian life. E. A. Payne rightly observed that in this way the hymn book provided for Dissenting churches what the Book of Common Prayer provided for the Anglican church.[34]

---

29 Horton Davies, *Worship and Theology in England from Andrews to Baxter and Fox, 1603-1690* (Princeton, NJ: Princeton University Press, 1970), 561.

30 Benjamin Keach, *Spiritual Melody, Containing near Three Hundred Sacred Hymns* (London: John Hancock, 1691). See J. R. Watson, *The English Hymn: A Critical and Historical Study* (Oxford: Oxford University Press, 1997), 111.

31 Isaac Marlow's *A Brief Discourse against Singing* (1690) offered five arguments against the singing of hymns, the most significant of which was that hymns were in effect no different than reading a written prayer. See Haykin, *Kiffin, Knollys and Keach*, 95.

32 Haykin, *Kiffin, Knollys and Keach*, 94.

33 Roger Hayden, *Continuity and Change: Evangelical Calvinism among Eighteenth-Century Baptist Ministers Trained at Bristol Academy, 1690-1791* (Chipping Norton, UK: Nigel Lynn, 2006), 159.

34 Earnest Alexander Payne, *The Free Church Tradition in the Life of England* (London: SCM Press, 1951), 79.

By the middle of the eighteenth century, evangelical hymnody was, perhaps, in its most productive period. The growing catalog of hymns for public worship included not only hymns by Congregationalist Isaac Watts (1674–1748), Anglican Augustus Toplady (1740–1788), and Methodists John (1703–1791) and Charles Wesley (1707–1788), but the hymns of Seventh-Day Baptist Samuel Stennett (1727–1795) and Particular Baptists Anne Steele (1717–1778), Benjamin Beddome (1717–1795), and John Rippon (1751–1836).[35] Ryland not only grew up in this rich age of hymnody, his experience of church life was saturated by it. The College Lane Baptist church in Northampton was so enthusiastic about hymn singing, it had its own "singing society." In 1762, Ryland Sr. recorded the articles of agreement for the group in his notebook. They stated:

> After deliberate consideration, we are convinced that singing of Psalms, hymns, and Spiritual Songs is an ordinance of God in the Christian dispensation and ought to be performed in the best manner to the Divine Honor and to the Edification of ourselves and others.[36]

Ryland Jr's remarkably rich environment—a family devoted to evangelical piety and intellectual depth, a diet of classical and theological literature, an ecumenical and gospel-centered relational network, and a local fellowship devoted to worship in word and song—amply furnished him to take up the pen to express praise in prose and verse.

"We Sing Thy Love": The hymns and verse of John Ryland

In such a context, it is no surprise that Ryland wrote and published his first hymn when he was sixteen.[37] Two years later, in 1771, he published an

---

35 For a concise treatment of the development of hymnody among Particular Baptists, see Hayden, *Continuity and Change*, 158–178.
36 Quoted in Hayden, *Continuity and Change*, 157.
37 Gordon, *Wise Counsel*, 129.

additional thirty-six hymns in *Serious Essays on the Truths of the Glorious Gospel*.[38] Ryland published several more in the *Gospel Magazine* throughout the 1770s.[39] While Isaac Watts' hymns formed the repertoire for many Baptist congregations, John Rippon recognized that Ryland's songs helped address the breadth of subjects needed in public worship. The first edition of his *A Selection of Hymns from the Best Authors* (1787) included four of Ryland's hymns alongside the previously unpublished work of numerous others. Eventually, seven others would appear in later editions.[40]

After his father's death in 1823, Jonathan Edwards Ryland (1798–1866) published two volumes of Ryland's works, the second containing 25 hymns.[41] The most extensive publication of Ryland's hymns, however, came with Samuel Sedgwick's collection entitled *Hymns and Verses on Sacred Subjects* (1862), which included 99 hymns and poetic compositions.[42] William Gadsby's *A Selection of Hymns for Public Worship*, first published in 1814 and expanded through 1930, retains the two most popular Ryland hymns, "O Lord I would delight in thee" and "Sovereign Ruler of the Skies."[43] In the nineteenth century, C. H. Spurgeon modified Rippon's

---

38 John Ryland, *Serious Essays on the Truths of the Glorious Gospel and the Various Branches of Vital Experience.* (London: J. Pasham, 1775).

39 Gordon, *Wise Counsel*, 129.

40 David W Music and Paul Akers Richardson, *I Will Sing the Wondrous Story: A History of Baptist Hymnody in North America* (Macon, GA: Mercer University Press, 2008), 52–53. Music writes, "The result was the most inclusive anthology to this time. About a quarter of the 588 hymns in the first edition were making their first appearance in print. Many others had been published only in the collections of the authors, and fewer than twenty percent of the items (110) had appeared in Ash and Evans's Bristol Collection, published less than two decades previously. By Rippon's own account, some 300 hymns received their first hymnal publication in his book." Rippon studied at the Bristol Baptist Academy under Caleb Evans (1737–1791) who along with John Ash (1724–1779) published *A Collection of Hymns Adopted to Public Worship* in 1769—the first Baptist hymn book.

41 Ryland, *Pastoral Memorials*.

42 Sedgwick, *Hymns and Verses on Sacred Subjects*. The library of Bristol College possesses a manuscript of 126 pages, which I was unable access for this essay and which contains 84 of Ryland's hymns that Jonathan Edwards Ryland gave to his niece Caroline Dent on the 107th anniversary of John Ryland's birthday (January 26, 1860).

43 See hymns 64 and 247 in Gadsby, Hart, and Philpot, *A Selection of Hymns for*

CHAPTER EIGHT

Selection for the people of the New Park Street Chapel, and retained four of Ryland's hymns.[44] Several of Ryland's hymns were included in the first American Baptist hymnal, published in 1843.[45] While some of his hymns are certainly "awful poetry" and "lack poetic worth," the appearance of Ryland's hymns in collections nearly a century after his death is evidence for how many people were moved by his verse.[46]

Public Worship. See also Robert W. Oliver, *History of the English Calvinistic Baptists, 1771-1892: From John Gill to C.H. Spurgeon* (Edinburgh: Banner of Truth Trust, 2006), 193.

44 The included hymns: "Psalm 130" (p. 104), "Sovereign Ruler of the Skies" (p. 150), "O Lord I would delight in Thee" (p. 431), and "Look down my soul on Hell's domains" (p. 541). See C. H. Spurgeon, *Our Own Hymn-Book: A Collection of Psalms and Hymns for Public, Social, and Private Worship* (London: Passmore & Alabaster, 1866). In the preface, Spurgeon wrote "Despite the judgment of many to the contrary we believe that the store of spiritual songs contained in these two volumes [Rippon's *Selection* and Watts' *Psalms and Hymns*] is not excelled even if equaled by any compilation extant and we should most probably have been very well content with those books had it not been for difficulties connected with the remarkably complex arrangement of their contents" (Spurgeon, *Our Own Hymn-Book*, v). Spurgeon's critique of Rippon is equally true of Sedgwick or the collection in *Pastoral Memorials*. It is very difficult to know which of Ryland's hymns besides those that were part of the Rippon or Gadsby collections were sung in corporate worship.

45 S. F. Smith and Baron Stow, *The Psalmist: A New Collection of Hymns for the Use of the Baptist Churches* (Boston, MA: Gould, Kendall, and Lincoln, 1843). Three hymns attributed to Ryland are included in this volume ("Gird thy Sword on, Mighty Saviour" [#868], "In all my Lord's appointed ways" [#812], and "O Lord I would delight in Thee" [#538]). The first is a selection of several stanzas from *Hymn XVI* in J. E. Ryland's collection in *Pastoral Memorials*. Though the hymn did not appear in Rippon's collection, Andrew Reed included it in his *The Hymn Book: Prepared from Dr. Watt's Psalms and Hymns and Other Authors with Some Originals* (London: Ward and Co., 1842), though there it is attributed anonymously. The second hymn is based on Ryland's longer hymn "When Abraham's Servant to Procure," which first appeared in the *Gospel Magazine* in May of 1775. The final hymn was first included in Rippon's *Selection* in 1798.

46 Haykin, *Kiffin, Knollys and Keach*, 96; Robert H. Young, "The History of Baptist Hymnody in England from 1612 to 1800" (Doctor of Musical Arts dissertation, University of Southern California, 1959), 84. John Julian's *Dictionary of Hymnology* recorded that 13 of Ryland's hymns were in common usage in 1907, though he noted that Ryland's hymns "lack poetry and passion and are not likely to be largely drawn upon for future hymnals" (John Julian, ed., *A Dictionary of Hymnology*, Rev. ed. [London: John Murray, 1908], 983–984). Ryland was in good company, however. Hayden uses the word "appalling" to describe some of Keach's lyrics: "Keach's efforts at hymn writing were very poor" (Hayden, *Continuity and Change*, 159).

Though none of his available works describe his motivation for hymn writing, two observations can be made.[47] First, it is evident that his hymns were the overflow of a heart that had tasted the goodness of God and seen his beauty. Ryland seemed to experience this everywhere—not only in the Bible and in the created world, but also (even) in classical literature.[48] Thus, much of his hymnody was attentive to raised affections and the importance of inward experience in singing:

Sweet was the hour and sweet was the place
But sweeter was the love:
When I first met the God of grace,
And did his kindness prove.

So comfortably did he speak
And swore eternal love:
Sure nothing could be half so sweet,
Except the joys above.
My soul began to sing at once

---

47 The sermons collected in *Pastoral Memorials*, however, do give a sense of Ryland's expectation that singing is to be part of worship in the church now and in the presence of God forever: "But when the nations of the redeemed are brought together, surely they will strive to out-sing the angelic hosts." See his "The Pleasantness of Religion," John Ryland, *Pastoral Memorials Selected from the Manuscripts of the Late Rev. John Ryland D.D. of Bristol with a Memoir of the Author in Two Volumes*, vol. 1 (London: B.J. Holdsworth, 1826), 124.

48 The collections contain several hymns that Ryland apparently wrote as a response to classical literature. The first hymn in *Pastoral Memorials* (#15 in *Hymns and Verses*), a triumphant song celebrating the absolute sovereignty of God, is based on Horace's *Epistles* I.1 "when you alone bear the burden of so many and such great responsibilities" (Ryland, *Pastoral Memorials*, 2:423). Hymn 16 in *Hymns and Verses* is inspired by Virgil's *Ecologue* and its description of Daphnis' epitaph: "A well-kept herd's guardian, more well-kept himself" (*Ecologue* V. 44). Daphnis was the "inventor" of pastoral poetry and Virgil's *Ecologue* is the great example of such in the Latin tradition. Ryland's "Thou Keeper of a lovely flock" is a beautiful hymn displaying Christ as the great shepherd (Sedgwick, *Hymns and Verses on Sacred Subjects*, 18). There is even a hymn, written near the end of his life, in imitation of "Icelandic Poetry" (Sedgwick, *Hymns and Verses on Sacred Subjects*, 102–103).

In strains unknown before.
I wanted then a seraph's voice;
To praise my Saviour more.[49]

Here Ryland surpasses the hymnody of Keach, who was "long on objective praise and doctrine," but not experimental.[50] Ryland, in contrast, frequently speaks in terms of Christian experience with a particular focus on the affections. Hall wrote that Ryland's love for Christ "was an awful love, such as the beatific vision may be supposed to inspire, where the worshippers veil their faces in that presence in which they rejoice with ecstatic joy."[51] Thus, Ryland's hymnody often expresses the delight in seeing and knowing Christ in Edwardsean language:[52]

If I from others differ aught
Lord, 'twas thy grace the difference wrought
If I one holy wish have known
Thy Spirit gave that wish I own.

I cannot pay the thanks I owe
For tasting once thy love below:

---

49   Hymn 2, written in 1775. Sedgwick, *Hymns and Verses on Sacred Subjects*, 2–3.
50   Haykin, *Kiffin, Knollys and Keach*, 84.
51   Robert Hall, Jr., *A Sermon Occasioned by the Death of the Rev. John Ryland, D.D.* in *WRH*, 5:56.
52   It is likely that Ryland was the first of the Fuller circle to discover Edwards. In his biography of Fuller, Ryland notes that he passed along sermons discussing the distinction between natural and moral ability to Hall in 1776 (John Ryland, *The Work of Faith, the Labor of Love, and the Patience of Hope, Illustrated in the Life and Death of the Rev. Andrew Fuller: Late Pastor of the Baptist Church at Kettering, and Secretary to the Baptist Missionary Society*, 2nd ed. [Charlestown, MA: Samuel Etheridge, 1818], 2, note 2). Ryland also includes Fuller's narrative describing his first encounters with Ryland and Robert Hall Sr. in 1776. Fuller notes that both Hall and Ryland were familiar with Edwards (*Work of Faith, the Labor of Love, and the Patience of Hope*, 28). In *Serious Remarks*, Ryland seems to indicate that his reading of Edwards preceded Hall's reading of the same (John Ryland, *Serious Remarks on the Different Representations of Evangelical Doctrine by the Professed Friends of the Gospel*, vol. 2 [Bristol: J.G. Fuller, 1818], 19).

Yet cannot rest 'till I, above
Shall feast forever on thy love.

The smallest drop of precious grace
Demands a ceaseless song of praise:
Yet largest draughts from mercy's store
But make me long and pant for more

The heav'nly sweets of holy joy
Always delight but never cloy;
More holiness, O Lord, impart,
Till I am holy as thou art.[53]

Clearly, other hymn writers also propelled Ryland into expressing in song such longings for Christ. In a hymn with strong resemblance to Anne Steele's "Thou Lovely Source of True Delight," Ryland writes:

Shine out, eternal sun,
Enflame my lukewarm soul;
Breathe heav'nly wind, until my spark
Blaze forth without control.

Reign, Savior! in my breast,
Unrivall'd and alone,
And hurl down ev'ry idol thence
That dares attempt thy throne.

Of all the things in heav'n
The love of Christ is best;

---

53 Hymn 5, written in 1775. Sedgwick, *Hymns and Verses on Sacred Subjects*, 7. See also hymns 4, 36, and 61.

CHAPTER EIGHT

And this till heav'n to me is given
I cannot, will not rest.[54]

Second, like Keach and many of his own contemporaries, Ryland saw the value of hymns as an aid to corporate worship, for the exposition of Scripture, and for the edification of the church.[55] Beginning with Keach, Baptist pastors developed the practice of writing hymns to accompany and reinforce sermons and for special occasions of public worship such as baptisms, celebration of the Lord's Supper and prayer meetings. Anglican John Newton, Ryland's close friend, was well known for these occasional hymns.[56] While Ryland also composed occasional hymns, he also wrote hymns from 24 books of the Bible.[57] Nearly half of the collected hymns are direct reflections on Scriptural text. It is likely that he often used these hymns to reinforce and celebrate the sermon text.[58]

Whether to raise affections for Christ, to celebrate Christian doctrine, or to reinforce the meaning of Scripture, singing was aimed to edify the church. Ryland wrote hymns to help the church corporately celebrate the

---

54   The first stanza of hymn 49 (no authorship date given) in Sedgwick, *Hymns and Verses on Sacred Subjects* reads: Thou sovereign of my soul/who unseen I adore/I trust thy love has reached my heart/but fain would love thee more (Sedgwick, *Hymns and Verses on Sacred Subjects*, 52–53). This is resonant of Steele's "Thou lovely source of true delight," published in 1760: "Thou lovely source of true delight/whom unseen I adore/unveil thy beauties to my sight/that I might love thee more." Several days before his own death, Ryland recited the lines of Augustus Toplady's "Anticipation of Glory": "When he makes his jewels up/not a saint shall wanting be/O my God, fulfill my hope/and with them reckon me" (Ryland, *Pastoral Memorials*, 2:83).

55   Watson, *The English Hymn*, 111; Haykin, *Kiffin, Knollys and Keach*, 83.

56   Hindmarsh, *John Newton and the English Evangelical Tradition*, 93, 258–260.

57   For hymns related to special meetings, see #52 "To be sung at a church meeting," #60 "For the Lord's Supper," #76 "A Baptismal Hymn," and on his friendship with Fuller, Carey, and Sutcliff, see #94 in Sedgwick, *Hymns and Verses on Sacred Subjects*.

58   Given the limited number of sermons available for consultation in this paper (the 150 available in the two volumes of *Pastoral Memorials*), it is difficult to say with certainty that this was his practice. Nevertheless, several hymns from *Hymns and Verses on Sacred Subjects* demonstrate a strong connection: 1) Sermon 4 on Deuteronomy 8:2 & Hymn 35; 2) Sermon 95 on Romans 15:30 & Hymn 77; 3) Sermon 139 on Hebrews 12:2 & Hymn 33; 4) Sermon 45 on Ezekiel 33:11 & Hymn 34.

glory of Christ (#11 "Kingdom of Christ"), remember his sovereign care (#28 "Sovereign Ruler of the Skies"), fan affections for him into flame (#27 "O Lord!, I would delight in Thee", #57 "To thee I lift my waking eyes"), comfort suffering friends (#13, "Lord, teach a little child to pray"), endure amidst various trials (#45 "Of trials I meet by the way", #69 "Our God how perfect is his way", #52), warn against the dangers of sin (#881 "Look down my soul on hell's domains"), and remember its mission to unevangelized millions (#10 "For the Success of the Gospel", #31 "Rejoice the Saviour Reigns").[59]

Ryland also had a keen sense of the Spirit's work, both preaching and writing hymns to inspire deeper delight in God's triune operations.[60] Ryland's deep passion for the evangelization of the lost, evidenced in his tireless efforts in the Baptist Missionary Society, permeate his hymns:

> From ev'ry nation, every tongue
> A remnant must to him belong;
> Nor can there be too vile a race,
> To furnish trophies of his grace.
>
> Exert that pow'r which could subdue
> The furious, slaughter-breathing Jew,
> And made him in thy cause become
> Victorious over Greece and Rome.

---

[59] Hymns are numbered and titled (by first line, unless titled) as they are in the index in *Hymns and Verses on Sacred Subjects*. The one exception, however, is #881 "Look down my soul on hell's domains" which appears in Spurgeon's *Our Own Hymnbook,* but does not appear in either *Hymns and Verses on Sacred Subjects* or *Pastoral Memorials*. When Andrew Fuller's young daughter was suffering from a terminal sickness, Ryland wrote a hymn entitled "teach a little child to pray" which she sang in the hours before her death (Hymn 13, Sedgwick, *Hymns and Verses on Sacred Subjects*, 15).

[60] Hymn 77, "The Love of the Spirit I sing," written in 1796 (Sedgwick, *Hymns and Verses on Sacred Subjects*, 81–82). For Ryland's theology of the Spirit see Michael Haykin, "'The Sum of All Good': John Ryland, Jr. and the Doctrine of the Holy Spirit," *Churchman* 103, no. 4 (1989): 332–353.

CHAPTER EIGHT

Now, Lord, before thy servants go,
Let God himself the trumpet blow;
Hasten the gospel jubilee,
Which bids a captive world be free.[61]

And Ryland sought to promote this vision beyond Broadmead Baptist. Beginning in 1785, Baptist congregations across the country had set aside the first Monday of the month to "unite in imploring" the special blessing of God for a revival of religion at home and "for the spreading of the gospel in foreign parts."[62] In 1798, Ryland recruited the ministers of the Independent, Methodist, and Presbyterian churches in Bristol to gather all of their people together once a month, rotating locations, "to show their union in one grand object, *the success of the gospel.*"[63] The chief difficulty they encountered, however, was that almost every congregation was using a different hymnbook. Ryland, therefore, set out to produce a hymn book for their congregations to share that would include a selection "with which each Congregation was best acquainted, that were most appropriate to our purpose" and that "might enable us to combine pertinence and variety." The 98-page hymn book begins with several hymns of prayer "imploring the Divine Presence and Aid in our Public Meetings." Further sections categorized hymns under the headings of "On Christian Fellowship,"

---

61   Hymn 10, Sedgwick, *Hymns and Verses on Sacred Subjects*, 13 written in 1795.
62   John Ryland, *Hymns Intended for the Use of United Congregations of Bristol at Their Monthly Prayer Meeting for the Success of the Gospel at Home and Abroad* (Bristol: N. Biggs, 1798), 3.
63   Ryland, *Hymns Intended for the Use of United Congregations of Bristol*, 3. Eight Bristol ministers were signatories to the prefatory letter: Joseph Bradford (c.1748–1808), a close friend of John Wesley who oversaw Bristol's "New Room"; John Sharp who was involved in opening both the Portland and Ebenezer chapels; John Prichard (1771–1814) who served Bristol's Portland Chapel and promoted missions work in Sierra Leone; William Moore a Methodist itinerant preacher and part of the Bristol Methodist Society; John Hey (1734–1815), pastor of Castle Green Congregational Church; Thomas Roberts (1780–1841) who later became pastor of Bristol's King Street Baptist Church which, in 1798, was the Methodist chapel in which Moore and Sharp were serving; Robert Cottam, a Methodist itinerant in 1798, who later returned to the Anglican church; and James Barnet, a junior colleague among the Methodist itinerants.

"Universal Praise," "For the General Spread of the Gospel," "For the Jews," "For the Revival of Religion at Home," "For the Nation," as well as hymns to be sung at the conclusion of the service. Testifying to the familiarity of Ryland's work, the following hymns of Ryland are among the book's forty-six hymns: "Here Assembled in Thy Name," "Hosanna to the King," "How Many Years Hath Man Been Driven," "Let Us Sing the King, Messiah," "Now Let the Slumbering Church Awake," and "Rejoice the Saviour Reigns."[64]

Conclusion

As a pastor, Ryland understood the formative importance of singing in the local church. Hymns brought the truth of Scripture to expression in fresh and memorable ways. Ryland also understood how the use of familiar hymns served the unity of the church by reminding Christians from different evangelical traditions of their shared convictions, calling, and mission. Underneath it all, Ryland saw poetic effort as the happy overflow of a life transformed by the glorious grace of God:

> Ah! I shall soon be dying,
> Time swiftly glides away;
> But on my Lord relying,
> I hail the happy day—
>
> The day when I must enter
> Upon a world unknown;
> My helpless soul I venture
> On Jesus Christ alone.
> He once a spotless victim
> Upon Mt. Calv'ry bled!

---

64 Ryland, *Hymns Intended for the Use of United Congregations of Bristol*, 62, 28, 52, 57, 42, and 55.

Jehovah did afflict him
And bruise him in my stead.

Hence all my hope arises,
Unworthy as I am
My soul most surely prizes
The sin atoning Lamb

To him by grace united
I joy in him alone
And now, by faith, delighted
Behold him on his throne

There he is interceding
For all who on him rest
The grace from him proceeding
Shall waft me to his breast.

Then with the saints in glory
The grateful song I'll raise
And chant my blissful story
In high seraphic lays.[65]

---

65   Hymn 12, Ryland, *Hymns Intended for the Use of United Congregations of Bristol*, 14–15.

9

Forty years of friendship: The letters of John Ryland, Jr. to John Sutcliff

LON GRAHAM

Introduction

One of the tasks of historians is to help those in the present understand the people, places, movements, and events of the past. The limitation of this pursuit presents itself readily: historians lack access to the space in which much of history takes place, which is in personal conversations and in-person interactions. Public records and published works are immensely helpful in shedding light on the past, but, if a person thinks over their own life, they must realize that some of the most important things in their life will be unknown and unknowable to future historians.

We are not left completely bereft, however, as historians can get close to that space through the study of private correspondence. In letters, people show at least some of the intimacy and private moments that are found in conversations and in-person interactions. For this reason, Grant Gordon's work as a historian has proven invaluable, as he has published and provided commentary upon vital correspondence which helps to shed light on

Baptist and evangelical history.¹ The present writer has benefited greatly from his scholarship and will remain indebted to him for paving the way.

In "Gordonian" style, then, the present essay will investigate previously unpublished correspondence between John Ryland Jr and one of his noteworthy friends, John Sutcliff. Ryland was the pastor of the College Lane Baptist Church in Northampton (1781–1793) and, later, the pastor of Broadmead Baptist Church in Bristol and the President of the Bristol Baptist Academy (1793–1825). Sutcliff served for most of his ministry as the pastor of the Baptist church in Olney (1775–1814). Along with William Carey, Andrew Fuller, and others, Ryland and Sutcliff founded the Baptist Missionary Society.

Ryland and Sutcliff met in 1773 and began their correspondence the same year. So important was their meeting that Ryland, when he revised his diaries later in life, kept an entry in which he recalled the date and occasion of his first meeting Sutcliff.² In addition, Ryland's younger contemporary Christopher Anderson spoke of the relationships of Ryland, Fuller, and Sutcliff in the most glowing terms as a kind of ideal Christian friendship, describing their union as being "a little band of brothers … who should leave behind them a proof of how much may be accomplished in consequence of the union of only a few upon earth in spreading Christianity."³ This essay will examine Ryland's side of the epistolary conversation,

---

1   See, for example, Grant Gordon, ed., *Wise Counsel: John Newton's Letters to John Ryland, Jr* (Carlisle, PA: Banner of Truth Trust, 2009); idem, "The Call of Dr John Ryland Jr," *Baptist Quarterly* 34.5 (January 1992): 214–227; and idem, "A Revealing Unpublished Letter of George Whitefield to John Collett Ryland," *Baptist Quarterly* 47.2 (April 2016): 65–75.

2   John Ryland, *Autograph Reminiscences*, Bristol Baptist College Archives, 47. The date was July 22, 1773. Ryland was only twenty years old, and Sutcliff was still at student at the Bristol Baptist Academy. Sutcliff had come to Ryland's hometown of Northampton to see Ryland's father, John Collett Ryland, who was then the pastor of the College Lane Baptist Church.

3   Quoted in Hugh Anderson, ed., *The Life and Letters of Christopher Anderson* (Edinburgh: W. P. Kennedy, 1854), 379; cf. Michael A. G. Haykin, "'A Little Band of Brothers': Friendship in the Life of Andrew Fuller—An Essay on the Bicentennial of His Death," *Journal for Baptist Theology and Ministry* 12.2 (Fall 2015): 2–3. To these three, Anderson adds William Carey and Samuel Pearce. Pearce is often added to these men,

as Ryland's letters are more numerous and available. It is admitted at the outset that this presents a limitation to the study. However, Ryland's letters are sufficient to show the kind of relationship the two men had. The twenty-five letters from Ryland to Sutcliff are contained in five different archives: the Angus Library and Archive, Regent's Park College, Oxford University; the John Rylands Library at the University of Manchester; the Beinecke Rare Book and Manuscript Library at Yale University; the American Baptist Historical Society in Atlanta, Georgia; and the Historical Society of Pennsylvania in Philadelphia, Pennsylvania. While some of these letters have been used in previous research and publications, they have never been brought together to give a more complete portrait of the relationship between these two men.[4]

---

though he died young and only a few years into the existence of the BMS, indicating the profound impact he had on those around him. For more on Pearce, see Andrew Fuller, *Memoirs of the Late Rev. Samuel Pearce, A. M.* (Clipstone: J. W. Morris, 1800); Samuel Pearce, *Missionary Correspondence: Containing Extracts of Letters from the Late Mr. Samuel Pearce, to the Missionaries in India* (London: Gardiner, 1814); Jason Edwin Dees, "The Way to True Excellence: The Spirituality of Samuel Pearce" (PhD dissertation, Southern Baptist Theological Seminary, 2015); Michael A. G. Haykin and Jerry Slate Jr, *Loving God and Neighbor with Samuel Pearce* (Bellingham, WA: Lexham Press, 2019).

4   Research into Ryland's correspondence, while not voluminous, is substantial. In addition to Gordon's work on Ryland, other studies of Ryland's correspondence include: L. G. Champion, "The Letters of John Newton to John Ryland," *Baptist Quarterly* 27.4 (October 1977): 157–163; Geoffrey F. Nuttall, "Letters from Robert Hall to John Ryland 1791–1824," *Baptist Quarterly* 34.3 (July 1991): 127–131; Timothy Whelan, "An Evangelical Anglican Interaction with Baptist Missionary Society Strategy: William Wilberforce and John Ryland, 1807–1824" in *Interfaces: Baptists and Others*, ed. David Bebbington and Martin Sutherland, Studies in Baptist History and Thought 44 (Milton Keynes: Paternoster Press, 2013), 56–85; Jonathan Yeager, *Enlightened Evangelicalism the Life and Thought of John Erskine* (Oxford: Oxford University Press, 2011), 150–153, 193–196; idem, "The Letters of John Erskine to the Rylands," *Eusebeia: The Journal of the Andrew Fuller Center for Baptist Studies* 9 (2008): 183–195; idem, "A Microcosm of the Community of the Saints: John Erskine's Relationship with the English Particular Baptists, John Collett Ryland and His Son John Ryland, Jr" in *Pathways and Patterns in History: Essays on Baptists, Evangelicals, and the Modern World in Honour of David Bebbington*, ed. Anthony R. Cross, Peter J. Morden, and Ian M. Randall (Didcot: The Baptist Historical Society, 2015), 231–254. Additionally, a few of Ryland's letters have been published, including: "A Letter from Dr. Ryland," *Baptist Quarterly* 12.6-7 (April-July 1947): 221–222; "Letter to Joseph Kinghorn," in *Joseph Kinghorn of Nor-*

CHAPTER NINE

The early letters

The available letters divide neatly into two groups: the early letters and the later letters. There are five early letters, and they encompass the years from 1773 to 1775. There is then a fifteen-year gap between extant letters.[5] The later letters, then, extend from 1790 to 1813, the year before Sutcliff died. The correspondence of Ryland and Sutcliff, thus, ranges over forty years and shows the depth of their friendship and how it developed over time. The following section will cover the changing ways in which Ryland divulged his spiritual struggles, how he counseled Sutcliff and others, and the hints that he gives of later interests and personal characteristics.

Ryland's expression of spiritual struggles

The early letters reveal much of young Ryland's spirituality, considerably more so than the later letters. Ryland's persistent evaluation of himself and his own spiritual state is overwhelmingly negative. In one letter, he writes that he is "more brutish than any man to think so little so seldom so slightly so superficially of precious *Jesus*."[6] He evaluates his own heart as "carnal" and his love "so dwindling" that he says that he hates himself for not loving God as he ought.[7] In other letters, he calls himself "a dead

---

wich, ed. by Martin Hood Wilkin (Norwich: Fletcher and Alexander, 1855), 183–185; "Letters of Dr. John Ryland to Dr. Stephen West," *Bibliotheca Sacra* 30.117 (January 1873): 178–187; "Mursell's Preparation for College," *Transactions of the Baptist Historical Society* 2.2 (October 1911): 74–76; Daniel T. Weaver and Michael A.G. Haykin, "A Significant Letter from John Ryland to Samuel Hopkins," *The Andrew Fuller Review* 3 (Summer 2012): 29–33.

5   Neither Ryland nor Sutcliff have had their published works collected, so there has never been a sustained push to gather all of their unpublished material. Because of this, there is a distinct possibility that there are more letters out there, but they have not been identified and made available for research. If any archivists or collectors have Ryland letters in their possession, please do not hesitate to reach out to the author.

6   John Ryland, "Letter to John Sutcliff," December 28, 1773, Angus Library and Archive, Regent's Park College, The University of Oxford.

7   Ryland, "Letter to Sutcliff," December 28, 1773.

dog the poorest of all poor creatures"[8] and a "poor cold hearted Wretch."[9] Similar expressions may be found in his revised diary, which covers the years 1766–1776. In one vivid passage in his diary, he recounts events in 1775, in which he writes of his own "dullness" and his fear of being "lukewarm" in his faith. He says that he has "often wished to keep away from our experience meetings" because he did not want the people to hear too often of his "less complaints"[10] and thereby be encouraged "to be satisfied with the same dull frame which their minister so often mentioned."[11] He goes on to offer a summary of the years 1775 and 1776 as having "many complaints of deadness."[12] This comparison with his diary is helpful because it sheds light on the growing closeness between the two men. If we understand Ryland's diary as a place where he honestly divulged his heart, then it may be concluded that he did not withhold his inmost spiritual feelings to Sutcliff.

It is interesting to note that this sort of self-flagellation, though not completely absent,[13] is largely missing in later letters. The reason for this is not entirely clear. While not averse to changes in theological conviction,[14] Ryland's understanding of human sinfulness remained largely the

---

8   John Ryland, "Letter to John Sutcliff," August 26, 1774, American Baptist Historical Society Archives, Atlanta, GA.
9   John Ryland, "Letter to John Sutcliff," May 9, 1775, Angus Library and Archive, Regent's Park College, The University of Oxford.
10 Ryland seldom wrote the word "heart." Rather, he drew a heart where the word would go. As seen in the quote above, this extended to words that have heart in them.
11 John Ryland, *Autograph Reminiscences*, Bristol Baptist College Archives, Bristol, 52.
12 Ryland, *Autograph Reminiscences*, 57.
13 He writes to Sutcliff about a sermon he preached for the Fast Day, "On the Fast Day I repeated last yrs. Sermn. 'I will that men pray every where &c. had no pleast. time myself, nor ever heard any observn. good or bad concerning it" (John Ryland, "Letter to John Sutcliff," March 10, 1794, Historical Society of Pennsylvania). Many preachers in Ryland's day and since may no doubt sympathize with him here.
14 Ryland famously changed his answer to the Modern Question, which he formulated like this: "Whether it be the duty of all men to whom the gospel is published, to repent and believe in Christ" (John Ryland, *The Work of Faith, the Labour of Love, and the Patience of Hope Illustrated; in the Life and Death of the Reverend Andrew Fuller* [London: Button and Son, 1816], 6). Early in his life, Ryland would have answered this in the negative, but he, along with Fuller and Sutcliff, came to embrace an affirmative answer to the query (John Ryland, *Serious Remarks on the Different Representations of*

same throughout his life. In a poem composed in 1817, when Ryland was sixty-four years old, he writes:

> From all the pow'r of sin
> I long to be set free;
> Reign ever blessed Lord within,
> Set up thy throne in me.[15]

Ryland did not, therefore, begin to think more highly of himself or human achievement in general.

It is possible that Ryland simply "grew out of" this sort of language. While not rejecting the substance of what he said, Ryland may have simply left behind the expressions as he grew older. It is known that Ryland looked at his earlier writings with some amount of embarrassment. In his revised diaries, he writes, "I did, for many years, keep a brief diary; in the former volumes of which are doubtless many childish things, which tho' they may have an humbling effect, when I survey them myself, yet would be of no use to another."[16] Ryland also mentions directing his family to burn his old diaries as well as his older poetry, and he says that he has "charge[d] my children and friends to do their utmost to prevent the re-publication of any verses printed before I was thirty years of age."[17] None of this is to say that he would have been embarrassed or ashamed of his letters; rather, it is to suggest that he did experience some growth in his personal literary expression, and that may extend to his early letter writing.

A second possible explanation for Ryland's change in expression is more intriguing. Second, it could be that there was something rhetorical

---

Evangelical Doctrine by the Professed Friends of the Gospel, 2 vols. [Bristol: J.G. Fuller, 1818], 2:8–26).

15 John Ryland, *Poems by John Ryland Junr, Vol. 1 (1778-1821)*, Bristol Baptist College Archives, Bristol, 39.
16 Ryland, *Autograph Reminiscences*, 1.
17 Ryland, *Autograph Reminiscences*, 2.

in Ryland's proclamations of his own sinfulness. David Parry explains the "Puritan ideals of godly communication" as earnest expression stemming from "doctrinal conviction, inward spiritual experience, and a heartfelt desire to persuade others."[18] While Ryland lived well after the Puritan era, he was nonetheless influenced by them.[19] It is possible, then, that this is an instance in which Ryland is showing the Puritan influence on himself. It is not that he is trying to show something that he is not to Sutcliff.[20] Rather, he is using conventional language to communicate his convictions and experiences to a new acquaintance. The later letters, coming as they do from a time when Sutcliff knew well who Ryland was and what he believed, do not require such a display, meaning that Ryland could change his rhetoric.

As negative as Ryland was toward himself, he did not extend such negativity to others. Indeed, with Sutcliff, Ryland is consistently encouraging. In one letter, Ryland responds to Sutcliff's complaint about his own inability, perhaps much like Ryland does, and Ryland responds, "Your sense of your own weakness need be no discouragement, your strength is in your head."[21] He goes on to compare a person young in the faith to one more mature, saying, "I rather think the difference between a babe in Christ and a strong man, is not in one having a fuller pocket (if I may so speak) of his own, the experienc'd christian has no more strength of his own than the youngest

---

18   David Parry, "'A Divine Kind of Rhetoric': Rhetorical Strategy and Spirit-Wrought Sincerity in English Puritan Writing," *Christianity and Literature* 67.1 (December 2017): 115.

19   In his memoir of John Ryland Jr., Jonathan Edwards Ryland, writes of Ryland Jr.'s "extensive acquaintance with the Puritan writers and their immediate successors" (J. E. Ryland, "Memoir," *Selected from the Manuscripts of the Late Revd. John Ryland, D.D. of Bristol: With a Memoir of the Author* [London: B. J. Holdsworth, 1828], 2:15). As an example of this, Ryland quoted John Owen with approval in his works. See John Ryland, "Sinful Doubts," *Pastoral Memorials*, 1:243; and *A Candid Statement of the Reasons which Induce the Baptists to Differ in Opinion and Practice from Their Christian Brethren*, 2nd ed. (London: Wightman and Camp, 1827), 24. He also referred to Owen as one of "the most eminent Nonconformists" (Ryland, *Serious Remarks*, 1:38).

20   Parry rightly insists that sincerity was a key Puritan ideal (Parry, "Divine Kind of Rhetoric," 114–115). Ryland's personal diary matches his private expression to Sutcliff, indicating that it was so with Ryland as well.

21   Ryland, "Letter to Sutcliff," August 26, 1774. "Head" here refers to Jesus.

convert, but he better knows where to go for it."²² For himself, Ryland tends to focus on his faults, but in his counsel for Sutcliff, he focuses on Christ. He is also optimistic about Sutcliff's prospects for usefulness in Olney, encouraging his friend, "If a man of a gospel spirit shou'd go there and determine to believe No Tales and labor by gentle degrees to undermine a party spirit and try to outdo Mr N. in Candor & Love for all that love Christ I believe he wou'd have a *good* prospect."²³ Ryland leaves no doubt that he believes the Sutcliff is that "man of a gospel spirit."

This adds nuance to Ryland's understanding of human sinfulness and complexity to his expressions of his own spirituality. While he is prepared to see himself in the most negative of lights, he does not extend that to his friends in need of counsel. Rather, he seeks to be an encouragement to them. He sees the best in others but the worst in himself.²⁴

Elements of later interests and characteristics

There are also hints in the early letters of issues and interests that would show themselves over and again in Ryland's life. First, there is a lesser-known

---

22 Ryland, "Letter to Sutcliff," August 26, 1774. As part of his counsel, Ryland recommends the letters of Newton to Sutcliff, saying, "I most earnestly recommend to you Omicrons Letters just printed. You will assuredly like them[.] there is one upon frames written to a friend of yours that it maybe will in part suit yourself." The friend of Sutcliff's mentioned is, in fact, Ryland himself. The letter was printed as "On a Believer's Frames" in the *Gospel Magazine* (April 1773): 185–191; cf. Grant Gordon, *Wise Counsel*, 33, n.1. The printed letter does not contain the name of the addressee, but, in a subsequent letter to Ryland, Newton says, "As I lately sent you a long letter by the Magazine, you will excuse a short one now ... I shall be glad if Omicrons Letter was acceptable to you" (John Newton, "Letter to John Ryland," May 10, 1773, Bristol Baptist College and Archive). The copy of the letter held at the Bristol Baptist College Archives is written in Ryland's handwriting, and he has written the word "on frames" in the margin, identifying to which letter Newton refers.

23 John Ryland, "Letter to John Sutcliff," November 12, 1774, John Rylands Library at the University of Manchester.

24 In his funeral sermon for Ryland, Robert Hall Jr. said that he "was ingenious in discovering reasons for thinking well of many who widely dissented from his religious views" (Robert Hall, Jr, "A Sermon Occasioned by the Death of the Rev. John Ryland," in *The Works of the Rev. Robert Hall, A.M.: With a Memoir of His Life*, ed. Olinthus Gregory, 3 vols. [New York: Harper, 1835], 1:217).

aspect of Ryland that is seen briefly in the letters: his love of history and concern with record keeping. When Ryland learns that Sutcliff was in Shrewsbury, he asks him to "enquire of your old folks who gather'd the baptist church at Shrewsbury, how long ago, first minister, his character, conversion, success, death, successor, &c. &c. if one cou'd get a good acc^t. of this sort from each particular baptist church 'twoud be very entertaining. I have begun trying for it."[25] This concern is reflected in other writings that Ryland produced. The Northamptonshire Record Office contains a document entitled "History of the Baptist Church in Northampton" written by him.[26] It is a factual recounting of the history of the College Lane Baptist Church. Other documents written by Ryland betray his interest in keeping records of even the most minute of events. For example, the Northamptonshire Record Office also contains something Ryland called his "Text Book," which is a record of every sermon he ever preached, complete with Scripture passage preached, place, date, and, at times, information pertinent to the occasion.[27]

There is also a brief look in the early letters into Ryland's growing understanding of catholicity, something for which he was known by his contemporaries.[28] He tells Sutcliff about the ministry of Rowland Hill,

---

25 Ryland, "Letter to Sutcliff," August 26, 1774. Commas were added to this quotation for ease of reading. They are not in the original.

26 This document was published in John Rippon, ed, *Baptist Annual Register, for 1801–1802* (London: Button and Conder, 1802), 713–720, 769–772, 983–986. The handwritten original is held by the Northamptonshire Record Office.

27 For example, on July 20, 1776, Ryland preached at what he called a "7 day" church in Stapleton, referring to Baptists who held to Saturday as the Christian Sabbath. He recounts the experience: "about 30 people, almost all mad or asleep" (John Ryland, "Text Book," July 20, 1776, Northamptonshire Record Office). Also, in January 1780, Ryland inserts a brief note about his marriage to Elizabeth Tyler: "J.R.j. married Jan. 12" (Ryland, "Text Book," January 12, 1780). Similarly, marking Elizabeth's death on January 23, 1787, Ryland inserts a thick black line.

28 See Hall Jr.'s assessment of Ryland's catholic attitude toward others: "No man was more remarkable for combining a zealous attachment to his own principles with the utmost liberality of mind towards those who differed from him; an abhorrence of error, with the kindest feelings towards the erroneous. He detested the spirit of monopoly in religion, and opposed every tendency to circumscribe it by the limits of party" (Hall, Jr

CHAPTER NINE

ordained by the Church of England but ministering in an independent chapel, writing that Hill was "bless'd abundantly among us last year 12 alarm'd whereof 8 stand well. He has just been here again—thousands attended."[29] Noting this apparently led Ryland to consider the propriety of Particular Baptists partnering with those outside of their denomination. In the same letter, he says to Sutcliff, "Tis the wisdom as well as the duty of the dissenters to be friendly with the <u>orthodox</u> Methodists."[30] It is likely, at this point in his theological development, and based on the context,[31] that "orthodox" here is a synonym for "Calvinistic." However, though he would never move from his Calvinistic convictions, Ryland would later partner with Arminians, preach in Methodist churches, and speak highly of Arminian missionaries.[32] In other words, his catholicity would broaden considerably after this point, but it is, nevertheless, important to note it in its early stages.

These things are important to recognize because they show that Ryland was "real" with Sutcliff. Though there may have been an element of rhetorical flourish in the letters, what we find in them is, nevertheless, a reasonably accurate portrait of Ryland, at least as he understood himself. Their friendship, at least from Ryland's side of it, was marked by honesty and a desire not to obfuscate but to truly divulge oneself to another.

The later letters

The letters from 1790–1813 are less personal and more informational, sharing intelligence from missionaries, mutual acquaintances, and life as

---

"A Sermon Occasioned by the Death of the Rev. John Ryland," 218).
29 Ryland, "Letter to Sutcliff," August 26, 1774.
30 Ryland, "Letter to Sutcliff," August 26, 1774.
31 Immediately following this sentence, Ryland writes of the Arminian Methodists, "As to the Weslytes both their Doctrin and Policy are inimical to the Dissenters and I think contrary to the Word of God."
32 For more on Ryland's catholicity, see Lon Graham, *"All Who Love Our Blessed Redeemer": The Catholicity of John Ryland Jr.*, Monographs in Baptist History 24 (Eugene, OR: Pickwick, 2022).

a leader among the Particular Baptists. The overall impression of these letters is that they show a friendship that has developed into a partnership. Ryland and Sutcliff are partners in leadership and mission. As such these letters say much about developing leaders from the students at the Academy, the promotion of Edwardsean theology, and the work of the Baptist Missionary Society (BMS), which will each be examined separately.

Academy students

Regarding the students of the Academy, some of Ryland's remarks to Sutcliff read like a teacher's evaluation. Of a "Watts of Frome," Ryland comments that his "Orthodoxy is suspected (but an amiable Man)."[33] Of another Watts, this one from Naseby, Ryland has a high opinion, but he notes that he "is at present unpopular thro the length of his sentences & dullness of Delivery,"[34] which is a less than glowing commendation. Of a man named Angus, Ryland declares that he "is awkward in his delivery—no great Genius."[35] In a more serious and sad case, Ryland relates the story of a student named Burnett, "who suddenly lost his reason, & tho't he was elected Member of Parliam*t*. for Wells."[36] Ryland takes responsibility for the man, who was not improving, though he confesses that he does not know how to help him. He writes, in a somewhat despondent tone, "He

---

33   Ryland, "Letter to Sutcliff," March 10, 1794. This is most likely Gabriel Watts (https://dissacad.english.qmul.ac.uk/sample1.php?parameter=personretrieve&alpha=2926; accessed December 11, 2021). Ryland does not specify the nature of the suspicion toward Watts.

34   Ryland, "Letter to Sutcliff," March 10, 1794. This is possibly Robert Watts (https://dissacad.english.qmul.ac.uk/sample1.php?parameter=personretrieve&alpha=2927; accessed 11 December 2021).

35   Ryland, "Letter to Sutcliff," March 10, 1794. This is James Angus, not the more famous Joseph Angus, who did not attend the Academy in Bristol (https://dissacad.english.qmul.ac.uk/sample1.php?detail=people&personid=2356; accessed 11 December 2021).

36   John Ryland, "Letter to John Sutcliff," January 26, 1807, Angus Library and Archive, Regent's Park College, The University of Oxford. This is Thomas Burnett, who came to Bristol from Paulton and left because of "bodily and mental affliction" (https://dissacad.english.qmul.ac.uk/sample1.php?detail=people&personid=2404; accessed December 11, 2021).

continues in a rather deranged state. I know not what can be done for him. His Mother is very poor. His Father in Law wicked—Paulton Ch. poor—he is not bad enough for S^t. Luke's, nor well enough to pursue his Stud^s, nor to get his bread by his trade as a shoemaker."[37] Finally, Ryland reveals some reservations with regard to Joshua Marshman, then a student at the Academy but one day to become one of the Serampore Trio, writing that he fears that Marshman "deals too much in sarcasms, which never do any good."[38]

Edwardseanism

Sutcliff and Ryland were, along with Andrew Fuller, committed to the theology of Jonathan Edwards and American New Divinity and sought to promote it to their fellow English believers. Both the early and late letters contain references to Edwards and his theological successors. In an early letter, Ryland asks if Sutcliff had ever seen Edwards on the affections, and, if so, what his thoughts were on the book. A later letter contains Ryland's handwritten copy of remarks on Archibald M'Lean by Jonathan Edwards Jr.[39] The remarks were not available to Sutcliff, but they were apparently important enough for Ryland to hand copy many pages of them in a letter.

That Ryland would write to Sutcliff on Edwardseanism is not surprising, but the way in which he writes is. In public, Ryland was a steadfast defender of Edwards and his theology. He summarized his own devotion to Edwardseanism in a sermon given on the occasion of Andrew Fuller's death, saying, "If I knew I should be with Sutcliff and Fuller to-morrow, instead of regretting that I had endeavoured to promote that religion delineated by

---

37 Ryland, "Letter to Sutcliff," January 26, 1807.
38 John Ryland, "Letter to John Sutcliff," July 27, 1810, Angus Library and Archive, Regent's Park College, The University of Oxford.
39 John Ryland, "Letter to John Sutcliff," July 26, 1801, Angus Library and Archive, Regent's Park College, The University of Oxford. The remarks by Edwards Jr. were contained in a letter from Edwards Jr. to Ryland, dated August 24, 1799, which is held at the Beinecke Rare Book and Manuscript Library. The only changes that Ryland makes have to do with pagination. When Edwards Jr. gives a page number for a quotation, Ryland changes it, indicating that they were working from different editions of the book.

Jonathan Edwards, in his Treatise on *Religious Affections*, and in his *Life of David Brainerd*, I would recommend his writings, and Dr. Bellamy's, with Dr. Whitaker's *Two Sermons on Reconciliation*, with the last effort I could make to guide a pen."[40] With Sutcliff, however, he shows that he did not receive the American Divinity uncritically. Ryland tells Sutcliff that he had sent two sermons by Samuel Hopkins to a friend, Thomas Scott, for Scott's critical remarks on them.[41] The reason for this, according to Ryland, was that he wants to "muster up the strongest Argumt^s. ag^t. him wherever he seems mistaken."[42]

This privately critical stance of Ryland toward American Divinity is seen in other private correspondence. To Hopkins himself, Ryland writes,

> Tho I wish to call no man M^r. on Earth, I w^d. be highly obliged to seek after Truth as after hid Treasure, & I think your writings have assisted me in the search, tho I must follow slowly wherein I see few footsteps before you, & may never fully accord with all you have written."[43]

Ryland also offers criticisms of Jonathan Edwards Jr.'s ideas about the sufferings of Christ not proving the equity of the law.[44] While Ryland could say that his "most sincere respect" for the elder Jonathan Edwards meant

---

40 John Ryland, *The Indwelling and Righteousness of Christ No Security against Corporeal Death, but the Source of Spiritual and Eternal Life* (London: Button and Son, 1815), 47. In the same sermon, he quotes a letter from Fuller to a similar effect: "We have some, who have been giving out of late, that 'If Sutcliff and some others had preached more of Christ, and less of Jonathan Edwards, they would have been more useful.' If those who talk thus, preached Christ half as much as Jonathan Edwards did, and were half as useful as he was, their usefulness would be double what it is" (Ryland, *Indwelling and Righteousness of Christ*, 34). Note that Fuller does not deny that they spoke much of Edwards.
41 John Ryland, "Letter to Sutcliff," January 28, 1795, The Isaac Mann Autograph Collection, James Marshall and Marie-Louise Osborn Collection, Beinecke Rare Book and Manuscript Library, Yale University.
42 Ryland, "Letter to Sutcliff," January 28, 1795.
43 John Ryland, "Letter to Samuel Hopkins," 1797, Historical Society of Pennsylvania.
44 John Ryland, "Letter to Jonathan Edwards Jr," June 29, 1787, Beinecke Rare Book and Manuscript Library, Yale University.

that "evry thing relative to him & his family seem'd a matter of importance,"[45] his devotion was not unquestioning but was possessed of at least some self-critical reflection.

Work of the BMS

Concerning the BMS, Ryland writes much to Sutcliff. He shared missionary intelligence, sharing accounts of raising money for the missions, and complains about the Church Missionary Society being mistaken as the only missionary society, mocking it as "*the* Society." While these are no doubt interesting and provide insight into the burgeoning missionary movement, the story of John Fernandez, which is told in these letters, is perhaps the most unique.

John was the son of Ignatius Fernandez, a Portuguese man who became a valuable part of the BMS mission in India. John was born in India and was, at first, helpful in the ministry there. Along with Felix and William Carey Jr., he helped open the first Sunday School in India.[46] He also translated a letter from "Four Hindoos" and "Several Hindoos at RamKristnopore."[47] William Ward said that he was "much pleased" with John's progress.[48]

It was decided, however, that Fernandez needed to spend time in England. In a letter from Ward transcribed by Ryland to Sutcliff, Ward says that Marshman wants Fernandez to go to the Academy in Bristol "to perfect himself in Greek, Latin &c."[49] Ward's earlier pleasure has become

---

45   John Ryland, "Letter to Jonathan Edwards Jr," June 29, 1787.
46   F. Deaville Walker, *William Carey: Missionary Pioneer and Statesman* (London: Student Christian Movement, 1926), 231; William Ward, "Journal, May-December 1803," *Periodical Accounts Relative to the Baptist Missionary Society* 2, no. 14 (London, 1804): 481.
47   Ram Mohun, Ram Rotton, Bydenaut, Krishno Presaud, "From Four Hindoos," trans. J. L. Fernandez, *Periodical Accounts Relative to the Baptist Missionary Society* 3, no. 16 (London, 1807), 196–197; Anonymous, "From Several Hindoos at Ramkristnopore," trans. J. L. Fernandez, *Periodical Accounts Relative to the Baptist Missionary Society* 3, no. 16 (London, 1807): 197–198.
48   Cited in F. G. Hastings, "Calendar of Letters, 1742–1831," *Baptist Quarterly* 6.6 (April 1933): 279.
49   John Ryland, "Letter to John Sutcliff," June 1806, Angus Library and Archive, Regent's

mixed with a bit of cynicism, however, as he confesses that he thinks Fernandez is coming to England to "*enlarge his mind*—by the sight of its superb buildings amazing shops, manufactures, arts, exhibitions &c &c by hearing Lect^s. on Natural Philosophy &c learning drawing, music &c by an intercourse wth English X^s.—seeing the crowded congregat^s. hearing the animating serm^s. and becoming acquainted with those who are forming those great & glorious plans that are to Christianize the world."[50] In other words, he is going to enjoy the many things that England has to offer a young man.

In that initial letter, Ward added some words that proved to be prescient. He warned that Fernandez "wants a firmness of character" and is "incapable of saying *No* with firmness to a companion."[51] As it turns out, neither Ward nor Marshman correctly predicted what Fernandez would do, and it would be far worse than either imagined. In the next letter that mentions Fernandez, written several years later,[52] Fernandez has proven to be more of a burden than they anticipated. Ryland writes, "I have just rec^d. a letter from Pilpin, by wch. I find Fernandez has given him the slip, or rather disappointed his expectation of meeting him at Newport to go with him to Leominster."[53] By the next year, Fernandez has left England, but his handlers are still discovering the problems he left in his wake.[54] Ryland writes that Fernandez cheated people out of money, having gotten ten pounds from a Mr. Roote of Portsmouth and giving him a draft for repayment that turned out to be fraudulent.[55] Ryland writes to Sutcliff soliciting advice on

---

Park College, The University of Oxford.

50   Ryland, "Letter to Sutcliff," June 1806. Ward has no problem with this. In the letter, he says "let him go" and experience all the sights and sounds that England has to offer. He even insists that the BMS support him while he is in England.
51   Ryland, "Letter to Sutcliff," June 1806.
52   Fernandez was only supposed to be in England for two years.
53   Ryland, "Letter to Sutcliff," July 27, 1810.
54   John Ryland, "Letter to John Sutcliff," October 1811, Angus Library and Archive, Regent's Park College, The University of Oxford.
55   Ryland, "Letter to Sutcliff," October 1811.

how to handle this issue with discretion.⁵⁶

In the aftermath of Fernandez's sojourn in England, letters were exchanged between Andrew Fuller, William Ward, William Carey, Ignatius Fernandez, and Ryland. They all express a certain exasperation with the young man as well as reticence to allow him to re-engage with the mission as he had before he left. In a letter from John Peter, copied by Ward to Ryland, he shares the thoughts of Carey and Marshman, who he says are "afraid he will be of no use in anything much less in the cause of God."⁵⁷ Carey confirms this in a letter to Ryland, stating that he "never approved of [Fernandez's] going to England," and giving a final update on Fernandez's fate: "He is now at Dinagepore where he will sink into perfect insignificance."⁵⁸

Ryland shared this information with few people,⁵⁹ but he trusted Sutcliff with the potentially embarrassing details of Fernandez's conduct in England. This demonstrates the depth of trust between the two men. Ryland felt perfectly safe in divulging this information to Sutcliff.

Conclusion

Naomi Tadmor, in her work on eighteenth-century friendship and family, noted the importance of friends in the context of religious and spiritual communities. The examples she adduced in favor of this contention were largely drawn from larger social groups, such as the Society of Friends.⁶⁰

---

56 Discretion marked the whole of Fernandez's sojourn in England. In the first letter to Sutcliff about Fernandez, Ryland writes, "Some part of what [Ward] says about [Fernandez] must not be seen by more than two or three" (Ryland, "Letter to Sutcliff," June 1806).

57 The provenance of this letter is convoluted. It was written by John Peter to William Ward, who copied it to Ryland, who then copied it in a letter to Fuller dated February 25, 1811. This letter is held at the Angus Library and Archive, Regent's Park College, The University of Oxford.

58 William Carey, "Letter to John Ryland," July 14, 1812, Northamptonshire Record Office.

59 Ryland tells Sutcliff that no more than two or three need to know the details (Ryland, "Letter to Sutcliff," June 1806).

60 The field of friendship studies is an important and growing area of historical research.

This study shows how one of those religiously-based friendships was carried on in private correspondence. The letters of Ryland to Sutcliff show a friendship between two young men that grew into a seasoned partnership in ministry. The early letters have the marks of youthful exuberance and expression, while the later ones demonstrate a settled ministry and united missionary vision cultivated over many years. All of the letters are marked by honesty, a concern for the other, and ministry-related concerns.

A sampling of this literature includes: Sandra Hynes, "Mapping Friendship and Dissent: The Letters from Joseph Boyse to Ralph Thoresby, 1680–1710" in *Varieties of Seventeenth- and Early Eighteenth-Century English Radicalism in Context*, ed. Ariel Hessayon and David Finnegan (London: Routledge, 2011), 205–220; Kenneth Loiselle, "Friendship and Loyalty in Early Modern Europe" in *Faces of Communities: Social Ties between Trust, Loyalty and Conflict*, ed. Sabrina Feickert, Anna Haut, and Kathrin Sharaf (Göttingen: V&R Unipress, 2014), 121–136; K. D. M. Snell, "Belonging and Community: Understandings of 'Home' and 'Friends' among the English Poor, 1750–1850," *Economic History Review* 65.1 (February 2012): 1–25; Naomi Tadmor, *Family and Friends in Eighteenth-Century England: Household, Kinship and Patronage* (Cambridge: Cambridge University Press, 2001), 167–215; Keith Wrightson, *English Society 1580–1680* (New Brunswick, NJ: Rutgers University Press, 1982), 47–73. In recent research on this topic, it has been noted that there is a dearth of case studies of actual friendships during these centuries. The present study will meet this need by showing the relationship between two prominent religious leaders from the time when they were young men and continuing throughout their lives. While space does not allow interaction with the literature on friendship, this article is meant as a resource for that ongoing conversation.

10

Faith and practice: Setting the "invisible" Lord "ever before me"

KEITH ALAN TILLMAN

Although John Ryland, Jr. (1753–1825) was considered a leader among the Particular Baptist during their transition from the high Calvinism of John Gill (1697–1771) to a more missional Calvinism of Jonathan Edwards (1703–1758), and he served as a prominent educator of Baptist clergy at Bristol Baptist College, he is relatively unknown to most modern Baptists. In the fall of 2012, in my first meeting with church historian Michael A. G. Haykin in Louisville, Kentucky, he introduced me to Ryland and encouraged me to read and research this wonderful pastor, author, revivalist and missional leader. What I discovered in Ryland was a man who was an extremely vital part of the English Particular Baptist and who played a major role in the formation of the Baptist Missionary Society, yet very little academic work had been done on Ryland's life and ministry. Through my initial reading about Ryland, I decided to engage in an in-depth look into the life, ministry, and spirituality of Ryland. It would be this pursuit of getting to know Ryland that introduced me to church historian Grant Gordon.

CHAPTER TEN

As I began to gather material on Ryland, Gordon's biography of Ryland in Haykin's *The British Particular Baptists: 1638–1910*,[1] first gave me insight into the man that would consume my time for the next few years and would be the subject of two dissertations through my seminary work at The Southern Baptist Theological Seminary.[2] While the biography of Ryland was extremely helpful, Gordon's article in *The Baptist Quarterly* concerning Ryland's "call" from the church at Northampton to Broadmead in Bristol demonstrated Gordon's passion for research and writing as he pooled information on Ryland from various church records, as well as letters penned between John Newton (1725–1807) and Ryland. As a budding researcher of church history, Gordon's compilation of these letters revealed to me the depth and richness of engaging historical figures of the church and mining these "treasure troves of wisdom" for modern application. For example, in his *Wise Counsel*, which was the publication of eighty-three letters from Newton to Ryland, Gordon demonstrated the wisdom of Newton's pastoral mentorship to the younger Ryland. As a pastor, it would be these letters that would influence my preaching, counseling, and pastoral care ministries, especially the way I deal with grief, particularly through Newton's counsel to Ryland concerning the "presence of Christ" in times of suffering. When Ryland's first wife, Elizabeth (d. 1787), died, Newton immediately penned a letter to his friend pointing him toward the narrative of 2 Samuel 12:22–23 regarding the death of David's son and David's faith through his grief. Newton wrote these words for the grieving Ryland: "You have received a wound, but faithful is the Friend who has wounded you … Your wound must be painful for a time, but the Lord will not leave you; he will condescend to visit you; he will, if I may so speak,

---

1 Grant Gordon, "John Ryland, Jr. (1753–1825)," in *The British Particular Baptist: 1638–1910*, ed. Michael A. G. Haykin (Springfield, MO: Particular Baptist Press, 2000), 2:77.
2 Keith Alan Tillman, "'He Worked Out His Salvation with Fear and Trembling': The Spirituality of John Ryland, Jr." (ThM dissertation, Southern Baptist Theological Seminary, 2014); Keith Alan Tillman, "'Seeing the Invisible God': John Ryland Jr.'s Spirituality of Triumphal Living in Christ" (PhD dissertation, Southern Baptist Theological Seminary, 2022).

dress your wound, till it be effectually healed."[3] Newton's encouragement to his young protégé was rooted in Scripture and the promise of God that his presence was continuous and faithful in the lives of his elect. He also reminded Ryland of a future "presence" with God and the anticipation of the "exceeding abundant and eternal weight of glory" that will be revealed to him in the last days.[4] For Ryland, the presence of Christ and the doctrine of the incarnation of the Son of God served as an important "evangelical truth" that would produce in him a "godly zeal" to both live out his faith as if Christ had truly "condescended to visit" with him, and to increase the effectiveness of his pastoral ministry, including those experiencing grief in the deaths of loved ones.

This essay will examine the direct bearing of Ryland's theological understanding of the presence of Christ in the believer's life, especially as it relates to the incarnation and deity of Christ. Ryland's spirituality, which he aptly called the "beauty of Christian experience,"[5] was affected by his understanding of the incarnation of Christ and the promise of his presence in the life of the church. He explained, "I set the Lord ever before me, as though I could see him that is invisible. I often think of my obligations to the Redeemer, remembering what he did and suffered for me. The life I live in the flesh, I live by the faith of the Son of God, who loved me, and gave himself for me."[6]

Ryland's spirituality of faith and practice: The essence of "true religion"
In a circular letter to the ministers and messengers of the Northamptonshire Baptist Association, Ryland asserted that godly zeal was the "fervor of true benevolence" towards a "beloved object," therefore, "exciting the

---

3   John Newton, *Wise Counsel: John Newton's Letters to John Ryland, Jr.*, ed. Grant Gordon (Edinburgh, U.K.: Banner of Truth Trust, 2009), 189.
4   Romans 8:18 (KJV).
5   John Ryland, "Separation from the World" in *Pastoral Memorials: Selected from the Manuscripts of the Late Revd. John Ryland, D.D. of Bristol: With a Memoir of the Author* (London: B. J. Holdsworth, 1828), 2:98.
6   Ryland, "Separation from the World" in *Pastoral Memorials*, 2:28.

subject" to vigorous activities for the good of the "beloved object."[7] Ryland argued that there was a "dutiful connection" between faith and practice, which he called the practice of "true religion."[8] He asked the messengers of the association and his readers whether faith in Christ and his possession of the believer make one "live differently" from the way one normally lives.[9] Faith in Christ, argued Ryland, produced a "true religion" that generated "holy affections" of the heart towards Christ. This devotion to Christ or "true religion," according to Ryland, begins internally, but works out externally, producing "devout exercises of the heart."[10] He said, "But if [holy affections towards Christ] be genuine, they will, in proportion to their strength, show themselves externally, and influence the whole conduct."[11] Ryland's affections towards Christ developed in him a spirituality of the external practice of faith, not necessarily out of burden or task, but from the "sincerity and strength" of his love towards Christ.[12] This devotion in his affections for Christ and his spiritual activities that demonstrated this love are clearly expressed in his sermon, "Obedience the Test of Love to God," where he declared, "Love to a creature will sweeten labor."[13] According to Ryland, living out the "sweet labor" that was initiated by great affections towards Christ was a product of God's love for mankind that was demonstrated through Scripture, including the doctrine of the incarnation of the Son of God. Ryland stated, "Never had God such another servant as his own incarnated Son."[14] For Ryland, this ultimate act of "self-denial and self-abasement" of the Son of God was the definitive example and

---

7   Ryland, "Godly Zeal Described and Recommended" in *Pastoral Memorials*, 2:392.
8   John Ryland, "Characteristics of Divine Revelation" in *Pastoral Memorials: Selected from the Manuscripts of the Late Revd. John Ryland, D.D. of Bristol: With a Memoir of the Author* (London: B. J. Holdsworth, 1826), 1:168.
9   Ryland, "On Devotedness to Christ" in *Pastoral Memorials*, 2:26.
10 Ryland, "Obedience the Test of Love to God" in *Pastoral Memorials*, 2:291.
11 Ryland, "Obedience the Test of Love to God" in *Pastoral Memorials*, 2:291.
12 Ryland, "Obedience the Test of Love to God" in *Pastoral Memorials*, 2:293.
13 Ryland, "Obedience the Test of Love to God" in *Pastoral Memorials*, 2:293.
14 Ryland, "Obedience the Test of Love to God" in *Pastoral Memorials*, 2:294.

motivation for the practice of true religion in the believer's life.[15] He believed that "doctrine and practice" were an important part of the believer's spirituality and championed this practice as an endearing quality within the spiritual life of a believer.[16]

As Ryland understood the doctrine of the incarnation, he argued that the gift of the incarnate Son of God was the most wonderful display of God's sovereignty that has ever been demonstrated[17] and that the doctrine of the incarnation was a worthy subject within the redemptive message of God and for the teaching of the proper aim of worship. In Ryland's "Confession of Faith" (1781),[18] he declared:

> I am fully assured that in order to affect this Salvation, God the *Son* was manifested in the Flesh, being born of a Virgin in whom he had been conceived by the Power of the Holy Ghost. Thus he who was from Eternity in the form of God assumed in Time the form of a Servant. Uniting absolute Divinity and real Humanity in his Person, he alone was a fit Mediator between God and Man.[19]

Ryland was amazed by the idea that God would "permanently unite himself to a created nature" or "that God should make himself visible to his creatures" in order to become the sacrifice for the sins of the elect.[20] He said, "If the guilt of man was so great, as to need to be expiated by the sacrifice of God's incarnate Son, surely the gift of Christ must be the most wonderful

---

15 Ryland, "Obedience the Test of Love to God" in *Pastoral Memorials*, 2:294.
16 Ryland, "The Unworthy Communicant" in *Pastoral Memorials*, 2:62.
17 Ryland, "On the Alleged Impiety of Calvinism" in *Pastoral Memorials*, 2:358.
18 John Ryland, "A Confession of Faith Delivered by John Ryland Jun of Northampton at His Ordination to the Pastoral Care of the Church in College Lane, June 8, 1781," in John Ryland, "MS Volumes of Miscellaneous Writings" n.d., 1–22 (Bristol Baptist College, Acc. No. 14884).
19 Ryland, "A Confession of Faith," 11–12.
20 Ryland, "On the Alleged Impiety of Calvinism" in *Pastoral Memorials*, 2:355.

instance of divine sovereignty that ever was, or can be conceived."[21] For Ryland, the incarnation of Christ and his atoning work for the elect was "an idea which would promote piety, and especially humility" in his life, and would be "the most powerful motive [for] … gratitude and obedience, the natural consequences of this doctrine."[22] Therefore, for Ryland, the doctrine of the incarnation and the atonement by Christ represented the greatest motive for spiritual formation. He voiced this same thought in a sermon focused on Romans 14:8. Ryland, utilizing Paul's letter to the church at Rome, expressed the foundation of his spirituality: "Whether therefore we live, or whether we die, we are the Lord's."[23] Ryland then asked, "Are you more his than others … and does the thought of being the Lord's influence you?"[24] In other words, Ryland believed that since Christ gave you "existence, and bestowed on you numberless mercies, surely he deserves some return," or "practical evidence," manifested in the life of the believer, thus demonstrating a "cordial gratitude" to God.[25]

In his sermon concerning the devotion to Christ, Ryland quoted the psalmist: "How precious are thy thoughts unto me, O God! How great is the sum of them!"[26] As Ryland reflected on the great doctrines of Scripture that encouraged him in the practice of "true religion" and the manifestation of the practical evidence of this new life through the incarnated Son of God, he gave a series of reactions that demonstrated the influence that Christ had on his life. He said:

> We do habitually aim at glorifying God, and do endeavor to make every other object subordinate to this grand and beloved design … We regard all he says as law; and wish fully to know his will in every

---

21 Ryland, "On the Alleged Impiety of Calvinism" in *Pastoral Memorials*, 2:358.
22 Ryland, "On the Alleged Impiety of Calvinism" in *Pastoral Memorials*, 2:358.
23 Romans 14:8 (KJV).
24 Ryland, "On Devotedness to Christ" in *Pastoral Memorials*, 2:26.
25 Ryland, "On Devotedness to Christ" in *Pastoral Memorials*, 2:26–7.
26 Ryland, "On Devotedness to Christ" in *Pastoral Memorials*, 2:27.

thing, that we may do it. We cheerfully resign ourselves to his disposal, and would have no will of our own, contrary to the will of God. What God loves, we love; what he condemns, we would forsake and mortify. We long to be absolutely free from all that he dislikes, to be holy as he is holy, and perfect as our Father in heaven is perfect. We would prefer the honor of God to our own honor, and the interest of Christ to every other interest.[27]

The influence of the incarnation of Christ, and Christ's presence in deity in the life of the believer, according to Ryland, produced a grand effect in the believer, thus answering the question of how one can obtain this "essence of the bliss" of longing to be with Christ and the hope of a continual pursuit of the presence of Christ.[28] In a description of Ryland's own spirituality, he stated, "I set the Lord ever before me, as though I could see him that is invisible."[29] Ryland described this invisible Christ as the catalyst for "holy activity" and the submission of "ourselves out to do good, honoring God with our substance, acting as stewards for him, imitating his beneficence, abounding in every good work."[30] Ryland asserted that as a spiritual practice, he often meditated on his "obligations to the Redeemer, remembering what he did and suffered for me. The life I live in the flesh, I live by the faith of the Son of God, who loved me, and gave himself for me."[31] For Ryland, there was no salvation apart from belief in the deity of Christ and the doctrine of the incarnation of the Son of God. Ryland argued that these doctrines demonstrated the true divinity of Christ and therefore demanded from the life of the followers of Christ a dedication to living out life as if this divine, invisible Christ were standing before them. The influence of the doctrine of the presence of Christ, past, present and

---

27 Ryland, "On Devotedness to Christ" in *Pastoral Memorials*, 2:28.
28 Ryland, "On Devotedness to Christ" in *Pastoral Memorials*, 2:28.
29 Ryland, "On Devotedness to Christ" in *Pastoral Memorials*, 2:28.
30 Ryland, "The Beauty of the Divine Image" in *Pastoral Memorials*, 1:104.
31 Ryland, "On Devotedness to Christ" in *Pastoral Memorials*, 2:28.

future, affected Ryland spiritually, and this influence was clearly demonstrated in his spiritual formation, as well as in his pastoral ministries.

Spiritual formation: "The mind of Christ"

The doctrine of the incarnation of the Son of God played an extremely prominent role in Ryland's spiritual formation because he was thoroughly convinced that God was most consistently and fully known through the person of Jesus Christ. In a letter to John Rowe (1764–1832), the English Unitarian minister, concerning the misplaced zeal of the Socinians, Ryland noted that God the Father required his church to "continually look unto Jesus" as the hope of the church and giver of "benefits."[32] Ryland's argument was that the presence of the Son of God in flesh was the hope of the church and the foundation of true religion. For Ryland, the "glorious idea" of true religion was found in God's calling for his followers to be "imitators of God" and to develop through discipleship the "mind of Christ."[33] In Ryland's *Christ, the Great Source of the Believer's Consolation*, he spoke of the believer's hope as being connected with the gift and revelation of the Son of God in his incarnation.[34] For Ryland, this revelation of the Son of God was a cause for worship of the Father for the "Scriptural evidence" of Christ's presence within the believer and the dwelling of the Son of God in their "hearts by faith."[35] This reflection of Christ's presence by Ryland was an important part of his spirituality, and he made it a practice to examine the connection between "evangelical truth and vital holiness" within the lives of followers of Christ.[36]

---

32 John Ryland, *The Partiality and Unscriptural Direction of Socinian Zeal: Being a Reply to the Rev. Mr Rowe's Letter, Occasioned by a Note Contained in a Sermon Entitled "The First Lye Refuted"* (Bristol, UK: Briggs and Cottle, 1801), 52.
33 Ryland, "The Mind of Christ" in *Pastoral Memorials*, 2:183.
34 John Ryland, *Christ, The Great Source of the Believer's Consolation; and the Grand Subject of the Gospel Ministry. A Sermon Occasioned by the Death of The Rev. Joshua Symonds* (London, 1787), 17.
35 Ryland, *Christ, the Great Source*, 17.
36 Ryland, "The Mind of Christ" in *Pastoral Memorials*, 2:183.

As for "evangelical truth," Ryland expanded on this thought by describing evangelical truth as "the richest discoveries of the gospel" that were designed for "practical purposes," that is, "the sublimest virtues of morality enforced by evangelical motives."[37] He argued that the "beauty and strength" of evangelical truth and vital holiness were lost if there was no connection between truth and holiness. In other words, the truth of Scripture applied in the mind of the believer should motivate true holiness in the life of the believer. For this reason, Ryland was committed to preaching Christ-centered sermons that reminded his audience that Jesus Christ "was the main subject of ministry," which many found to be "salutary and efficacious."[38] For Ryland, a Christ-centered spirituality was developed by the transformation of his mind through Scripture, and this developed in him a desire to imitate Christ and to develop the character of Christ in his life.

The spirituality of the imitation of Christ. In his sermon, "The Mind of Christ," Ryland focused on Paul's words to the church at Philippi: "Let this mind be in you, which was also in Christ Jesus."[39] He began this sermon by declaring, "Surely it is a glorious idea of true religion, that it calls us to be imitators of God: and it is a blessed advantage that evangelical religion presents to us the example of God incarnate, who was found in fashion as a man, and exemplified the most difficult duties, in such circumstances as most powerfully to recommend them."[40] In Ryland's mind, the incarnation of the Son of God was of infinite importance for the spiritual formation of the believer, as it "contains all that is valuable on earth, and stands connected with all that is glorious in heaven."[41] Ryland understood that by the self-emptying birth of the Son of God, humanity now had before them the spiritual model of God in the flesh and the means of living out the new life.

---

37 Ryland, "The Mind of Christ" in *Pastoral Memorials*, 2:183–84.
38 Ryland, "The Preaching of the Cross" in *Pastoral Memorials*, 2:47.
39 Philippians 2:5 (KJV).
40 Ryland, "The Mind of Christ" in *Pastoral Memorials*, 2:183.
41 Ryland, "The Criminality of Selfishness" in *Pastoral Memorials*, 2:190.

While Ryland understood that it would be impossible to imitate Christ in all of his attributes, miracles, and especially in his works of atonement, he did nevertheless champion Christ as the prime example of obedience to the Father and argued for a spirituality of imitation.[42]

For Ryland, godliness included "the knowledge … and [the] imitation of God."[43] He understood the knowledge of God to include God's attributes and moral character, as well as the "knowledge of God in Christ."[44] In other words, one could not know God without knowing Christ. Ryland also spoke of the imitation of the moral perfections of Christ as being a particular activity of godliness. He said, "Oh, what a honor, to be called to imitate God! What an additional advantage have we, from the example of Christ!"[45] Ryland explained this advantage of the presence of Christ in the spiritual formation of the church by noting that God cannot humble himself, yet he has commanded his followers to be humble. Ryland noted that Paul "proposed Christ Jesus as an example of humility, or lowliness of mind," yet, according to Ryland, "humility cannot properly be predicated of the divine nature."[46] Ryland's argument was that God, by nature and "according to truth," can condescend, but he cannot be humble because he cannot in his divine nature think "nothing less than the highest opinion of himself."[47] It was in the incarnation of the Son of God, "having assumed human nature," that true humility could be displayed and exercised by Christ for the formation of true religion within a believer.[48] Ryland stated that Christ's humility was "unspeakably enhanced by the dignity of [Christ's] person" and that "never was any heart so lowly as that of our Lord Jesus."[49] It was

---

42 Ryland, "The First and Second Adam" in *Pastoral Memorials*, 2:71.
43 Ryland, "Godliness and Contentment" in *Pastoral Memorials*, 2:215.
44 Ryland, "Godliness and Contentment" in *Pastoral Memorials*, 2:216.
45 Ryland, "Godliness and Contentment" in *Pastoral Memorials*, 2:216.
46 Ryland, "The Mind of Christ" in *Pastoral Memorials*, 2:184.
47 Ryland, "The Mind of Christ" in *Pastoral Memorials*, 2:184.
48 Ryland, "The Mind of Christ" in *Pastoral Memorials*, 2:184.
49 Ryland, "The Mind of Christ" in *Pastoral Memorials*, 2:184.

the presence of the Son of God in the flesh on this earth that demonstrated to the believer the mindset of a follower of Christ, and if Christ did not come in the flesh, according Ryland, then true humility was "spoiled."[50]

The character of Christ. For Ryland, the application of evangelical truth to the life of the believer was a calling or "glorious idea" of true religion, and this pursuit of evangelical truth defined the life of Ryland. He was convinced that there was "great beauty in true holiness" and that this beauty stemmed from believers being conformed to the character of Christ.[51] Ryland proclaimed that there was "nothing on earth" or in heaven that was "so lovely," and this beauty of Christ's character "makes saints and angels lovely, and the more of it we possess the more lovely we are."[52] For this cause, Ryland believed that true piety towards God and the possession of the beauty of Christ's character were founded upon having the "mind of Christ" through the study of evangelical truth. Ryland realized that "all evangelical truth is of a holy tendency, and is either misunderstood, or you do not enter into the spirit of it, if it does not regulate your tempers and influence your lives."[53] Therefore, he believed that spiritual growth through evangelical truth was the foundation of living out the mind of Christ in this world, and to him this mind of Christ was founded upon the evangelical truths of Scripture. As he said, "Nothing can so happily promote beneficence, integrity, and equity towards men, and piety towards God, as evangelical truth."[54] Hence, Ryland warned the church not to neglect evangelical truths or to neglect the practice of these truths because they would be in danger of having a "dead faith."[55] For Ryland, Christ was our valuable example of living out life according to the "mind of Christ," for

---

50   Ryland, "The Mind of Christ" in *Pastoral Memorials*, 2:184.
51   Ryland, "The Beauty of the Divine Image" in *Pastoral Memorials*, 1:103.
52   Ryland, "The Beauty of the Divine Image" in *Pastoral Memorials*, 1:103.
53   Ryland, "On Godly Zeal Descried and Recommended" in *Pastoral Memorials*, 2:403.
54   Ryland, "On Godly Zeal Described and Recommended," in *Pastoral Memorials*, 2:403.
55   Ryland, "Indecision in Religion" in *Pastoral Memorials*, 1:49.

Christ's mind was "dead to the world, and altogether heavenly."[56]

Assurance and faith: "The presence of Christ"

As Ryland was expositing the Apostle John's words concerning Jesus' removing himself bodily from the presence of his disciples, Ryland noted the promise of Jesus: "I will not leave you comfortless. I will come unto you."[57] For Ryland, the presence of Christ, both in his incarnation for the atonement and in his spiritual relationship for comfort with his earthly disciples after the ascension, was an important part of his compassion ministries as a pastor. In 1796, Ryland was asked to give the "Charge" at the pastoral ordination of William Belsher of the Baptist church at Silver Street in Northampton. He reminded Belsher that there would be times when God's people would enter into adversity, and that it was the pastor's responsibility to this people to be their caregiver.[58] Ryland opened his sermon with Moses' words as found in the Book of Numbers: "Have I conceived all this people? have I begotten them, that thou shouldest say unto me, carry them in thy bosom, as a nursing father beareth the sucking child, unto the land which thou swearest unto their fathers?"[59] Ryland compared the work of a pastor with the calling and care that God entrusted to Moses over the people of God in the wilderness. This pastoral work, according to Ryland, must be infused with the promise from Christ that he was continually present in the life of the believer.

---

56   Ryland, "The Mind of Christ" in *Pastoral Memorials*, 2:186.

57   Cited in John Ryland, *The Promised Presence of Christ with his People: A Source of Consolation Under the Most Painful Bereavements. A Sermon Delivered at the Baptist Meeting-House, Cannon-Street . . . Occasioned by the Death of the Rev. Samuel Pearce*," 2nd ed. (London: Clipstone, 1800), 15.

58   John Ryland, *The Duty Ministers to be Nursing Fathers to the Church to Regard Ministers as the Gift of Christ: A Charge Delivered by the Rev. John Ryland, D. D. of Bristol; and a Sermon by The Rev. S. Pearce, M. A. of Birmingham, in the Dissenters Meeting-house, Angel Street, Worcester; at the Ordination of the Rev. W. Belsher, to the Pastorate of the Baptist Church, meeting in Silver Street, in the same city; Together with an Introductory Address, by the Rev. G. Osborn, and also Mrs. Belsher's Declaration of Religious Sentiments* (London, 1796), 17.

59   Numbers 11:12 (KJV).

In John Newton's 1787 letter to Ryland upon the death of Ryland's wife, he wrote such encouraging words about the presence of Christ during suffering that they served as a great example to a young Ryland of the importance of the language or words used by the pastor in times of grief. It was evident from the many letters that Newton wrote Ryland in their thirty-nine years of friendship that Ryland learned much from him in terms of pastoral care. In Ryland's sermon at the death of his friend and fellow pastor, Samuel Pearce (1766–1799), he told Pearce's church, "So deeply am I sensible of the loss sustained by this church in general, not to say by the nearest relative of my dear departed brother, that on a partial view of their circumstances, I could not be surprised were some now present, ready to exclaim, 'Is there any sorrow like unto our sorrow, wherewith the Lord has this day afflicted us?'"[60] Ryland, knowing the suffering of both the church and Pearce's family, interjected into his sermon the biblical doctrine of Christ as husband of the church, giving care in times of suffering. Ryland declared:

> Surely they who drank with him [Pearce] the deepest out of his cup of affliction, could find no savor of the curse, no, not at the bottom; nor would they drink the bitter, without tasting also of the sweet, which was not sparingly dropt into it, but copiously infused. And after such proofs and illustrations of the divine fidelity, I cannot but believe, that she [Pearce's widow] who needs them most of all shall find farther stores of consolation laid upon for her relief: since God her Maker is her husband, who giveth the songs in the night.[61]

Ryland described how Pearce, while serving as pastor of this church, often recommended Christ's presence as "ground encouragement" on which the church could depend.[62] As Christ promised to not leave the disciples

---

60   Ryland, *The Promised Presence of Christ*, 15.
61   Ryland, *The Promised Presence of Christ*, 16.
62   Ryland, *The Promised Presence of Christ*, 17.

in their time of suffering, so Ryland reminded the church that this "same respect to his whole church in every age" was available to them so that they could "safely rely on his gracious promise, as his very apostles."[63] Ryland's language in this sermon was infused with the understanding of the presence of Christ, and this understanding was the source of a great hope and consolation to the church that would sustain them in their times of grief.

The language of presence. In Ryland's "Confession of Faith," he declared that he was "convinced of the existence of God"[64] and knew that this assured faith in God's existence was an important piece of "great spirituality."[65] He said, "We must live as seeing the invisible God … impressed with a deep sense of the work of spiritual things."[66] This blessed assurance of the existence of God fueled Ryland's theology regarding a future presence of God, as well as an experience and expectation of the current presence of God. Ryland was conscious of the church's "continued enjoyment of [Christ's] spiritual presence, and divine influence."[67] Ryland asserted:

> We fully ascertain this privilege to be included in the text, by comparing this promise, I will come unto you, with those declarations, recorded by Matthew, which admit of no solution without the acknowledgement of Christ's proper divinity: "Where two or three are gathered together in my name, there am I in the midst of them. And lo I am with you always to the end of the world."[68]

For Ryland, the divinity of Christ, along with his continued presence, was the source of the believer's joy, even in the midst of suffering. One final

---

63   Ryland, *The Promised Presence of Christ*, 17.
64   Jonathan M. Yeager, ed., "A Baptist's Beliefs: John Ryland, Jr.," in *Early Evangelicalism: A Reader* (Oxford: Oxford University Press, 2013), 294.
65   Ryland, "Triumphing in Christ" in *Pastoral Memorials*, 2:77.
66   Ryland, "Triumphing in Christ" in *Pastoral Memorials*, 2:77.
67   Ryland, *The Promised Presence of Christ*, 22.
68   Ryland, *The Promised Presence of Christ*, 22.

way Christ fulfilled his promise of eternal presence, according to Ryland, was that "at the end of the world," Christ will "come again, and receive them to himself; that where he is, there they may be also."[69]

Ryland's confidence in the eternal presence of God was an encouragement in his own life, which he made apparent in his confession. He said, "We must have a strong confidence in the all-sufficiency of Christ to support and defend us, and to carry on his own interest, being persuaded that he will be exalted in his own strength, will overcome all his foes, fulfill all his counsel, gather in all his people, and make them eternally happy."[70] This confession in the eternal presence of God developed in Ryland a language that made its way into his pastoral care, which was evident in his consoling use of the phrase "presence of God" in his funeral discourses.

A notable example of this was found in Ryland's comforting words to the church at Birmingham where Pearce pastored. Ryland said to the Church, "Yes, beloved, we are authorized to make a general application of this word of consolation; and must affirm, that the promised presence of the blessed Redeemer is the best source of comfort to all his people, in every time of trouble."[71] Ryland was so convinced in the comfort that this doctrine of "presence" brings to the church that he challenged the church at Birmingham to reflect on Pearce's earthly ministry, but also to realize that Pearce's "affections were evidently and eminently in heaven."[72] Ryland also reminded them that when Pearce knew that he was going to die, "he could not promise to come again" to the church, but he believed that the "presence of his great Master, as to his divine nature," would be the sufficient comfort to sustain the church "by his departure."[73] Ryland continued, "The spiritual presence of Christ could make up for the want of his bodily presence, to those who knew what it was to enjoy the latter; it must then

---

69   Ryland, *The Promised Presence of Christ*, 23.
70   Ryland, "Triumphing in Christ" in *Pastoral Memorials*, 2:77.
71   Ryland, *The Promised Presence of Christ*, 17.
72   Ryland, *The Promised Presence of Christ*, 25.
73   Ryland, *The Promised Presence of Christ*, 25–26.

assuredly be sufficient to supply the absence of any under-shepherd."[74] For Ryland, the presence of Christ and the hope of his return were the greatest comfort of the grieving church and were more than sufficient in their lives to bring complete effectual healing in their time of grief.

Ryland called upon Pearce's church, in their mourning for the loss of their pastor, to "reflect that if Christ should come unto you, according to this gracious promise, he will communicate unto you, more largely, the supply of his Spirit. And shall not this fit you for every duty, support you under every pressure, and ensure you the victory over every spiritual enemy?"[75] For Ryland, the language of the "presence of Christ" as both a present help in times of grief and as a future hope of the promised eternal presence with Christ was a consistent teaching point for the church, especially for those who were suffering.

Presence of Christ: "The source of earthly consolation"

When Samuel Pearce was nearing death, he entreated Ryland to preach his funeral using John 14:18: "I will not leave you comfortless. I will come unto you."[76] For both Pearce and Ryland, "the promised presence of the blessed Redeemer is the best source of comfort to all his people, in every time of trouble."[77] Pearce wanted to leave his church with an anticipation of the comforting presence of God, no matter the extent of the grief they felt upon this earth. Ryland accomplished Pearce's wishes by presenting the assurance of the fulfillment of Christ's promise that He would not leave His disciples "comfortless," a reference to the ministry of the Holy Spirit of God, and that He would return again for His church.[78] Ryland told the church, "Let then the expectation that this promise will be accomplished,

---

74 Ryland, *The Promised Presence of Christ*, 26.
75 Ryland, *The Promised Presence of Christ*, 35.
76 John 14:18 (*KJV*).
77 Ryland, *The Promised Presence of Christ*, 17.
78 Ryland, *The Promised Presence of Christ*, 20.

moderate your sorrows."[79] In other words, Ryland encouraged the church to "moderate" or restrain their grief by contemplating the promises of God for consolation. He continued, "It is the presence of Christ which constitutes the perfected felicity of our dear departed friend: but Christ is really present with his church upon earth also."[80] As the church was to moderate its sorrows, it would find its "felicity" or happiness in the presence of God on this earth.

Another example of Ryland comforting others through Christ's promise of his presence is found in his message to the grieving congregation at Bedford when their pastor, Joshua Symonds (1739–1788), died. Ryland began his sermon for Symonds' church with an encouragement to remember that Christ was the "great source of the believer's consolation."[81] In order to bring this church comfort, Ryland chose Colossians 1:27–28 as his base text: "Christ in you, the hope of glory."[82] Ryland said, "The text is the language of inspiration, and points out infallibly to us all, the only ground of every Christian's hope, and the noblest theme on which every preacher should insist."[83] The message of "Christ in you," according to Ryland, revealed to the church that "none of the fallen race of Man can entertain a rational hope of glory, but what must be founded on Christ alone, that Anointed Saviour who died without the gates of Jerusalem, who lives and reigns in glory now, and lives and reigns within the breast of every sincere believer."[84] Therefore, there was great comfort to the church, which was grieving the loss of their pastor, in the understanding that there was only one hope, Jesus Christ, and his Spirit "lives and reigns" in the life of true believers in Christ.

As a pastor, Ryland understood that in order to deal with grief, the

---

79   Ryland, *The Promised Presence of Christ*, 40.
80   Ryland, *The Promised Presence of Christ*, 40.
81   Ryland, *Christ, the Great Source*, 1.
82   Colossians 1:27 (*KJV*).
83   Ryland, *Christ, the Great Source*, 4.
84   Ryland, *Christ, the Great Source*, 4.

church must comprehend that their hope was not in this world, and that they were not left alone in this world. Therefore, he spoke to them about the presence of God and the truth that the Spirit of Christ indwells every "sincere believer," thus revealing to the church "the account given us of what Christ is to the church."[85] Ryland stated, "By [Christ's] obedience unto death, he rendered the bestowment of future glory, upon lost, guilty sinners, perfectly consistent with the divine character, and the honour of God's moral government. They who were exposed to everlasting contempt, on account of the dishonour they had cast upon their maker, may now hope for everlasting glory."[86] In other words, Ryland argued that the presence of incarnated Son of God, the "maker" of all things, brought about a restoring of the relationship between God and sinners, thus ensuring a future "new hope," which was everlasting. It was of this future hope Ryland reminded the church at Bedford in order to bring assurance and consolation during their time of grief.

Presence of Christ: "The source of eternal bliss"

When Benjamin Francis (1734–1799), pastor of the Church at Shortwood, died, Ryland preached his funeral message utilizing 1 Thessalonians 4:17–18: "So shall we ever be with the Lord. Wherefore, comfort one another with these words."[87] Ryland's pastoral care for this church was based on Paul's phrase: "shall we ever be with the Lord." Ryland held that the life-giving presence of the Lord, which he described as "within the breast of every sincere believer," had its root in the "stronger attractions of heaven" because "to be with Christ was still far better, than all the bliss, which even a Christian could enjoy below."[88] Therefore, for Ryland, a belief in the

---

85 Ryland, *Christ, the Great Source*, 8.
86 Ryland, *Christ, the Great Source*, 13.
87 1 Thessalonians 4:17–18 (KJV).
88 John Ryland, *The Presence of Christ the Source of Eternal Bliss: A Funeral Discourse Delivered December 22, 1799 … The Death of the Rev. Benjamin Francis, A. M.* (Bristol: Ann Bryan, 1799), 4.

eternal communion between God and the believer was the greatest source of the believer's happiness on earth. He said, "The presence of the Lord is evidently represented as the very essence of their bliss."[89] This eternal "celestial bliss,"[90] which was "the state of the Saints in glory," [91] was held in the promised eternity of the presence of Christ. It was here that Ryland introduced a connection between the happiness of the living Church with the anticipation of the presence of Christ throughout eternity. In other words, Ryland believed one cannot truly have joy or happiness in the present life without a convincing faith in eternal life with Christ.[92] In Francis' funeral discourse, Ryland sought to deliver to the church an anticipation of the eternal bliss found in an everlasting communion with the eternal Christ.

First, Ryland reminded the church that "they who are for ever with the Lord, enjoy an uninterrupted sense of his divine excellencies and glorious perfections."[93] Ryland assured the church that their departed pastor could now "see [Jesus] as he is,"[94] that is, in all his perfections because he "now possessed a just and full acquaintance with the divine character."[95] This was only accomplished, according to Ryland, when one saw God "face to face."[96] The anticipation of this "face to face" encounter with God was a source of the believer's "eternal bliss" or happiness in Christ. It was never truly realized until one was "for ever with the Lord."[97] Yet it was here that Ryland reminded the church that their "extacy [sic] of joy" was in the presence of Christ and "that they shall derive everlasting blessedness from the uninterrupted contemplation of his perfections."[98]

---

89 Ryland, *The Presence of Christ the Source of Eternal Bliss*, 7.
90 Ryland, *The Presence of Christ the Source of Eternal Bliss*, 9.
91 Ryland, *The Presence of Christ the Source of Eternal Bliss*, 9.
92 Ryland, "Christ the Only Source of Eternal Happiness" in *Pastoral Memorials*, 1:310.
93 Ryland, *The Presence of Christ the Source of Eternal Bliss*, 10.
94 Ryland, *The Presence of Christ the Source of Eternal Bliss*, 10.
95 Ryland, *The Presence of Christ the Source of Eternal Bliss*, 10.
96 Ryland, *The Presence of Christ the Source of Eternal Bliss*, 11.
97 Ryland, *The Presence of Christ the Source of Eternal Bliss*, 11.
98 Ryland, *The Presence of Christ the Source of Eternal Bliss*, 19.

A second encouragement was that those believers who have already died have entered into a "perfect union with [Christ]."[99] Ryland's stated, "Your own happiness consists in connexion and communion with God, in union with Christ and conformity to him; and so does the happiness of others."[100] This was to say that the eternal bliss by which Ryland was encouraging these grieving churches was only found in a union whereby "the believer is now so 'joined unto the Lord,' as to be 'one spirit' with him, and to 'have the mind of Christ.'"[101] For Ryland, union with Christ was an important aspect of receiving all of the benefits of God, including "His intrinsic glory being displayed to [the believer's] enlightened understanding."[102] Ryland said that Christ "must dwell in your hearts; abide in your affections, as truly as the bridegroom dwells in the heart of the bride."[103] Yet, for those who were "for ever with the Lord," this union was demonstrated through a "continual and uncloying community with [God]."[104] Ryland's point was that there were no "impediments" to true fellowship with God through eternal union with Christ.

A third point of encouragement from Ryland directed the church to anticipate being perfectly conformed to the image of God. Ryland stated, "But as a believing sight of Jesus has, even in this life, a transforming efficacy, so the full enjoyment of his presence, in the world above, shall instantly complete the blessed transformation."[105] For Ryland, this completion of earthly sanctification was a point of joy for the believer. To be present with the Lord, face to face, brought a fullness of possession by the Holy Spirit of the believer's soul.[106] Ryland called this the "state of perfection" although

---

99   Ryland, *The Presence of Christ the Source of Eternal Bliss*, 10
100 Ryland, "Enlarged Desires Satisfied" in *Pastoral Memorials*, 1:95.
101 Ryland, *The Presence of Christ the Source of Eternal Bliss*, 11.
102 Ryland, *Christ, the Great Source*, 11.
103 Ryland, *Christ, the Great Source*, 11.
104 Ryland, *The Presence of Christ the Source of Eternal Bliss*, 12.
105 Ryland, *The Presence of Christ the Source of Eternal Bliss*, 13.
106 Ryland, *The Presence of Christ the Source of Eternal Bliss*, 13.

he did not ascribe to "absolute perfection," for he understood this "state of perfection" to be progressive. He said, "For every fresh discovery of God will assuredly have a corresponding impression on the heart," yet without any earthly obstacles, biases, errors or sins to distort these "fresh" discoveries of God.[107]

The premise that to be present "for ever with the Lord" brings "eternal bliss" was a major theme in Ryland's funeral discourses. He encouraged a great anticipation for this "face to face" encounter with God within the hearts of his hearers. He maintained that the brethren who had already entered "into the joy of the Lord," that is, who were in the presence of the Jesus Christ, "participate with him of that ineffable bliss which he derives from the enjoyment of his Father's love. They rejoice in his exaltation, and in a manner, enjoy it with him, as though they sat down with him on his throne."[108] Ryland believed that it was only through the presence of God that the church truly found its consolation and comfort in this life, and it was only by this same presence of God that the church would find its joy and eternal bliss. He remarked, "From the whole, we should learn, not to sorrow for those who have died in the Lord, as those who are without hope." Rather, Ryland said, "They are safe and happy. The fruit is gathered for life eternal."[109] The presence of God was a main focus for Ryland, and he utilized this encouraging thought on multiple occasions to bring comfort to churches who had lost their pastor.

Godly zeal: "The influence of the love of Christ"

For Ryland, godly zeal was a direct response to the "kingdom of God among men," who took on the "arduous task" of suffering for the cause of the Father, and Ryland never allowed any opposition to deter him from his task, "even the reconciliation of transgressors to God."[110] In the 1792

---

107 Ryland, *The Presence of Christ the Source of Eternal Bliss*, 14.
108 Ryland, *The Presence of Christ the Source of Eternal Bliss*, 13.
109 Ryland, "The Death of the Aged Believer" in *Pastoral Memorials*, 1:65.
110 Ryland, "Godly Zeal Described and Recommended" in *Pastoral Memorials*, 2:409.

Baptist Association circular letter, Ryland exclaimed:

> We beseech you, holy brethren, partakers, of the heavenly calling, consider the Apostle and High Priest of our Profession, Christ Jesus. Let the excellency of his cause, the ardor which he himself hath shewn in it, the personal obligations you are under to him, and blessings derived from him to all his people, excite your zeal to the uttermost—Reflect on the original dignity which he eternally possessed, and consider the depth of humiliation to which he condescended for your sakes.[111]

This work of reconciliation was accomplished, argued Ryland, by Christ condescending and applying his salvation to the heart of his elect. It was this condescension of the Son of God in the flesh that birthed in Ryland's heart a zeal for the things of God. He stated, "And can you be languid and lukewarm in the service of such a friend? Let his love, his dying love, constrain you to imitate his example, and exert yourselves in his interest."[112] Ryland implored his hearers to consider the love of Christ towards the church through his incarnation and to allow Christ's zeal for the cause of the Father to fuel the church's zeal for "further advancement of his cause."[113] It was not that God needed the assistance of the church to fulfill the mission of Christ. Instead, according to Ryland, "he honors you by employing you in his service."[114]

Godly zeal through opposition. Ryland often experienced opposition in his ministry, especially from the Socinians and others who rejected the deity of Christ. Robert Hall, Jr. (1764–1831), in his funeral sermon for Ryland, portrayed his character as having a "certain timidity of spirit,"[115] yet it

---

111 Ryland, "Godly Zeal Described and Recommended" in *Pastoral Memorials*, 2:409.
112 Ryland, "Godly Zeal Described and Recommended" in *Pastoral Memorials*, 2:410.
113 Ryland, "Godly Zeal Described and Recommended" in *Pastoral Memorials*, 2:409–10.
114 Ryland, "Godly Zeal Described and Recommended" in *Pastoral Memorials*, 2:410.
115 Robert Hall Jr., *A Sermon Occasioned by the Death of the Rev. John Ryland, D.D.:*

never caused him to shrink from speaking out against doctrinal errors nor to neglect his leadership qualities that would have affected many in that generation. In his 1792 letter to the Baptist Association, Ryland stated, "Let the greatness of the opposition that is made to the reign of God on earth stir you up to the more ardent zeal." In other words, the opposition to the deity of Christ and his presence on this earth should empower the believer with "ardent zeal" to continue to advance the cause of Christ.[116] Ryland believed that opposition to Christ merely demonstrated that the "hosts of hell" were actively "engaged on the side of sin," and it reminded Ryland of his former position as an "active" enemy of "the blessed Saviour."[117] Ryland challenged the ministers and messengers of the Northamptonshire Baptist Association by stating, "Let reflection upon your former servitude rouse you to assert that glorious liberty wherewith Christ has made you free. Be at least as active for the best of masters, as you were once for the worst of tyrants."[118] Godly zeal, therefore, should be the fruit of opposition because it reminds the believer of Christ's work of "pardon and recovery," and it should "stimulate" the believer to "activity in glorifying [God]."[119] He also stated that this opposition allowed the believer to engage in combat against "principalities and powers," who "once lorded it over you. But Omnipotence is on your side. Through your God you may do valiantly, for he shall tread down your enemies for you."[120] For Ryland, godly zeal was increased in his spiritual life through supernatural opposition and allowed him to experience spiritual warfare "in the name of Jesus."[121]

Godly zeal for the state of mankind. As Ryland was finishing his thoughts concerning godly zeal and opposition, he stated, "Carry on the war in the

---

Preached at the Meeting Broadmead, Bristol, June 5th, 1825 (London: Hamilton, Adams, and Co., 1825), 35.
116 Ryland, "Godly Zeal Described and Recommended" in *Pastoral Memorials*, 2:410.
117 Ryland, "Godly Zeal Described and Recommended" in *Pastoral Memorials*, 2:410.
118 Ryland, "Godly Zeal Described and Recommended" in *Pastoral Memorials*, 2:410.
119 Ryland, "Godly Zeal Described and Recommended" in *Pastoral Memorials*, 2:410.
120 Ryland, "Godly Zeal Described and Recommended" in *Pastoral Memorials*, 2:410.
121 Ryland, "Godly Zeal Described and Recommended" in *Pastoral Memorials*, 2:410–11.

name of Jesus into the empire of your adversary. Through the Spirit you shall mortify the deeds of the body, and obtain farther conquests over your in-bred foes. And you are warranted to labor and hope to be the instruments of rescuing others from the prince of darkness, that are now led captives by him at his will."[122] For Ryland, when one considered the "divine nature" of the Son of God incarnate and his moral character in the flesh, compared to the "miserable state of mankind," there was a godly zeal for evangelism and missions that ensued.[123] Ryland encouraged his readers to give "serious attention" to the writings of William Carey (1761–1834) on "the state of the heathen world," and published sermons by Andrew Fuller (1754–1815) and John Sutcliff (1752–1814) in *Jealousy for the Lord of Hosts, and the Pernicious Influence of Delay*.[124] Ryland asserted that these works, "if you have any feelings in your souls," will "excite your compassionate concern for your brethren of the human race, who sit in darkness and the shadow of death."[125] Having an ardent zeal for the salvation of mankind was part of Ryland's spirituality. He was committed to missions and a zeal for the salvation of Muslims, Roman Catholics, Eastern Orthodox, nominal Protestants, which he considered to all be "poor miserable heathens."[126] In other words, Christ's actions demonstrated his zeal for the Father, his authority over the Jews, and his zeal for the worship of God. True godly zeal, according to Ryland, promoted the divine honor of God and "strenuously" opposed "all that would dishonor God."[127]

---

122 Ryland, "Godly Zeal Described and Recommended" in *Pastoral Memorials*, 2:411.
123 Ryland, "Godly Zeal Described and Recommended" in *Pastoral Memorials*, 2:411.
124 Ryland, "Godly Zeal Described and Recommended" in *Pastoral Memorials*, 2:411. For the sermons, see John Sutcliff and Andrew Fuller, *Jealousy for the Lord of Hosts: And, the Pernicious Influence of Delay in Religious Concerns. Two Discourses Delivered at a Meeting of Ministers at Clipstone, in Northamptonshire, April 27, 1791* (S.l., 1791).
125 Ryland, "Godly Zeal Described and Recommended" in *Pastoral Memorials*, 2:411.
126 Ryland, "Godly Zeal Described and Recommended" in *Pastoral Memorials*, 2:411.
127 Ryland, "Christ an Example of Zeal" in *Pastoral Memorials*, 2:294.

Conclusion

When one examines the contemporary church, especially in Western culture, it is apparent that most Christians are not genuinely interested in church history as a source of their personal spirituality. Yet, church historians like Grant Gordon consistently demonstrate to the modern church, the importance of the spiritual life of men like John Ryland, Jr. and his spirituality of "faith and practice." Even in Ryland's seventieth year of life, as his health and strength began to fail, he was consistent in his ministry and he labored "more exclusively to the church at Broadmead, the College, and those religious and benevolent objects in the West of England whose claims pressed upon him."[128] His benevolent spirit and commitment to the gospel, which were demonstrated in his life, continued to be his moniker as his life began to fade. For Ryland, "true religion is internal" and produced "affections" for God and for humanity that flow from the "devout exercises of the heart."[129] All throughout his writings, Ryland demonstrated his genuine faith in Christ by his encouragement to the church to participate in the eternal activities that were derived from their love for and adoration of Christ, including the divine works of Christ. Ryland demonstrated how the doctrines of the incarnation and the presence of Christ were applied to various areas of his ministry and to his own Christian life. His life provides the contemporary believer with examples of the source of true godly zeal and the practical implications of this biblical doctrine. In the final reflections of his sermon "Christ an Example of Zeal," he expressed the results of the doctrine of the incarnation of the Son of God and the humility he demonstrated in the flesh. Ryland stated, "Oh! May we look to the author and finisher of faith, for an increase of faith, love, and zeal!"[130]

---

128 James Culross, *The Three Rylands: A Hundred Years of Various Christian Service* (London: Elliot Stock, 1897), 88.

129 Ryland, "Obedience the Test of Love to God" in *Pastoral Memorials*, 2:291.

130 Ryland, "Christ an Example of Zeal" in *Pastoral Memorials*, 1:296.

11

Herman Witsius Ryland (1759-1838) & the evangelical conversion narrative[1]

CHRISTOPHER W. CROCKER

"The Lord knoweth them that are His" (2 Timothy 2:19). Herman Witsius Ryland (1759–1838, hereafter HWR)[2] came from a family of Baptists that included a father and brother who were notable Particular Baptists in England. As such the perennial question of salvation and of having assurance

---

1   Grant Gordon is an important pioneer in the studies of John Ryland Jr. through his publication of John Newton's letters to John Ryland Jr. entitled *Wise Counsel* (2009). I became acquainted with Gordon and his work as I built upon his, and many other pioneer studies, to undertake to write a critical biography of Ryland for my PhD (2014–2018). One sub-story that emerges in *Wise Counsel*, and which was of interest to my research, was the relationship between John Ryland Jr. (JRJ) and his youngest brother Herman Witsius Ryland (HWR). This short essay seeks to explore that relationship, and others connected to it, through the lens of the evangelical conversion narrative. Was HWR converted? This essay is in honour of a man who has modelled what it means to be a pastor-scholar.

2   The main biographical work on HWR is as follows: James H. Lambert, "Ryland, Herman Witsius" in the *Dictionary of Canadian Biography*, vol. 7, University of Toronto/Université Laval, 2003– (http://www.biographi.ca/en/bio/ryland_herman_witsius_7E.html; accessed May 7, 2025).

of this by adhering to a Puritan-evangelical conversion narrative, was of the utmost importance to this family culture. HWR was—seemingly—the family exception to this conversion narrative, his other siblings all professing evangelical faith. Notable evangelical figures such as evangelical Anglican John Newton (1725–1807) and Particular Baptist John Ryland Jr. (1753–1825, hereafter JRJ), all sought to carry on the discipling influence of HWR's sincere though eccentric father, John Collett Ryland (1723–1792), but to uncertain ends. This essay will consider the life of HWR in light of the Puritan-evangelical conversion narrative, his unique context, along with uncited letters between the Ryland brothers, to consider whether he ever came to adhere to such a narrative or what his spiritual narrative may have been. Particular emphasis will be given to his politics (or politicking), religion, and character. This essay will survey portions of his life, but with a focus on this spiritual narrative as expressed in the pastoral interest shown toward him by the likes of Newton and his brother.

Before proceeding, what is the Puritan-evangelical conversion narrative? The Puritans, and the evangelicals who followed them, stressed an applied theology of conversion, an experimental or experiential religion of the heart. Mere mental assent to doctrine was not what made someone a Christian but rather a personal response to the Gospel; this transformed someone from sinner to saint. This internal change was marked by external evidence. In his preface to *The Religious Affections* (1746), a book written to aid in discernment in the face of the revivals seen in the First Great Awakening, Jonathan Edwards (1703–1758) wrote, "What are the distinguishing qualifications of those that are in favour with God, and entitled to his eternal rewards? Or, which comes to the same thing, What is the nature of true religion? and wherein do lie the distinguishing notes of that virtue and holiness, that is acceptable in the sight of God?"[3] Sixteenth- and seventeenth-century Puritans, such as William Perkins (1558–1602), had shown themselves physicians of the soul, like cartographers, mapping the

---

3   Jonathan Edwards, *A Treatise concerning Religious Affections* (Edinburgh: John Gray, 1772), iii.

soul, or the *ordo salutis* (e.g., Perkins' *Golden Chain*). In his work *The Evangelical Conversion Narrative* (2005) Bruce Hindmarsh notes: "For Puritans salvation had its own proper syntax. And by the late sixteenth century this syntax had been carefully parsed."[4] JRJ compressed this narrative into what may be described as three distinct phases: convicted, convinced, and comforted: convicted or awakened to the reality of sin, convinced of the need of salvation in Christ alone through faith alone, and finally comforted that the Gospel promises had been effectually applied to the believer by the Spirit.[5]

HWR was born into a family and church culture steeped in a commitment to this ethos in 1759. Whether it was in Warwick or Northampton is unclear. The Rylands had moved to Northampton in October, 1759. He was named after his father's favourite Dutch theologian, Herman Witsius (1636–1708), who wrote on the relationship between the biblical covenants. HWR's early years of education and spiritual nurture were at the hands of his father who not only pastored College Lane Baptist Church in Northampton but also operated a successful Dissenting Academy for boys.[6] Here HWR had opportunity to be acquainted with notable Christian leaders in his father's circle such as John Newton, George Whitefield, and Rowland Hill, not to mention those families connected with the academy and his father's ever-widening evangelical network. Though the list of Ryland's scholars[7] does not name HWR as one of his father's students it is almost certain that he received his preliminary education here, including French (see below).[8]

---

4 Bruce D. Hindmarsh, *The Evangelical Conversion Narrative: Spiritual Autobiography in Early Modern England*. (Oxford: Oxford University Press, 2005), 13–15 and Mark Noll, *The Rise of Evangelicalism* (Leicester: IVP, 2005), 35.

5 Christopher Crocker, "The Life and Legacy of John Ryland Jr. (1753-1825): A man of considerable usefulness—an historical biography." (PhD dissertation, University of Bristol, 2018), 61–62, 60–66.

6 For more, see Crocker, "Life and Legacy of John Ryland Jr.," 54.

7 "The Rev. John Collett Ryland's Scholars," *Northamptonshire Notes and Queries*, n.s., 1.6 (January 1926): 18–31.

8 For example, his brother JRJ is also not listed but is known to have studied and then

It is interesting that of the family members mentioned by JRJ, and even his father, HWR seldom featured. This is possibly because he was the youngest child, or perhaps some sort of "black sheep" of the family, since his biographer, Lambert, described his nature as "combative."[9] This may have put HWR at odds with the dramatic and strong personality of his father. A 1775 comment by John Newton to JRJ, to pass along his regards to his "brothers," means that in that year HWR was still at home. With the onset of the American Revolution and HWR's eventual service in that conflict, it is possible that in 1776, at the age of 17, he sought opportunity and further education in the army (maybe even serving or being trained in England until he did deploy early in the next decade). Other possibilities as to his activity include education, apprenticeships, or work in a location such as London. He certainly was in London at some point prior to his departure for America, as Newton said that HWR "often" attended services at St. Mary Woolnoth in London where Newton served as rector.[10] What is known is that beginning in 1781 he enjoyed a long and rather successful career as a civil servant. In 1781, during the final stages of the Revolutionary War, he arrived in New York where he served as the assistant deputy-paymaster-general of the British army. When the war ended in 1783, he returned to England with the commander-in-chief, Sir Guy Carleton (1724–1808). In a short time HWR had done well positionally to distinguish himself and become acquainted with senior British officials.

Already in his short career HWR had embarked on two courses very different from his family, both religiously and militarily. As the Test Act was not repealed for Dissenters to serve in senior government and military posts until 1828 it is likely HWR began frequenting Anglican churches to advance his career as a civil servant. Though a friend to evangelical Anglicans such as James Hervey, Ryland Sr. was still a principled Baptist. Though

---

assisted in the academy.
9   Lambert, "Ryland, Herman Witsius."
10 Grant Gordon, ed., *Wise Counsel: John Newton's Letters to John Ryland Jr.* (Edinburgh: Banner of Truth Trust, 2009), 163, which cites Letter 33, dated January 17, 1785.

a son conforming to Anglicanism would have troubled the elder Ryland, this would have been compounded by his politics. That he served in the British Army against the Americans was viewed by his father as aiding tyranny. His father had described the British conflict as "a crusade against the liberty of the subject and the rights of man."[11] At a time when the British stepped up their offensive against the Americans he said to fellow Baptist minister Robert Hall Sr. (1728–1791), "If I were general Washington … we would swear by Him that sits upon the throne, and liveth for ever and ever, that we would never sheathe our swords whilst there was an English soldier in arms remaining in America: and that is what I would do, brother Hall."[12] Baptists, who had endured much persecution at the hands of the state church in the previous century, were still, during the 1770s and 1780s, unsympathetic toward it. Yet, HWR went still further by not only serving in the army but later coming to embrace a politics that was anathema to his father (albeit after his death). Lambert has described HWR's politics as that of a "colonial tory, suspicious of democracy, popular politicians, and colonial ways, a defender of aristocracy and the royal prerogative, nostalgic for the mother country."[13] These divergent paths and views in politics and religion within the family will be illustrated further.

Despite one's politics (Newton's politics, an evangelical Anglican, were "Jesus is Lord"), and HWR's role as a civil servant in the establishment, Newton and JRJ were mutually, and chiefly, concerned about his spiritual life. Upon his return to London after the war HWR did not frequent St. Mary's but did call upon Newton. Newton informed JRJ on January 17, 1785:

Your brother called on me to tell me he had lost your letter and last Wednesday he called again and brought it. He stayed and dined with

---

11 William Newman, *Rylandiana: Reminiscences relating to the Rev. John Ryland* (London: George Whiteman, 1835), 194–5.
12 Newman, *Rylandiana*, 194.
13 Lambert, "Ryland, Herman Witsius."

me then, and we had a good deal of talk. I did all in my power to assure him that I shall be glad to see him whenever he comes; the ice is broken between us. I put Mr Soam Jenygs [sic] book on the internal evidence of Christianity in his pocket, which he said he would return soon, and then we shall perhaps have more talk. I like him well, and shall be glad indeed if the Lord is pleased to make me anyway useful to him.[14]

Newton sought to present the gospel to HWR, whom he did not believe to be converted. As a means of evangelism he gave him *A View of the Internal Evidence of the Christian Religion* (1776), an apologetic work written by Soame Jenyns (1704–1787) who was a Christian politician. Another interaction between Newton and HWR at this time sheds further light:

Your brother Witsius was several times with me before he left London, we had some interesting conversation, and he seemed to like to visit me. A while ago I received a letter from him, it was written in French, and was indeed a French letter.15 He expressed his thanks for civilities received, in higher terms than they deserved, but it was entirely in the complaisant style,16 without touching upon any points which we had conversed upon. I have been much engaged, and have not yet answered him, but perhaps I may, when wind and tide are favourable for writing. If I do, I must return him plain England for his polite French.[17]

This account speaks to HWR's continued interest in Newton, some meaningful gospel conversation, yet a reticence on HWR's part to reflect deeply or personally. After the war many soldiers struggled to find

---

14   Gordon, *Wise Counsel*, 163, from Letter 33, dated January 17, 1785.
15   This mastery of French would serve him well in his later career.
16   I.e. a form of flattery.
17   Gordon, *Wise Counsel*, 170, citing Letter 34, which is dated March 31, 1786.

employment. Throughout 1786, HWR was living with JRJ's family in Northampton.[18] This would have placed HWR under many indirect gospel influences, whether the gentle nature of JRJ afforded direct opportunities to speak to his brother is unknown. He may even have still been in Northampton when his sister-in-law, Elizabeth, died in January 1787. From the locations revealed in his letters in fonds held in the Canadian Archives, he also appears to have lived in Enfield with or near his father (December 1791–March 1792) and then in Blackfriars, London (March to Aug 1792).[19]

After a lapse of time, HWR was, by 1793, still seeking another advantageous government position. JRJ used Newton's connections within the influential Clapham Sect[20] to relay a letter respecting his brother to Mr. Thornton,[21] "When I have done this," Newton wrote, "I have done all in my power."[22] Whether through this letter or not, Herman found employment as secretary to Guy Carleton, now Lord Dorchester, the Governor of Lower Canada.[23] Upon hearing this news through a correspondence with JRJ, Newton commented, "I am glad you hear well of Mr Witsius. When you write give my love to him. I pray the Lord to give him those blessings, which Lord Dorchester cannot bestow."[24] Newton hoped HWR would find satisfaction in the gospel and not in worldly pursuits (cf. Matthew 6:33). Not long after going to Lower Canada, the evangelical Anglican William Wilberforce (1759–1833), a mutual friend of Newton and JRJ, published a best-selling work, *A Practical View of the Prevailing Religious System*

---

18   Gordon, *Wise Counsel*, 169-184, *passim*
19   Herman Witsius Ryland Family Fonds, Library and Archives Canada (https://data2.archives.ca/pdf/pdf001/p000000047.pdf; accessed May 7, 2025).
20   The Clapham Sect was an informal group of influential and wealthy evangelical Anglican politicians, businessmen, clergy and laity.
21   Henry Thornton or his brother Samuel, who were both influential politicians and businessmen, and Evangelicals.
22   Gordon, *Wise Counsel*, 283, Letter 60, dated March 28, 1793.
23   The Canadian province of Quebec was previously known as Lower Canada from 1791–1841.
24   Gordon, *Wise Counsel*, 311, Letter 65, dated May 2, 1794.

of Professed Christians, in the Higher and Middle Classes in this Country, Contrasted with Real Christianity (1797). In a country with much religious nominalism, Wilberforce sought to contrast nominal or cultural Christianity with the real Christianity of the Scriptures. This apologetical book may fairly summarize HWR's faith from an evangelical perspective, especially in light of what will be considered below. It is interesting to note the many indirect connections HWR had with Wilberforce, including the first Lower Canadian bishop, Jacob Mountain (1793–1825), who was acquainted with the Prime Minister William Pitt, who was a close friend of Wilberforce.

HWR's religion and politics were closely intertwined. On the Legislative Council of Lower Canada and in the church, he established an "excellent rapport" with the Jacob Mountain. With the Bishop, HWR shared a preoccupation in advancing Anglicanism in the colony. For less pious reasons than Mountain, HWR saw religion as a political vehicle (a point that caused tensions between these otherwise allies). He said, "In a political point of view it is immaterial whether the mass of the People be Protestants or Papists, provided the Crown is in full possession of the Patronage of the Church, but a House of Assembly composed of Men differing in Religion language and manners from those of the Parent State is the most powerful engine of mischief that can be devised in a conquered Province … unless counterbalanced by an adequate influence and authority on the part of the Crown."[25] This did not mean HWR approved of Catholicism. To his liberal outlook, Roman Catholicism was "a religion which sinks and debases the human mind."[26] As such, one of his personal objectives, which coincided with the general views of the English party, was to "gradually to undermine the authority and influence of the Roman Catholic Priest." To diminish Catholicism, advance the English party, and bring cohesion to the province, HWR counselled Mountain to urge the government to make the Church of England prestigious. This would give credence to the bishop "in the eyes

---

25 Lambert, "Ryland, Herman Witsius."
26 Lambert, "Ryland, Herman Witsius."

of French Canadians who are accustomed to see ... shew and splendour." Lambert noted that HWR privately envisaged a "Protestant Church establishment ... [with] as much *splendour* and as little *power* as possible."[27] No doubt his voice helped Mountain's decision to erect the prominent cathedral edifice of Holy Trinity, which opened in 1804. However, being on the wrong side of provincial politics, his cathedral pew was given away in 1812 when a new governor removed his secretarial role while HWR was in England lobbying the government on provincial matters. Thus, in his religion, like many statesmen of his day, he was pragmatic rather than principled, any principles flowing from his liberalism. The religious diet he would have received from Mountain was that of a high churchman with a deep spirituality, though never as missional as many of his priests who came from the Society for Propagating the Gospel (SPG).[28]

Although interested and engaged in religion, HWR's primary interest was in politics (and indeed politicking). Lambert observes, "As a Georgian office holder Ryland was typical in his insatiable hunger for posts and pensions for himself and his sons; he was less so, perhaps, in his scrupulous honesty and evident competence."[29] Lord Dalhousie, with whom he was in favour, disliked "the grasping at places" of which HWR practiced.[30] His politics, as a colonial Tory and member of the English party, have already been noted. Interestingly his politics and that of the Canadian party sprang from a similar source—the knowledge that their future lay in the province. He was fighting for his vision to become dominant. The offices he came to occupy, and the short tenure of the Governors, made someone of

---

27 Lambert, "Ryland, Herman Witsius."
28 Thomas R. Millman, "Mountain, Jacob," in *Dictionary of Canadian Biography*, vol. 6, University of Toronto/Université Laval, 2003–(http://www.biographi.ca/en/bio/mountain_jacob_6E.html; accessed May 7, 2025).
    The SPG had been founded in 1701 largely to minister to British colonists and not to evangelize. It was not overtly evangelical as the Church Missionary Society (1799) would be; however, it did take a certain expansionist mentality to minister in remote areas of the Empire.
29 Lambert, "Ryland, Herman Witsius."
30 Lambert, "Ryland, Herman Witsius."

CHAPTER ELEVEN

HWR's character and experience highly, though discreetly, influential in government. This can be seen in his relations with governors, public figures, bishops, etc., within British North America and in Britain combined with the roles in which he served. The following chart surveys the many political positions he held over the course of his 45 year career in Lower Canada (including wages):

Executive Position	Legislative Council	Other	[Lt.] Governor & Relationship
Secretary to the Governor (£200) 1793–1812 (1799 an increase to £1000 in several steps)			Lord Dorchester (In Favour) Robert Prescott (In and then out of Favour)
	Clerk (£100 + fees) 1796–1838 [Took leave from 1798–99 to go to England to seek the recall of Prescott. From 1813 his fees were increased to match his former role as secretary. His son, George Herman, assisted him the last 17 years and assumed the role upon his death.]		Lt. Gov. Robert Shaw Milne (In Favour) Lt. Gen Sir James Henry Craig (In Favour) Sir George Prevost (In and then out of Favour) Sir Gordon Drummond (In Favour) Sir John Coape Sherbrooke (In Favour) Lord Aylmer (In Favour) Lord Kempt (In Favour) Lord Gosford (In Favour) Lord Dalhousie (In Favour)
		Crown Chancery 1802+ £100 in 1802, £300 in 1804	
		Treasurer and Secretary of the Jesuit Estates 1811–1826 when ended £150	

198

Given the influential posts he occupied, and the political views he held, HWR is known to be a cause in the Lower Canadian Rebellion of 1838 in which French Canadians reacted against the political establishment in their demand for a responsible government.[31]

What can also be seen in the above chart is his wealth. When his brother, as a leading Baptist minister and principal was making £200/annum, HWR was earning around £1550 plus fees. Though apparently his scrupulous honesty produced severe financial restraint in his latter years (he also spent a considerable amount to have his children educated in England), he lived quite comfortably. For instance, in 1805 he acquired a "small Estate" in nearby Beauport, which he added to substantially in 1813. In *A Topographical Description of the Province of Lower Canada* (1815), Joseph Bouchette, described the property as being comprised of "two handsome stone dwelling-houses with gardens and summer-houses, surrounded by a wall; from their singularly beautiful situation, and the rich prospect they command over the basin of Quebec and surrounding distant objects, they obtain much notice."[32] Here the usually-public man enjoyed time with his family. In November, 1830, in lieu of backpay owing him, he was awarded 2,205 acres of land in Chester and Tingwick townships.[33]

Largely because of his part in colonial affairs which lead to the 1837 Rebellion, HWR has also been vilified in the historiography of this era (though his non-introspective character also produced an unrealistic caricature as well). Such views are observed through the lens of his contemporaries. His sometimes nemesis, the Roman Catholic Bishop Plessis, said that he was "an astute diplomat and good enough when one knew how to approach him," but also that he was "not a man one could pump." Matthew Bell, a businessman, militia officer and politician, described him in 1825 as "a bullying old servant of the Public." In 1821, Sir James Kempt spoke

---

31   Lambert, "Ryland, Herman Witsius."
32   Joseph Bouchette, *A Topographical Description of the Province of Lower Canada* (London: W. Faden, 1815), 423.
33   Lambert, "Ryland, Herman Witsius."

of how his "*Sanguin temperament*" lead him to social excesses. Lambert summarizes his character, as celebrated by his friends and despised by his enemies: "His friends lauded his discretion, loyalty, and generosity; his enemies reproached his secretiveness, 'duplicity,' and pettiness. His only humour was biting sarcasm."[34] Linked to his politics, he looked down on all colonials, which is a reason that he sent his children to be schooled in England.

From an evangelical perspective, a cursory review of HWR's religion, politics and character does not boast much comfort. He looked, in Newton's sentiment, to earthly things for that which they could not give him, including seeing religion as a means to an end, politicking, grasping after positions and money, and a character that was a mixture of vice and virtue. Interestingly, his mastery of French, educational liberalism, honesty, and competence are all probably a debt to his father. Despite this want of comfort, he continually seemed connected with Evangelicals or evangelical sympathizers in Quebec and particularly within his own family and connections. For example, on a visit to England in 1799 to lobby for the recall of Prescott, JRJ wrote Newton asking whether there was anything he could do, through his contacts, to aid his brother. Newton could not extend this favour, but did tell JRJ, "Your brother Witsius called at my house twice. The first time I was out, and the second time just going out. He promised to call again, but I have not yet seen him, though I suppose it was three months since."[35] Likewise, HWR maintained an acquaintance with John Rippon, who spoke with pastoral concern to JRJ about his brother.

In 1825, the high churchman Jacob Mountain died and was replaced by Charles J. Stewart (1775-1837). His father had been converted under Whitefield and his sister was a friend of Wilberforce and a disciple of Isaac Milner (1750-1820). He committed himself to missionary work in Lower Canada through one of Mountain's recruiting tours of Britain. He was

---

[34] Lambert, "Ryland, Herman Witsius."
[35] Gordon, *Wise Counsel*, 358, citing Letter 70, which is dated July 22, 1799.

supported by the SPG. "So unusual an undertaking in a man of family and independence," according to a sister of the bishop, "could not by the world in general be attributed to any but an enthusiast and a methodist."[36] Yet when he arrived in Quebec and met with a number of prominent men, including HWR, he "laid all fears to rest" (this reveals HWR's dislike of Evangelicals).[37] Still his pre-episcopal ministry was lively and successful and upon becoming bishop he was a cheerful supporter of Canadian missions and building churches. It is unknown the precise relationship the two men would have had; however, if still attending services, it is highly probable that HWR would have sat under Stewart's ministry. Regardless of the bishop's religious convictions and the political compatibility of the two,[38] it is difficult to imagine the Evangelical Revival, which accelerated post-1790, escaping HWR's notice, nor the rise in evangelical Anglican clergy within the church from a despised minority to, in Eugene Stock's estimation by mid-nineteenth century, "indisputably the strongest force in the country."[39]

Though HWR continued to have contact with Evangelicals in England and sympathizers such as Stewart in Canada, it is in the familial interaction between HWR and his brother, JRJ, where evangelical influence was, if not the strongest, the longest preserved. Not only did HWR live with the Rylands for a time in Northampton, he also frequented their home in Bristol on occasion and appears to have been very close to them. Around 1808, HWR sent his son, William Ryland, to England to be educated. In a letter between JRJ and his nephew, JRJ states that William probably had no recollection of their former visit to Bristol (1793 or 1799?). He introduced himself and the fact that HWR had entrusted JRJ to forward funds for his education to his tutor, a Rev. Thomas Pickersgill of Bishopton, Ripon,

---

36   Thomas R. Millman, "Stewart, Charles James" in *Dictionary of Canadian Biography*, vol. 7, University of Toronto/Université Laval, 2003– (http://www.biographi.ca/en/bio/stewart_charles_james_7E.html; accessed May 7, 2025).
37   Millman, "Stewart, Charles James."
38   Stewart was more tolerant of other denominations and less vocal in his support of the clergy reserves (Millman, "Stewart, Charles James").
39   Eugene Stock, *History of the Church Missionary Society* (London, 1899), I, 38.

Yorkshire.[40] A close friend of HWR (presumably nearby), a Col. Dalton, was to watch out for William. JRJ affectionately spoke of all of these things and asked him to write, inquiring about his welfare. After sharing about a recent letter from HWR and the state of William's family in Lower Canada, JRJ spoke of the state of William's cousins. He ended his letter with a familial benediction:

> May the ever blessed God keep you from all evil, and grant you to grow up to be a comfort and credit to your dear parents and a blessing to society. I hope you will diligently apply to your studies, and pray to the Almighty for his blessing.
> My dear William
> Your affectionate Uncle
> John Ryland.[41]

This conclusion is expressive of JRJ's spiritual interest in his nephew and is in keeping with other letters that were exchanged between the two.[42] William Deane Ryland went on to become an Anglican rector of Hinton and Steane, Northamptonshire. He is known to have published a letter to the Archbishop on reforming the Book of Common Prayer.[43] Here he based his suggested reforms upon Scripture but chiefly reason. Given the times, it may be said from this document that he was a progressive churchman.

---

40 That he was listed as a subscriber to a book written by Rev. John Shepherd, a churchman, on the Book of Common Prayer may suggest HWR safely placed his children beyond the reach of an evangelical education. See John Shepherd, *A Critical and Practical Elucidation of the Book of Common Prayer* (London: R&R Gilbert, 1817), 49.

41 HWR Fonds, John Ryland, Letter to William Ryland, October 25, 1808, H-2959, images 160–162.

42 HWR Fonds, John Ryland, Letter to William Ryland, April 14, 1810, H-2959, image 205.

43 W. D. Ryland, *A Letter to the Lord Archbishop of Canterbury on Certain Alterations which are required in the Liturgy and Offices of the Church of England. (A Tract for Men of Common Sense)* (London: William Edward Painter, n.d.).

The second known work that he produced was a "Plain and Scriptural"[44] defence of the Church of England, often cited during the Gladstonian debates about disestablishment.[45] While interesting documents, they are not of the genre of evangelical literature and thus, the fact that HWR's son entered the ministry is inconclusive as to whether Evangelicalism made any inroads into this branch of the family.

Writing to "The Honourable H. W. Ryland" of Quebec, JRJ informed his brother of Andrew Fuller's death (with the inference he was known to him). He forwarded an account of his children's education (now at least three, including Ann and George), which totaled a costly £426 (the price to be paid for non-colonial education). He wrote of family news, the ill health of their sister Mrs. Dent and their brother James, and how HWR's daughter was at their home in Bristol. All of this intelligence came from seeing some of HWR's children while JRJ had been in London after George had just arrived (along with Mr. D [Col. Dalton?] and Miss W, Ann's tutoress). He ended his letter, "We pray that ever blessing may attend you all. I am my dear brother, yours affectionately, John Ryland."[46] Such remarks bespeak the closeness they enjoyed in temporal matters and JRJ's longstanding spiritual concern. This is the last known correspondence between the two but as is evident in these letters there existed a loving trans-Atlantic relationship between these brothers and a deep interest of JRJ for his brother's children. Further to this, fully in keeping with HWR's liberalism, there is a donation to the museum at the Bristol Baptist Academy in 1822 of "A North American Calumet, or Pipe. By the Hon. H. W. Ryland, of Quebec."[47] Clearly HWR took an interest in his brother's activities, if only from an

---

44   W. D. Ryland, *A Plain and Scriptural Defence of the Honours and Dignities of the Church of England*, 2nd ed. (London: John Cochran, 1834).

45   E.g., see *The Church Defence Handy Volume* (London: The Church Defence Institute, 1892).

46   HWR Fonds, John Ryland, Letter to H. W. Ryland, July 1815 (received September 1815), H-2959, images 585–586.

47   "Museum donation, A North American Calumet, or Pipe. By the Hon. H. W. Ryland, of Quebec," *Bristol Education Society* (1822): 46.

educational perspective.

A man well surrounded or at least in reach of Evangelicals, HWR seems to have lived his life in light of the gospel very much like Felix in the Book of Acts (though arguably more religiously refined): being sympathetic and even interested in it, yet ultimately holding it, or rather Christianity, as a card for personal gain. The limited works on HWR probe little into his spiritual beliefs, let alone his spiritual state. Given the great circle of Evangelicals with whom he was acquainted and their concern for him, it was but a natural question to ask whether he ever conformed to the evangelical conversion narrative. Nothing here suggests from his religion, politics or character that he was ever convicted or convinced; we have no comfort here. Yet, like Felix, we do not know how the story ended and again there is 2 Timothy 2:19.

III.
Evangelical Issues

Olaudah Equiano (1745–1797),
the frontispiece to *The Interesting Narrative of The Life of Olaudah Equiano, or Gustavus Vasa, the African* (London: T. Wilkins, 1789), vol. I.

12
Slavery, the slave trade, and Christians' theology[1]

IAN SHAW

Through the seventeenth to the nineteenth centuries, Christians in North America and Britain, shaped by diverse factors, took various and shifting positions in regard to slavery and the slave trade. Since the middle of the last century there have been a number of writers who have endeavoured to explain occasions such as the abolition of the slave trade in Britain in 1807 in terms of social and economic determinants rather than those of a moral and specifically Christian character.[2] In this essay I reflect on the

---

1   This essay first appeared in two parts in *Foundations* 86 (Summer 2024) and 87 (Winter 2024), which is an international journal of evangelical theology published by Affinity. It has been edited slightly for this Festschrift. Used by kind permission.
2   There are numerous accounts of the history of the slave trade and slavery, and the movements that led to their abolition. D. Richardson, *Principles and Agents: The British Slave Trade and its Abolition* (New Haven, CT: Yale University Press, 2022) and W. Hague, *William Wilberforce: the Life of the Great Anti-Slave Trade Campaigner* (London: Harper, 2008) offer variously focused and helpful sources. John Coffey has made a major contribution to how Christians have played a part in that history: "Evangelicals, Slavery & the Slave Trade: from Whitefield to Wilberforce," *Anvil* 24.2 (2007): 97-119; " 'Tremble, Britannia!': Fear, Providence and the Abolition of the Slave Trade, 1758–1807," *English Historical Review* 127, no. 527 (2012): 844-881; "Difficult histo-

theological themes that framed how those who engaged with the slave trade and slavery thought, spoke, and acted. The picture is not complete. The most severe omission is the central contribution made by black Evangelicals through these centuries, people such as Lemuel Haynes, Jupiter Hammon, and Phillis Wheatley.[3] But it is instructive and sometimes chastening to understand the grounds of the endeavours of white Evangelicals to hold a consistent Christian stance in regard to slavery. They did so in the ways they:

1. Grasped the implications for slavery of a Christian view of human nature.
2. Drew varying consequences for a Christian doctrine of God's providence.
3. Believed, in some cases, that slavery was a national sin and hence raised the likelihood, if not repented, of national judgement, and,
4. In some cases, regarded slavery as a deep hindrance to the gospel, and its abolition as promising gospel prosperity.

Human nature

Michael Haykin says that "what it means to be human" was "*the* central ethical dilemma for eighteenth–century, transatlantic British society, namely, the ethics of running the slave-trade and of owning slaves," and it was only

---

ries: Christian memory and historic injustice," *Cambridge Papers* (Cambridge: Jubilee Centre, 2020; https://www.cambridgepapers.org/difficult-histories-christian-memory-and-historic-injustice/). I have outlined the history: "Evangelicals, Slavery and Colonialism in the 18th and 19th Centuries" in *Wrestling with Our Past: Papers Read at the 2022 Westminster Conference* (Stoke on Trent: Tentmaker Publications, 2023).

3 I address the lives and significance of these and other black evangelicals in *Christians and Slavery* (Leominster: DayOne Publications, forthcoming). T. M. Anyabwile helpfully threads part of the story of black evangelical engagement with slavery in his account and assessment of African theology: *The Decline of African American Theology* (Downers Grove, IL: InterVarsity Press, 2007).

resolved when this question was answered.⁴ Among the key themes in the preaching of the Particular Baptists towards the close of the eighteenth century, for example, the inherent equality of all human beings should appear first. Thus, it appeared as the title page image of a sermon by James Dore.⁵ Their arguments sometimes were very general. John Beatson referred to the "benevolent spirit of the gospel," saying, "Are we not under obligation to exercise the offices of kindness, independent of complexion, language, colour, religion, or any other tie than that strongest of relations—one common nature?"⁶ Robert Robinson made clear he believed that "the enfranchisement of slaves is one act of justice naturally proceeding out of evangelical doctrine."⁷

Robert Hawker (1753-1827), a vicar in Plymouth, published two relevant items. *The Injustice of the African Slave Trade, Proved from Principles of Natural Equity* was a sermon given in January 1789 at the height of the lobbying for the abolition of the slave trade. He later published *An Appeal to the Common Feelings of Mankind on Behalf of the Negroes, in the West-India Islands* in the form of "A Letter to William Wilberforce."⁸ He concludes that the African slave trade "is the most palpable violation of all equity, and an outrage to every law of nature, reason, and religion."⁹ The memorial to William Knibb, Baptist missionary to Jamaica early in the nineteenth century, outside Falmouth Baptist Chapel quotes Knibb's words:

---

4 M. Haykin, "To promote ... cordial affection for our neighbor": Abraham Booth & the fight against the slave trade" (Unpublished lecture, c.2019), page 1. For the bulk of this lecture, see M. Haykin, " 'To promote ... cordial affection for our neighbor': Abraham Booth and his sermon against the slave trade and slavery" in *"The First Counsellor of Our Denomination": Studies on the Life and Ministry of Abraham Booth (1734–1806)*, ed. Michael A.G. Haykin with Victoria J. Haykin (Springfield, MO: Particular Baptist Press, 2011), 80–102.

5 In M. E. Roe, ed., *Preaching Deliverance to the Captives: Particular Baptist Sermons on the Abolition of the Slave Trade* (Privately Published, 2021).

6 Roe, ed., *Preaching Deliverance to the Captives*, 110.

7 Roe, ed., *Preaching Deliverance to the Captives*, 53.

8 M. E. Roe, ed., *Let the Oppressed Go Free: Robert Hawker on the Slave Trade and Slavery* (Southampton: The Huntingtonian Press, 2021).

9 Roe, ed., *Let the Oppressed Go Free*, 34-35.

> The same God who made the white made the black man. The same blood that runs in the white man's veins, flows in yours. It is not the complexion of the skin, but the complexion of character that makes the great difference between one man and another.[10]

Dore perhaps had most to say on this theme. He cites the Magna Carta, the Bill of Rights, the Petition of Rights, and the Coronation Oath, waxing lyrical: "And shall we be tenacious of liberty at home, and rule with the iron rod of slavery abroad? How inconsistent! How preposterous!"[11] On the British trade he says, "You are men: respect humanity."[12] Of "the prince upon the throne, the peasant in the cottage, the proud European Lord, and the poor Negro slave," we "all spring from one common stock. We took our rise from Adam, we all descended from Noah; we are all brothers and sisters, members of one great family. Let us *love as brethren, be pitiful, be courteous.*"[13]

> Are not men naturally free? Is not liberty the gift of God to every man? And can we trample on the sacred rights of the humankind without invading the prerogative of heaven? There are natural rights which belong to men, as men … Civil government is then only conducive to general happiness when it protects men in the enjoyment of their natural rights, such as their right to their lives, their liberty, the fruit of their labour, and to the use, in common with others, of air, light and water.[14]

---

10   Cited Alan Jackson, "William Knibb, 1803-1845, Jamaican missionary and slaves' friend," *The Victorian Web* (2003; https://victorianweb.org/history/knibb/knibb.html; accessed May 5, 2025).
11   Roe, ed., *Preaching Deliverance to the Captives*, 88.
12   He cites Proverbs 22:2; Malachi 2:10; and 1 Peter 3:8 to prove his point.
13   Roe, ed., *Preaching Deliverance to the Captives*, 83.
14   Roe, ed., *Preaching Deliverance to the Captives*, 83-84.

Some in his church wrote him a letter praising his "repeated exertions to advance the cause of Humanity and Universal Freedom" and asking for "a Course of Lectures on the principles of Non-conformity, and of civil and religious Liberty."[15]

In passing, this raises the complex question of whether and in what ways the Enlightenment shaped, knowingly or unknowingly, the thinking of Christians campaigning against slavery. The Southern theologians R. L. Dabney, J. H. Thornwell, and those who shared their thinking, appeared to have seen a close intertwining, and one that was wholly inimical to a Christian position. Thornwell held the conviction that "Opposition to Slavery has never been the offspring of the Bible. It has sprung from the visionary theories of human nature and society; it has sprung from the misguided reason of man; it comes as natural, not as revealed truth."[16] Dabney took the view that the Abolitionist agenda was of rationalistic origin.

Yet, the question is not simple. Considering the position in the late eighteenth century in America, Mark Noll says of Samuel Hopkins' opposition to slavery that he "did not find the origin of his reform in the Revolutionary philosophy or even in the equalitarian principle imbedded in the Declaration of Independence. Rather, he exploited the Declaration and the Revolution to support a conviction about equality already arrived at on other grounds. These grounds were religious, and they stemmed from the Great Awakening of the 1740's."[17] Hence, he "did not derive his attack on slavery from libertarianism but merely used that ideology to drive home points determined by prior theological commitments." It was his "religious conviction itself rather than its translation political or social ideology which

---

15 Roe, ed., *Preaching Deliverance to the Captives*, 71, note.
16 J. H. Thornwell, *Relation of the Church to Slavery* in *The Collected Writings of James Henley Thornwell*, ed. John B. Adger and John L. Giradeau (Richmond: Presbyterian Committee of Publication, 1973), IV, 393.
17 M. A. Noll, "Observations on the Reconciliation of Politics and Religion in Revolutionary New Jersey: The Case of Jacob Green," *Journal of Presbyterian History* 54.2 (1976): 229.

defined his concept of righteousness."[18] It would be possible to develop a similar argument with regard to others who used the language of liberty and human rights, although it may be the case that evangelicals in the late eighteenth century found it difficult to foresee the intellectual direction of travel that bore full fruit in 1789 with the onset of the French Revolution.

Perhaps it is in the voice of John Newton that the most telling, because most personal, words can be heard. He challenged assumptions about ethnicity and human nature. Pressed on this point in his evidence to the House of Commons in 1790, he was asked "what conclusions did you form respecting the capacity of the Negroes, compared with that of other men in the same period of society?" He replied, "I always judged that with equal advantages they would be equal to ourselves in point of capacity. I have met with many instances of real and decided natural capacity among them."[19]

The very title of Abraham Booth's sermon—*Commerce in the Human Species*—signaled his central argument:

> … be the station of an *innocent* Negro ever so obscure, his poverty ever so great, his manners ever so rude, or his mental capacities ever so contracted, he has an equal claim to personal liberty with any man upon earth. For the rights of humanity being common to the whole of our species, are the same in every part of the world. For though they are ignorant of the true God, and unacquainted with our concern to promote their happiness; yet they are men, they are brethren of the human race: agreeable to that saying. *God hath made of one blood all nations of men.*[20]

It was at this point that Booth took sharp issue with his fellow-Baptist, William Rogers of Philadelphia, in a letter of 1795, where he takes

---

18 Noll, "Observations," 233.
19 *House of Commons Sessional Papers for the Eighteenth Century.* Select Committee, 1790.
20 Roe, ed., *Preaching Deliverance to the Captives*, 178.

expressions from Rogers and responds. His irony is scathing when, on Rogers' phrase, "We are *all citizens*," he says, taking a constantly-cited text, and reasoning from human nature,

> That is, we who have the happiness and honour of wearing not black, or mulatto,[21] but white skins, possess liberty, personal, civil and political; are capable of acquiring large property, and are eligible to the first honours in the federal government ... It is indeed asserted in an old book, now but little regarded, "That God made of one blood all the nations of men," but we, the genuine sons of liberty, will never be persuaded that our blood is specifically the same with that which flows in the veins of a black or mulatto.[22]

John Rippon's 1807 verses following the ending of the slave trade included:

> Let charity, benevolence,
> And every smiling grace,
> In golden links of brotherhood
> Unite the human race.[23]

Telling applications of this biblical principle can be found in numerous writings. William Carey, for example, writes:

---

21   This term, offensive to us today, was much used in the Southern States to describe persons of mixed white and black ancestry, especially a person with one white and one black parent. It is analogous to how "Eurasian" is used now in parts of Asia.

22   Abraham Booth, "Original Letter from the Rev. Abraham Booth of London, to the Rev. Dr. William Rogers of Philadelphia," *The Christian's Penny Magazine* 3, no. 129 (1834): 374–375.

23   John Rippon, "The day has dawn'd, Jehovah comes," Stanza 3 (https://www.cpdl.org/wiki/index.php/The_day_has_dawn%27d,_Jehovah_comes_(William_Tansur); accessed May 6, 2025).

CHAPTER TWELVE

Barbarous as these poor heathens are, they appear to be as capable of knowledge as we are; and in many places, at least, have discovered uncommon genius and tractableness; and I greatly question whether most of the barbarities practised by them, have not originated in some real or supposed affront, and are therefore, more properly, acts of self-defence, than proofs of inhuman and blood-thirsty dispositions.[24]

James Montgomery gave it expression in his poem, "The West Indies":

Is he not *Man*, though knowledge never shed
Her quickening beams on his neglected head?
Is he not *Man*, though sweet religion's voice
Ne'er bade the mourner in his God rejoice

---

24 William Carey, *An Enquiry into the Obligations of Christians, to Use Means for the Conversion of the Heathens. In Which the Religious State of the Different Nations of the World, the Success of Former Undertakings, and the Practicability of Further Undertakings, are Considered* (Leicester, 1792), 63-64.
  This argument was not new-born in the late eighteenth century. Cotton Mather wrote to similar effect a hundred years earlier, when he said, "It has been cavilled, by some, that it is questionable Whether the Negroes have Rational Souls, or no. But let that Brutish insinuation be never Whispered any more." (Cotton Mather, *The Negro Christianized. An Essay to Excite and Assist that Good Work, the Instruction of Negro-Servants in Christianity*, ed. Paul Royster [1706; Electronic Texts in American Studies, 28; https://digitalcommons.unl.edu/etas/28]). We may note also that Samuel Rutherford referred to "nature's law" when he insisted in his *Lex Rex*, "A man being created according to God's image, he is *res sacra*, a sacred thing, and can no more, by nature's law, be sold and bought, than a religious and sacred thing dedicated to God." (*Lex Rex* ["The Law and the Prince"; https://www.monergism.com/thethreshold/sdg/rutherford/LexRex%20-%20Samuel%20Rutherford.pdf]). Richard Baxter wrote similarly of Africans: "they are of as good a kind as you, that is, they are reasonable creatures as well as you, and born to as much natural liberty," and concluded, "how cursed a crime it is to equal men to beasts!" (*Baxter's directions to slave-holders, revived* [https://quod.lib.umich.edu/e/evans/N34072.0001.001/1:3?rgn=div1;view=fulltext; accessed May 6, 2025], pages 4-5). Samuel Sewall, in 1700, wrote, "It is most certain that all Men, as they are the Sons of Adam, are Coheirs; and have equal Right unto Liberty, and all other outward Comforts of Life." (*The Selling of Joseph: A Memorial* (1700; available at https://digitalcommons.unl.edu/cgi/viewcontent.cgi?article=1026&context=etas; accessed May 6, 2025).

Is *he* not Man, by sin and suffering tried?
Is *he* not Man, for whom the Saviour died?
Belie the Negro's powers:—In headlong will,
Christian! thy brother thou shalt prove him still.[25]

We have seen how John Newton challenged assumptions about ethnicity and human nature in ways that were central to the Christian response to slavery. Countering suggestions that "African women are negroes, savages, who have no idea of the nicer sensations which obtain among civilized people," he responded to the House of Commons committee:

> I dare contradict them in the strongest terms. I have lived long, and conversed much, among these supposed savages. I have often slept in their towns, in a house filled with goods for trade, with no person in the house but myself, and with no other door than a mat; in that security, which no man in his senses would expect in this civilized nation, especially in this metropolis, without the precaution of having strong doors, strongly locked and bolted. And, with regard to the women, in Sherbro, where I was most acquainted, I have seen many

---

25 James Montgomery, "The West Indies" (1807) in *The West Indies, and Other Poems* (London: Longman, Hurst, Rees, Orme, and Brown, 1818), 22-23.
    Poetry was a powerful voice in both the UK and USA. J. G. Basker, *Amazing Grace: An Anthology of Poems About Slavery, 1660-1810* [New Haven; London: Yale University Press, 2002]) provides a magisterial collection of such poetry, with 400 titles from more than 250 different writers. In addition to William Cowper and James Montgomery, we should mention the Puritan, Michael Wigglesworth (1631-1705), as well as Jupiter Hammon (1711-1806), Phillis Wheatley (c.1753-1784) ("In the context of slavery in English literature, Wheatley is the most important figure of the eighteenth century," Basker, *Amazing Grace*, 170), the pious Bostonian, Jane Dunlap (fl.1765-1771), Lemuel Haynes (1753-1833), Hannah More (1745-1833), Olaudah Equiano (c.1745-1797) and Timothy Dwight (1752-1817). Even B. B. Warfield tried his hand, with the ironic short piece, "Wanted: a Samaritan." The life and coming to faith of Olaudah Equiano can be read in Y. Taylor, *I Was Born a Slave: An Anthology of Classic Slave Narratives* (Chicago, IL: Lawrence Hill Books, 1999), Volume I.

CHAPTER TWELVE

instances of modesty, and even delicacy, which would not disgrace an English woman.[26]

He insisted, in similar terms:

> I have often been gravely told, as a proof that the Africans, however hardly treated, deserve but little compassion, that they are a people so destitute of natural affection, that it is common among them for parents to sell their children, and children their parents ... But ... I never heard of one instance of either, while I used the coast.[27]

He was asked, "What opinion have you formed of the temper and disposition of the Negroes?" He gently reminded the committee that it would be as impossible to give "a general character" of people in Africa as it would be of the people of Europe, but that of the area he was familiar with—Sierra Leone: "The people ... are in a degree civilized, often friendly, and may be trusted where they have not been previously deceived by the Europeans. I have lived in peace and safety among them, when I have been the only white man among them for a great distance."[28]

Newton often made unfavourable comparisons with the Europeans encountered by the tribes of Africa. He recalls, "The most humane and moral people I ever met with in Africa were on the River Gaboon [sic], and they were the people who had the least intercourse with Europe at the time." He had heard these people actually speak against the slave trade, and asked to illustrate, said,

> One man of consequence said, "If I was to be angry, and to sell my boy, how should I get my boy back again, when my anger was gone

---

26 *House of Commons Sessional Papers.*
27 John Newton, *Thoughts Upon the African Slave Trade* (1788; http://www.gutenberg.org/cache/epub/68056/pg68056-images.html; accessed May 5, 2025).
28 *House of Commons Sessional Papers.*

away?" For the same reason they would not use firearms in their petty quarrels, though they had them, for they said, "If I kill a man when I am angry, I cannot bring him back to life when my anger is over."[29]

Providence

What are we to make of appeals to the hand of God's providence in the order of society in general, and domestic slavery in particular? We cannot make good sense of these arguments without recognising that understandings of God's providence were being used in several quite different ways.

In some cases, Christians were referring to the way that God orders society in general, or one's life in particular. John Newton spoke in this way, when looking back on the time he had worked in the slave trade:

> I felt greatly the disagreeableness of the business. The office of a gaoler, and the restraints under which I was obliged to keep my prisoners, were not suitable to my feelings; but I considered it as a line of life which God in His providence had allotted me, and as a cross which I ought to bear with patience and thankfulness till He should be pleased to deliver me from it. Till then I only thought myself bound to treat the slaves under my care with gentleness, and to consult their ease and convenience so far as was consistent with the safety of the whole family of whites and blacks on board my ship.[30]

However, the problem with some appeals to providence is that they sound little different to an appeal to custom and practice and a justification of the *status quo*. Calvin remarks on this:

> Naturally, if men's judgements were just, custom would be based on those that are sound. The reverse, however, has often been the case,

---

29 *House of Commons Sessional Papers.*
30 Cited Josiah Bull, *John Newton of Olney and St. Mary* Woolnoth (London: The Religious Tract Society, [1868]), 61.

because whatever the majority was seen to do acquired the force of customary law. Now men's lives have never been so well ordered that most men like the best things. Thus, the individual faults of the many have produced collective error, or rather a common conspiracy in evil, which these worthies would now pass off as law.[31]

William Wilberforce constantly referred to God's providence over and in his life. A small sample of extracts from his spiritual journals will suffice. In a letter to his mother soon after word of his conversion had become more widely known, he said, "It would merit no better name than desertion … if I were to fly from this post where Providence has placed me."[32] On September 4, 1796, he gave thanks for "My being providently engag'd in the Sl: Trade Business, thro' what we call accident, I remember well how it was. What an honourable Service."[33] On February 22, 1807, shortly before the passing of the bill outlawing the slave trade, he wrote:

> Never surely had I more cause for gratitude than now, when carrying the great object of my life, to which a gracious Providence directed my thoughts twenty-six or twenty-seven years ago, and led my endeavours in 1787 or 1788. O Lord, let me praise Thee with my whole heart … Oh may my gratitude be in some degree proportionate.[34]

At the high point of his life, April 5, 1807, he recorded, "How wonderful are the ways of Providence! The Foreign Slave Bill is going quietly on."[35]

We may think of this primarily as observing God's providence working

---

31 John Calvin, "Prefatory Letter to Francis 1" in his *Institutes of the Christian Religion*, trans. Robert White (Edinburgh: Banner of Truth Trust, 2014), xxviii.
32 *William Wilberforce: His Unpublished Spiritual Journals*, ed. M. McMullen (Fearn, Ross-Shire: Christian Focus, 2021), 52.
33 *William Wilberforce*, ed. McMullen, 214.
34 *William Wilberforce*, ed., McMullen, 327.
35 *William Wilberforce*, ed., McMullen, 319.

for good through the life of a Christian. The southern theologians appealed to providence in a rather different way, seeing it as a demonstration of *national* providence. Thornwell was confident that providence had given the South slavery.[36] In the eyes of Benjamin Palmer, slavery was a "great providential trust" that should be not only conserved but perpetuated.[37] In America at least, Dabney argued that slavery was "the righteous, the best, yea, the only tolerable relation."[38] Kelly's criticism of Dabney and his fellow advocates of slavery is the least that can be said:

> Dabney was not overly biblical on this subject; on the contrary, he did not go as far as the Bible should have taken him. Like all other fallen men, including theologians, he had blind spots where his devotion to the culture made it difficult for him to interpret the will of God … Undoubtedly Dabney's greatest blind spot in this whole matter was … his underestimation of the power of the gospel in the life and culture of the blacks (which can make saints, leaders, and heroes of them as well as of any other people).[39]

Calvin wisely observed that "Although providence, when correctly understood, is an enormous help in confirming faith, there are very few who rightly comprehend or reflect on it."[40] He concludes that "our heart is resolved on this: nothing will happen that God has not ordained,"[41] but

---

36 J. H. Thornwell, *Sermon on National Sins* in *Collected Writings of James Henley Thornwell*, IV, 541.
37 See Thomas Cary Johnson, *The Life and Letters of Benjamin Morgan Palmer* (Richmond, VA: Presbyterian Committee of Publication, 1906), 217.
38 R. L. Dabney, *A Defence of Virginia, [and Through Her, of the South,] in Recent and Pending Contests Against the Sectional Party* (New York: E. J. Hale & Son, 1867), 25.
39 D. F. Kelly, "Robert Lewis Dabney" in *Reformed Theology in America: A History of Its Modern Development*, ed. D. F. Wells (Grand Rapids, MI: William B. Eerdmans, 1985), 214 and 226.
40 Calvin, *Institutes*, 499.
41 Calvin, *Institutes*, 502.

this does not remove the need for prudence and caution. That would be to "muddle heaven and earth."[42] For example, he rejects the position of those who hold that "whatever does happen they so ascribe to God's providence that they disregard the person who does the deed."[43] While Calvin does not address the question of slavery, he gives several case examples that may be thought analogous. For example, "If a child lets his father die without helping him, he could not, they argue, have resisted God who had decreed that this should happen." His conclusion is that "[a]ccordingly they turn all vices into virtues, on the grounds that these serve the ordinances of God!"[44]

Carter, writing as a black Reformed Christian, and on God's providence, insists that

> the biblical understanding of God's sovereignty demands accepting the kidnapping and subsequent enslavement of Africans in America was according to his eternal and sovereign will. This must never be lost to us as we seek to resolve areas of racial tension and animosity in the church. If God is sovereign ... then we must acknowledge that it pleased God to bring Africans to the land of America. It pleased him to use the hands and wills of sinful men to do so ...
>
> Yet even though God ordained that Africans be brought to America in the hollow of slave ships this in no way absolves the Euro-American establishment of their responsibility for those horrors and subsequent degrading atrocities.[45]

He knows that some will ask, "Did this providence of God have to be worked out on the bruised and battered backs of African men and women? Did they have to bear the brunt of his bitter rod, that his purposes be

---

42 Calvin, *Institutes*, 502.
43 Calvin, *Institutes*, 503.
44 Calvin, *Institutes*, 503.
45 A. J. Carter, *Black and Reformed: Seeing God's Sovereignty in the African-American Christian Experience* (Phillipsburg, NJ: P&R Publishing, 2016), 103-104.

revealed?," and he replies, "Who could know why God's providence had to be so bitter? Who could venture to explain God's ways of infinite knowledge, unsearchable wisdom, and unfathomable mercy?"[46]

National sin and judgement

John Coffey refers to "the intense providentialism of the early British abolitionists."[47] When one turns to "abolitionist texts … here one finds an insistent testimony to human fear of divine wrath."[48] He suggests we should understand this as a *judicial* providentialism—the belief that God rewarded or punished nations according to their moral character and actions. He says that this was held by a very wide range of theological positions, yet "Evangelicals held these common biblical convictions with a peculiar intensity."[49]

A profoundly significant aspect of the Christian response to slavery and the slave trade was the way in which they applied the Bible to make sense of how slavery had been present and often unchallenged by the church for many years. Paul's sermon to the Greeks at Athens was a central passage. That God "hath made of one blood all nations of men for to dwell on all the face of the earth" (Acts 17:26, KJV) was often quoted, and verse 30—"the times of this ignorance God winked at; but now commandeth all men everywhere to repent" (KJV)—was central to how they interpreted their times.

Jonathan Edwards had appealed to the same verse, as did John Newton, saying, "What I did, I did ignorantly." We find the same appeal in George Bourne (1780–1845), an English-born American abolitionist Presbyterian minister, in his 1816 work *The Book and Slavery Irreconcilable*.[50]

---

46   Carter, *Black and Reformed*, 110.
47   Coffey, "Tremble, Britannia!," 845.
48   Coffey, "Tremble, Britannia!," 845.
49   Coffey, "Difficult histories," 108.
50   Bourne was known for his unyielding stance that may not have made easy allies. E.g. "Slavery is the Golden Calf … the Balaam, … the Achan … the Delilah … the Bathsheba … the thirty pieces of silver … that *love of the present* world, for which Demas

However, the Particular Baptists applied it in a distinctive way, arguing that in effect God *had* "winked at" Christians during the years of the Gospel age when they had not understood or appreciated the evils of slavery. They used this argument to give urgency to the challenge of slavery in their own immediate times.[51] Once accepting that they no longer lived in the times of ignorance the implications appeared clear. Slavery was a sin—a national sin—and to continue in such sin would incur God's judgement. Convinced as they were that Britain was at risk of so continuing, national repentance was called for and acts consistent with repentance.[52]

Wilberforce returned to the point year after year. In his celebrated 1789 speech, he began with a statement of collective guilt ("we are all guilty"). "In April 1791, he brought his three-hour speech to a climax by warning Parliament not to forget 'the bounty of Providence' or the 'day of retribution', and vowing 'Never, never will we desist till we have ... released ourselves from the load of guilt.'"[53] Newton wrote to Wilberforce in 1804:

> Though I can scarcely see the paper before me, I must attempt to express my thankfulness to the Lord, and to offer my congratulations to you for the success which he has so far been pleased to give to your

---

forsook the Apostles' doctrine and fellowship," and "slavery must be the *acme of all impiety*; consequently, it is *impossible* that a *Slave-holder* can be a *sincere Christian*" (*The Book and Slavery Irreconcilable* [Philadelphia: J. M. Sanderson and Co., 1816], 19, 53). He happily endorsed the saying that "a rough truth is better than a smooth falsehood" (*Book and Slavery*, 7). A. D. Strange traces the slavery debates in the successive General Assemblies of the Presbyterian church over this period and later. See his *Empowered Witness: Politics, Culture, and the Spiritual Mission of the Church* (Wheaton, IL: Crossway, 2024).

51   Jonathan Edwards, Jr. and others in America also applied the verse in this way, and it is probable that the Particular Baptists were aware of this.

52   John Wesley also warned of God's judgement, but of the individual. He addresses slave owners, "Is there a *God*? You know there is. Is He a Just *God*? Then there must be a state of Retribution A state wherein the Just *God* will reward every man according to his works. Then what reward will he render to You? O think betimes! Before you drop into eternity!" (*Thoughts Upon Slavery*, 4th ed. [Dublin: W. Whitestone, 1775], 24).

53   Coffey, "Tremble, Britannia!," 862.

unwearied endeavours for the abolition of the slave trade, which I have considered as a millstone, of itself sufficient, to sink such an enlightened and highly favoured nation as ours to the bottom of the sea.[54]

Alexander McLeod, writing in America around the same time, linked the matter to God's judgement:

O America, what hast thou to account for on the head of slavery! … Thou hast made provision for increasing the number and continuing the bondage of thy slaves. Thy judgments may tarry, but they will assuredly come … Even real Christians, the guilt of whose sins is removed through the atonement of Jesus, but who have learned the way of the heathen so far as to confirm to the wicked practice of buying, selling and retaining slaves, have a right to expect severe corrections.[55]

Perhaps we find the clearest account of national sins and national judgement in the sermons of Charles Spurgeon. To give but two examples from 1866 and 1859:

I am not among those, as you know, who believe that every affliction is a judgment upon the particular person to whom it occurs … but we do nevertheless very firmly believe that there are national judgments, and that national sins provoke national chastisements. As

---

54 Newton's position on this matter was not entirely constant. Ten years before he wrote this letter, and speaking in the context of an expected invasion of Britain by France, he preached a sermon on 'The Imminent Danger and the Only Sure Resource of this Nation,' on February 28, 1794, the day appointed for the national fast, in which he said of the African slave-trade, "I do not rank this among our national sins, because I hope, and believe, a very great majority of the nation earnestly long for its suppression."

55 Alexander McLeod, *Slavery Unjustifiable: A Discourse* (New York: T & J Swords, 1802), 19-20.

CHAPTER TWELVE

to individuals, their punishment or reward is reserved for the next state; but nations will not exist in the next world: there is no such thing as a judgment of nations, as such, at the last great day; that will be the judgment of individuals one by one. The trial and punishment of nations takes place in this state, and it is here that we are to look for the judgment of God upon national sin.[56]

There is a weighing time for kings and emperors … For nations there is a weighing time. National sins demand national punishments … The guilt they incur must receive its awful recompense in this present time state … So likewise, shall it be with the nations that now abide on the face of the earth. There is no God in heaven if the iniquity of slavery go unpunished. There is no God existing in heaven above if the cry of the negro do not bring down a red hail of blood upon the nation that still holds the black man in slavery.[57]

Warning again of such judgement in a sermon on March 6, 1881, which was entitled "Jesus at a Stand" and which was based upon Mark 10:49, Spurgeon says:

I have feared and trembled for my country of late lest the Lord Jesus should depart from it and take away the candlestick out of its place. More than two hundred years ago George Herbert said, when he looked upon the declining state of godliness in England,

---

[56] C. H. Spurgeon, "The Voice of the Cholera" that he preached on August 12, 1866. See https://www.spurgeon.org/resource-library/sermons/the-voice-of-the-cholera/#flipbook/; accessed May 6, 2025.

[57] C. H. Spurgeon, "The Scales of Judgement" that he preached on June 12, 1859. See https://www.spurgeon.org/resource-library/sermons/the-scales-of-judgment/#flipbook/; accessed may 6, 2025.

> Religion stands a-tiptoe in our land,
> Ready to pass to the American strand[58]...

> At times our Lord, as judge among the nations, arises to visit the sins of a people upon them. Patience makes room for justice, and Providence determines that guilty nations shall be scourged ... No man can read our history without perceiving that among guilty nations we hold a sorrowful place; for we have had more light than any other people and have sinned against it full often.[59]

Spurgeon was taking an argument that the Particular Baptists had used. For example, John Beatson believed that nations and empires have presence only in this world, and hence "such collective bodies of men must, in their national capacity, either be punished in this world or not at all."[60] Robert Robinson likewise said, "The sins of individuals are not punished here, for this to them is only a state of trial: but collective bodies submit here in a state of rewards and punishments, and if there be such a thing as national sin, that is it, assuredly, which the legislature makes its own. I fear, I fear, the African slave trade is of this kind."[61] James Dore also said that they would "learn that national crimes are productive of national judgement."[62] Beatson felt this perhaps more strongly than any of his contemporaries. He asked, what if "instead of making any reparation ... the nation that was guilty reduced the whole to system, and regulated it by law," they should have every reason to expect God's punishment. Quoting from Jeremiah 50:33, that Babylon "took them captives, held them fast; they refused to let

---

58 Spurgeon is quoting from the poem "Religion Westwards Bent" by George Herbert (1593-1633).
59 C. H. Spurgeon, "Jesus at a Stand." See https://www.spurgeon.org/resource-library/sermons/jesus-at-a-stand-2/#flipbook/; accessed May 6, 2025.
60 Roe, ed., *Preaching Deliverance to the Captives*, 124-125.
61 Robert Robinson, *Slavery inconsistent with the Spirit of Christianity* (Cambridge: J. Archdeacon, 1788), 20.
62 Roe, ed., *Preaching Deliverance to the Captives*, 77.

them go,"[63] he asks if Britain has not acted very much like Babylon.[64]

Slavery and gospel prosperity

A further theme in the theological position of some who spoke and acted against slavery and the slave trade was to counter the arguments of those who saw slavery as a means of bringing people under the sound and influence of the gospel. Samuel Sewall had resisted it in the following way, taking the selling of Joseph by his brothers as his text: "Evil must not be done, that good may come of it. The extraordinary and comprehensive Benefit accruing to the Church of God, and to Joseph personally, did not rectify his brethren's Sale of him."[65] Richard Baxter, referring to the way slaves were treated, asked, "Doth not the very example of such cruelty … directly tend to teach them to hate Christianity, as if it taught men to be so much worse than dogs, or tygers?"[66] The New England Puritan, John Eliot, also was forceful, saying, "It seemeth to me that to sell them away for slaves is to hinder the enlargement of his kingdom … to sell away souls from under the light of the Gospel into a condition where their souls will be utterly lost, so far as appeareth unto man?"[67]

But it was among the Particular Baptists that the strongest case would be made.[68] Carey recorded how the freeing of slaves "may prove the happy means of introducing amongst them the gospel of our Lord Jesus Christ."[69] Yet in so doing, those who take the gospel "must be very careful not to resent injuries which may be offered to them, nor to think highly of themselves,

---

63 He suggests Jeremiah 50 and 51 "merit perusal."
64 Roe, *Preaching Deliverance to the Captives*, 126.
65 Sewall, *The Selling of Joseph*.
66 Baxter, *Baxter's directions to slave-holders, revived*, page 5.
67 *Letter from John Eliot Protesting against Selling Indians as Slaves* (https://www.native-newenglandportal.com/node/18119; accessed May 6, 2025). This letter was written on August 13, 1675.
68 In this connection, Coffey quotes Drescher saying, 'the take-off of British abolitionism coincided almost exactly with the revival of the British missionary movement' (Coffey, 2020: 105).
69 Carey, *An Enquiry into the Obligations of Christians*, 79-80.

so as to despise the poor heathens, and by those means lay a foundation for their resentment, or rejection of the gospel."⁷⁰

James Dore insisted that "the slave trade works against the fulfilment of gospel promises." "Is it probable that the poor Negro will cordially embrace Christianity while they view it in such a horrid light in the lives of professed Christians? … What ideas must the Negroes form of that system of religion which, they naturally suppose, tolerates barbarity?"⁷¹ Beatson, in closing his message, linked it to the prosperity of the Gospel.

> Can the Gospel be recommended to the attention of men, while you are thus buying and selling them as though they were brutes? To be depriving a people of their natural liberty, and at the same time preaching to them of spiritual liberty, would appear such gross hypocrisy … If ever then you mean to spread the Gospel of peace, wipe off this stain of infamy from the Christian name.⁷²

John Liddon spoke of how the trade "prevents the introduction of Christianity into Africa, and naturally must excite strong prejudices against it amongst a people who have no idea of that strange distinction we are often obliged to make between the principles of Christianity, and the conduct of those who call themselves Christians."⁷³ He later says, "if they judge the

---

70   Carey, *An Enquiry into the Obligations of Christians*, 75-76.
71   Roe, ed., *Preaching Deliverance to the Captives*, 90-91. I have not addressed the question of whether preaching about slavery was, as some suggested, bringing "politics" into the pulpit. The Particular Baptists offered a defence of their approach, though others were careful to deal with slavery on days other than Sunday. Roe discusses their approach in the preface to his book (*Preaching Deliverance to the Captives*). A. Barnes expresses a position that may be thought helpful. Slavery "should be introduced into the pulpit, not in its political aspect, but in its bearings on religion, as one of the causes which hinder the progress and triumph of Christianity in the world; and in the same way it should be approached in our religious literature … (I)n this respect it should have a place, just as anything else has that hinders the progress of the gospel of Christ' (*The Church and Slavery* [Philadelphia: Parry and McMillan, 1857], 156-157).
72   Roe, ed., *Preaching Deliverance to the Captives*, 134-135.
73   Roe, ed., *Preaching Deliverance to the Captives*, 189.

Christian religion by the conduct of those who call themselves Christians, and who are their oppressors, they must suppose it to be of all others the worst religion, to justify such enormities."[74] Even if the Christian faith is taught by consistent Christians, and yet rejected, that does not justify action against such people. "The only arms (Christ) ever authorised his disciples to use were wisdom and innocence."[75]

"[N]either the missionary societies nor their individual agents set out with the intention of challenging the structures of colonial society."[76] Most took the initial position that "the gospel would so ameliorate the condition of the slaves that slavery would ultimately wither away."[77] But the realities of the field forced many to take more or less explicitly political stances. This was increasingly illustrated in the life of William Knibb, the Baptist missionary in Jamaica. Addressing the committee of the Baptist mission in 1832, he said, "I daily and hourly feel … that the questions of colonial slavery and of missions are now inseparably connected; that British Christians must either join with me in an attempt to break the chain with which the African is bound, or leave the work of mercy and the triumphs of the Redeemer unfinished." He insisted on the connection and takes an immediatist position:

> Feeling … as I do, that the African and the creole slave will never again enjoy the blessings of religious instruction, or hear of the benefits of

---

74 Roe, ed., *Preaching Deliverance to the Captives*, 197. The behaviour of slave holders who professed the Christian faith acutely embittered Frederick Douglass, perhaps the most famous freed slave of the nineteenth century. He wrote, "Were I to be again reduced to the chains of slavery, next to that enslavement, I should regard being the slave of a religious master the greatest calamity that could befall me. For of all slaveholders with whom I have ever met, religious slaveholders are the worst. I have ever found them the meanest and basest, the most cruel and cowardly, of all others." (*Narrative of the Life of Frederick Douglass: An American Slave* [Boston: Anti-Slavery Office, 1846], 77-78).

75 Roe, ed., *Preaching Deliverance to the Captives*, 197.

76 B. Stanley, *The Bible and the Flag: Protestant Missions and British Imperialism in the Nineteenth and Twentieth Centuries* (Leicester: Inter-Varsity Press, 1990), 90.

77 Stanley, *The Bible and the Flag*, 90.

that gospel which Christ has commanded to be preached among all nations, and which he has so eminently blessed in Jamaica, unless slavery be overthrown, I now stand forward as the unflinching and undaunted advocate of immediate emancipation.[78]

The hopefulness of the Particular Baptists was captured in John Rippon's composition of "A song in prospect of the Abolition of the Slave Trade," written for a sermon on Psalm 68:31, on March 27, 1807. It included this stanza:

The day has dawned, Jehovah comes
To crush oppression's rod;
Now Ethiopia soon shall stretch
Her hands to thee, O God![79]

Present Challenges

The challenges this history of the theologies adopted by those who opposed, or sometimes supported, slavery lie outside this essay, but entail questions such as these:

1. Can we gain lessons from the history of slavery regarding the involvement of Christians/churches—as Christians and as churches—in political level interventions?
2. How may Christians keep close to God while being publicly involved?

---

78 J. H. Hinton, *Memoir of William Knibb: Missionary in Jamaica* (London: Houlston and Stoneman, 1849), 147 and 148.

79 Rippon, "The day has dawn'd, Jehovah comes," Stanza 1. The stance taken in the eighteenth century often was linked to apparently millennial hopes for the future of the gospel. I have not explored this beyond the implications within the material quoted. Carey, in his characteristically contemporary way, links this to technological progress in his day, such as the invention of the mariners' compass, though he emphasises that even "the longest intercourse with Europeans" by itself would never achieve "happy effects" for the gospel (*An Enquiry into the Obligations of Christians*, 67-68).

3. What position should Christians take on questions of reparations and restorative justice?
4. How and what should Christians take care to remember?
5. What lessons should we learn when Christians disagree?
6. How should we understand and respond to instances in history when Christians fall short?
7. How should we approach and apply the Bible's teaching on slavery?[80]

---

[80] The endeavours of writers such as John Murray (*Principles of Conduct* [Grand Rapids: Eerdmans, 1957]) on the ordinance of labour and his Appendix D, "The Presbyterian Church in the USA and Slavery"; the commentaries of George Knight III, *The Pastoral Epistles* (Grand Rapids: Eerdmans, 1992); and the discussions by Douglas Kelly ("Kelly, "Robert Lewis Dabney"), are helpful, yet also illustrate the hazards sometimes encountered in this area. One of the most significant efforts to understand the teaching of Scripture was made more than 200 years ago, by Alexander McLeod (*Slavery Unjustifiable*). An important recent contribution to how Scripture was understood by the Presbyterian church in nineteenth-century America has been made by Alan Strange (*Empowered Witness*).

13

In what sense was Canada a Christian land after the American Revolution?

MARK NOLL

When American patriots rose up in 1775 to throw off the yoke of British tyranny, bold spokesmen for the patriot cause made forthright claims about God's choice in the struggle. Abraham Keteltas, a Presbyterian minister from New England, was carried away by enthusiasm, but still representative, when in 1777 he declared that the conflict under way with Britain was "the cause of truth, against error and falsehood, ... the cause of pure and undefiled religion, against bigotry, superstition, and human inventions. ... In short, it is the cause of heaven against hell—of the kind Parent of the universe against the prince of darkness, and the destroyer of the human race."[1] Even secular-leaning Founding Fathers were caught up in the same interpretive spirit—for example, Benjamin Franklin and Thomas Jefferson,

---

1   Abraham Keteltas, *God Arising and Pleading his People's Cause; or, the American War in Favor of Liberty, against the Measures and Arms of Great Britain, Shewn to be the Cause of God* (Newbury-Port, MA: John Mycall for Edmund Sawyer, 1777), 30.

who proposed for the Great Seal of the new United States scenes from the Exodus with the people of God led by pillar and cloud.[2]

Whether Americans have ever been able actually to create a society where Christian values dominated has of course remained a controversial question. After a half-century of independence, foreign opinion was mixed. Famously, Mrs. Frances Trollope saw almost nothing to recommend about the religious character of the United States.[3] By contrast, and even more famously, Alexis de Tocqueville concluded after his visit in the early 1830s that "there is no country in the world where the Christian religion retains a greater influence over the souls of men than in America." One key to de Tocqueville's conclusion was his sense that, in contrast to Europe, citizens of the United States had succeeded in crafting a successful version of modern Christianity: "the character of Anglo-American civilization ... is the result ... of two distinct elements, which in other places have been in frequent disagreement, but which the Americans have succeeded in incorporating to some extent one with the other and combining admirably. I allude to the *spirit of religion* and the *spirit of liberty*."[4]

During the half-century after 1776, Canadians could be defined as the North Americans who maintained more traditionally European attitudes toward the "spirit of liberty" and the practice of Christian faith. Unlike the Americans, they retained standards much closer to patterns of the old world. Many of them, however, were eager to insist that their path—as much or more than the American path—resulted in a better understanding of Christianity and a better application of Christian norms to society. For the most part, religious and civic leaders in the various sub-regions that would one day make up the Dominion of Canada avoided the extravagant claims of special divine mission that were common in the states during

---

2   Derek H. Davis, *Religion and the Continental Congress, 1774-1789: Contributions to Original Intent* (New York: Oxford University Press, 2000), 138-40.
3   Frances Trollope, *Domestic Manners of the Americans* (many eds., first published 1832).
4   Alexis de Tocqueville, *Democracy in America* (1835, 1840), ed. Thomas Bender (New York: Modern Library, 1981), 182, 35-36.

the Revolution. They also tended to make more modest claims about the Christian character of the societies taking shape north of the American border. Yet, if in efforts to specify God's role in their societies Americans were sometimes guilty of hyperbole and Canadians guilty of understatement, it does not mean Canadians were less concerned about defining themselves as "under God" or trying to shape their societies by Christian standards.

The case for considering Canadian history, *ca.* 1775 to 1815, as marked by a distinctly Christian character depends upon at least four observations. First, leading Canadians felt it was an explicit Christian duty *not* to revolt from the mother country. Second, Canadian leaders felt they had a Christian plan (or multiple Christian plans) to organize Canadian society on the principle of loyalty to Britain. Third, in the years after the thirteen colonies broke away, responsible Christian churches expanded slowly but steadily in Canada. Fourth, in these same years recognizably Christian ideals exerted observable influence on the social order—and arguably to a greater degree than in the United States.

While it is admittedly a speculative historical exercise to judge the Christian character of any nation, it may not be entirely foolish to ask in what sense Canada was a Christian land after the American Revolution, particularly given the strong claims of Americans about the Christian character of their national experiment. Even granting the severe limits of a "preliminary probe" based mostly on secondary sources, pursuing this question may serve to advance comparative understanding of U.S. and Canadian history, and it may encourage others who are better qualified to venture more responsible comparative judgments about the religious character of these two North American societies. This exercise is also a fitting tribute to Grant Gordon whose many contributions to the church and the academy include an important book on a Baptist pastor active in Canada in the immediate post-Revolutionary years.[5]

---

5   Grant Gordon, *From Slavery to Freedom: The Life of David George, Pioneer Black Baptist Minister* (Wolfville, NS: Acadia Divinity College, 1992).

CHAPTER THIRTEEN

It was a Christian duty not to revolt

When 50,000 or so of the perhaps 100,000 Loyalists who were driven out of the new United States arrived in Nova Scotia and what would soon become Upper Canada, they naturally brought with them an abiding commitment to Britain and British institutions. For many of these Loyalists, Christian reasons supported their regard for King George III as a friend instead of a despot, to view Parliament as a source of order rather than corruption, and to define freedom as loyalty to Britain instead of disloyalty.[6] As important as Christian Loyalism was for the future of Canadian society, however, strong Christian motives had been at work in Canada's two main regions well before the exiles arrived.

Quebec, with a solid majority of Canada's approximately 250,000 inhabitants (1785), had been under British jurisdiction for less than fifteen years when the Revolutionary War began.[7] Its nearly complete French and Catholic population might have been supposed to harbor the kind of grudges against Britain that could have turned it toward the patriot cause. Leaders of the Continental Congress certainly thought so when in 1775 they dispatched a delegation to Canada that included Benjamin Franklin and the Rev. John Carroll, who would later become the first Catholic bishop in the United States. The purpose of the delegation was to show Quebec that its interests lay with the new United States against what George Washington had described in a public memo to the Canadians as "the hand of tyranny."[8] The delegation failed utterly in this attempt. Moreover, the firm loyalty that Quebec maintained to the British crown sprang at least substantially from religious motives. The Bishop of Quebec, Jean-Olivier Briand, had earlier participated in a series of successful negotiations with

---

6   On Christian support for Loyalism, see Mark A. Noll, *Christians in the American Revolution*, 2nd ed. (Vancouver, BC: Regent College Publishing, 2006), 103-122.

7   This paragraph follows George A. Rawlyk, ed., *Revolution Rejected, 1775-1776* (Scarborough, ON: Prentice-Hall, 1968), 55-128.

8   George Washington, "Address to the Inhabitants of Canada" (Sept. 1775) in *The Papers of George Washington*, ed. W. W. Abbot; *Revolutionary War Series: June-September 1775*, ed. P. C. Chase (Charlottesville, VA, 1985), I, 461-462.

Britain that cemented his loyalty to George III and that made him gravely suspicious of American overtures.[9] Britain had allowed Briand to be consecrated as bishop in 1766; local officials in Canada had blunted proposals from London to convert Catholics into Protestants and force the use of English; most importantly, in the Quebec Act of 1774 Britain gave Canadian Catholics broader rights and privileges than had ever been accorded to any Catholics under its authority. This Act, which by its concessions to Quebec Catholicism so powerfully spoke to American patriots of Britain's intolerable practice of tyranny, had convinced most Quebeckers of Britain's magnanimity. The result of the surprisingly harmonious incorporation of Catholic Quebec into the Protestant British Empire was firm Quebec opposition to any thought of joining with the American rebels. During the American invasion of Canada in 1775-1776 a few *habitants* and Montreal merchants did join with the patriots, but most Quebeckers held firm under Bishop Briand. Briand even went so far as to threaten excommunication against those who helped the invaders; excommunication was in fact the edict he issued against Father Carroll for daring to support the American effort at winning over Quebec.

In the wake of Briand's sharply stated Loyalism, Britain remained unusually accommodating to the Catholics under his care. When in 1791 a Constitutional Act divided British North America into Lower Canada (Quebec) and Upper Canada (Ontario), one of the reasons was a concession to Quebec's Catholic leaders who wanted to preserve a sphere of Catholic authority over against the rapid British and Protestant settlement of Upper Canada. At the outbreak of the French Revolution in 1789, some Quebec Catholics even saw the direct hand of providence as having preserved their loyalty to Britain during the American War. That loyalty seemed now to be protecting Quebec's Catholics from the ravages sweeping over France as it had already protected them against the strongly anti-Catholic sentiments

---

9   A good survey is Lucien Lemieux, *Histoire du catholicisme québécois: Les XVIIIe et XIXe siècles: Tome 1, Les années difficiles (1760-1839)* (Montréal, QC: Boréal, 1989), 14-32.

at loose in the new United States.[10]

In Nova Scotia, there was a very different reason for turning aside from the American Revolution. As George Rawlyk and other historians have suggested, religious revivalism seems to have absorbed so much energy during the war years that little was left over for political insubordination.[11] Even though a majority of Nova Scotia's still small population had come from New England—and had brought along that region's strong Protestant religious affiliations tinged with republican ideology—Nova Scotia remained neutral during the war. Some of the neutrality came from the fact that Halifax became a major garrison for the British army and navy. Some also came from the persuasive apolitical preaching of Henry Alline, the peripatetic revival preacher who sparked the "New Light" awakening in that colony. Alline preached with great effect in Nova Scotia from the time of his own conversion in 1775 until his early death from tuberculosis in 1784. His all-or-nothing spirituality combined with an ethic rooted in mystical piety to inoculate Nova Scotians against political enthusiasm.

For both Nova Scotia and Quebec, in sum, Christian motivations of different sorts undergirded a refusal to join the American Revolution. Quite apart from latter-day judgments about the morality of the Revolution assessed by traditional just war criteria, the Canadian circumstances of 1776 offered a counter-Christianity to the patriot faith that so wholeheartedly embraced independence.

There was a Christian plan to organize a loyal Canadian society

With the arrival of the Loyalists and then significant migration from England and Scotland, leading Canadians articulated a clear vision for a

---

10   Peter M. Doll, *Revolution, Religion, and National Identity: Imperial Anglicanism in British North America, 1745-1795* (Cranbury, NJ: Fairleigh Dickinson University Press, 2000), 255.

11   George A. Rawlyk, *Ravished by the Spirit: Religious Revivals, Baptists, and Henry Alline* (Kingston, ON: McGill-Queen's University Press, 1984); Maurice W. Armstrong, *The Great Awakening in Nova Scotia, 1776-1809* (Hartford, CT: American Society of Church History, 1948).

distinctly Christian nation, but with a definition for Christianity differing significantly from the kind that was taking shape in the United States. This vision came mostly from Anglican leaders—who were influential beyond their numbers in Nova Scotia, Upper Canada, the areas of Quebec opened up for settlement from the United States, and within Catholic Quebec as well. It pictured a unified ideal whereby church and state worked harmoniously with each other under God to ensure order, promote freedom, generate prosperity, and honor Christianity. In contrast to the "Christian republicanism" of the U.S., this conception of order was hierarchical and aristocratic; prosperity was not to be pursued heedlessly in the American fashion; and Christianity was defined as much by ritual and catechesis as by revival and voluntarism. Perhaps most importantly, freedom meant positive liberty to enjoy a good life, not negative liberty to do what you pleased.[12]

In a perceptive essay published more than fifty years ago, S. F. Wise identified influential advocates of this ideal as Charles Inglis of Nova Scotia and John Strachan of Upper Canada.[13] Inglis was named the Anglican Bishop of Nova Scotia in 1787, the first bishop appointed for the colonial new world. Earlier he had served as rector of Trinity Church, New York, until he was forced into exile at the end of British rule, which Inglis had supported with sermons, practical services, and a well-reasoned but futile response to Tom Paine's ardent call for revolt, *Common Sense*. Scottish-born John Strachan arrived in Upper Canada on the last day of 1799 after study in his native land with Thomas Chalmers, Scotland's leading Presbyterian and a strong advocate of Christendom, whose views on church-state cooperation Strachan would implement as an Anglican in Canada. Strachan rapidly became a major figure in the Canadian Anglican church, an influential voice in

---

12   Michael Ducharme, *The Idea of Liberty in Canada during the Age of Atlantic Revolutions, 1776-1838*, trans. Peter Feldstein (Montreal, QC; Kingston, ON: McGill-Queen's University Press, 2014).

13   S. F. Wise, "Sermon Literature and Canadian Intellectual History," *Bulletin of the United Church of Canada* 18 (1965): 3-18.

government, a stout defender of Canada against American invasion during the War of 1812, a promoter of education at all levels, and eventually the first bishop of Toronto.

In their conception of a Christian society, Inglis and Strachan promoted what was, in effect, Christendom for the new world. They tried to establish a version of the benevolent Christian monarchism that, as depicted in a recent work by J. C. D. Clark, retained considerable influence in Britain at least into the early 1830s.[14] This picture, as summarized by Wise, stressed "the connection between church and state, the relative perfection of the British constitution, the delusiveness of projects of reform and the suicidal dangers of listening to innovators." Strachan outlined the ideal to which this social vision pointed when in 1810 he published a flattering account of the aging George III, which was meant to strengthen the loyalty of the Quebecois and recent immigrants from the U.S. in anticipation for what Strachan feared might soon be an invasion from south of the border: "Were we to model our lives by the conduct of our sovereign, corruption and venality would hide their heads, and all would be cheerfully obedient to the laws. Instead of pride, cruelty, and oppression, Christian charity would reign, each would embrace his fellow subject as a brother deserving of his confidence and friendship."[15] The evils against which Strachan warned were the same ones that American Christian republicans attacked; his antidote, in contrast to the Americans, was a commitment to tradition, history, and deference to proper authority.

Books by Peter Doll and J. I. Little have demonstrated how widespread and influential this conservative conception of Christian social order remained through the first decades of the nineteenth century. Doll has shown how seriously a broad sweep of Canadian Anglicans contended for

---

14   J. C. D. Clark, *English Society, 1660-1832: Religion, Ideology, and Politics during the Ancien Regime*, 2nd ed. (New York: Cambridge University Press, 2000).

15   John Strachan, *A Discourse on the Character of King George the Third, Addressed to the Inhabitants of British America* (1810), in *John Strachan: Documents and Opinions*, ed. J. L. H. Henderson (Toronto, ON: McClelland and Stewart, 1969), 29.

a new-world instantiation of Richard Hooker's classical Anglican ideal of a "unity between church and state, the identity of spiritual and temporal interests and values."[16] This vision was promoted with relative success by Inglis in Nova Scotia, by the first Anglicans in Upper Canada, and among English-speaking Loyalist refugees arriving in both the Maritimes and Upper Canada. It was also advocated in French Quebec by British imperial officials and their Anglican allies, yet quite gently and without resorting to harsh expedients when the Quebecois resisted.

More surprisingly, Little has made a good case for viewing the American emigrants who settled in Quebec's Eastern Townships as being strongly influenced by this largely Anglican ideal of social order, even though only a small proportion of these settlers were themselves Anglicans. Quebec's Eastern Townships had been previously uninhabited land lying between the St. Lawrence River and the state borders of Vermont and New Hampshire, east of Montreal and south of Quebec City, which was opened to settlement in 1792. Most of the early settlers who streamed into the region were from New England; few were Anglicans by tradition; and quite a few were caught up in the fervent Methodist revivals that swept through the region from the late 1790s onward.[17] In other words, this was not a propitious environment for a high-church, monarchical, and traditional conception of Christian social order. But as Little shows, persistent Anglican clergy, cooperating major landowners, Protestant immigrants from the North of Ireland, and also pioneering Wesleyan Methodists arriving from Britain soon succeeded in moderating American republicanism and instilling a cautious, conservative approach to family, politics, and religion. What Little calls "the conservative, pro-imperial message of the Anglican Church" was one of the major factors that forged "the values and institutions of a

---

16 Doll, *Revolution, Religion, and National Identity*, 262.
17 On these revivals, see George A. Rawlyk, *The Canada Fire: Radical Evangelicalism in British North America, 1775-1812* (Kingston, ON: McGill-Queen's University Press, 1994).

country in which 'peace, order, and good government' became the basis of the constitution."[18]

Much the same process was at work in the new settlements of Upper Canada, with a population that grew rapidly after the Constitutional Act of 1791. By 1812, about 60% of the 75,000 inhabitants of this province had arrived from the United States; about 20% were British immigrants and 20% were Loyalists exiled from the U.S. Jane Errington and George Rawlyk have pointed out that Upper Canada almost from the start constructed a relatively cautious, relatively conservative society that was influenced in roughly equal parts by the British-Loyalist heritage and the American migrants. Significantly, however, most of the Americans were New Yorkers or New Englanders of a Federalist bent—that is, Americans who occupied the most traditional and most publicly religious segment of the new nation's political spectrum and who were influenced by the Congregational establishments that remained in Massachusetts, Connecticut, and New Hampshire. With this kind of American immigrant, it was relatively easy to absorb conservative Federalist culture into the broadly conservative, monarchical, and loyal conception of Christian social order taking shape in Upper Canada.[19]

The specifically Anglican cast to this Canadian version of Christian society would fade from the 1830s, if not before. None of the Canadian provinces ever came through with the full establishment for which Anglicans agitated. The best they could ever obtain was informal support from the provinces and some income from the "clergy reserves," land that the provincial governments set apart to support religion. In addition, when leaders of the Oxford Movement came to denounce church establishment in Britain after the Catholic Emancipation bill of 1829, Anglican support for a specifically Canadian Christendom declined. Yet, if Canadian Anglicans

---

18 J. I. Little, *Borderland Religion: The Emergence of an English-Canadian Identity, 1792-1852* (Toronto, ON: University of Toronto Press, 2004), 281.

19 Jane Errington and G. A. Rawlyk, "The Loyalist-Federalist Alliance of Upper Canada," *American Review of Canadian Studies* 14 (1984): 157-176.

were always forced to share revenue from the clergy reserves with other denominations, if they could not convince Catholics in Quebec to trade their own pattern of a Christian *ancien régime* for an Anglican pattern, and if they never successfully transplanted a full-scale Hanoverian establishment on this side of the Atlantic, their efforts still made a difference. Imported Anglican ideals of church-state harmony exerted some effect directly; they also influenced Presbyterians, Methodists, and even Baptists to accept more ties to public projects and less insistence on absolute freedom than prevailed in the U.S. More factors than just the activity of Anglicans were at work in producing the strong churchmanship, moderate evangelical theology, and willing cooperation with government that came to characterize Canadian Protestant life.[20] And of course the presence of a strongly Catholic Quebec lent an ongoing European orientation to the geographical center of Canada that had no parallel in the U.S. The upshot of developments in the years after the American Revolution resulted in different patterns of social and religious organization in Canada and the United States. Judged by its own ideals, the Canadian pattern was no less distinctly Christian than the voluntaristic, democratic, and entrepreneurial pattern that came to characterize the United States.

Responsible Christian churches expanded slowly but steadily
Careful study would be required to compare the scale and pace of church expansion in Nova Scotia and the two Canadas versus that in the early

---

[20] John Webster Grant, *A Profusion of Spires: Religion in Nineteenth-Century Ontario* (Toronto, ON: University of Toronto Press, 1988); Marguerite Van Die, *An Evangelical Mind: Nathanael Burwash and the Methodist Tradition in Canada, 1839-1918* (Kingston, ON: McGill-Queen's University Press, 1989); William Westfall, *Two Worlds: The Protestant Culture of Nineteenth-Century Ontario* (Kingston, ON: McGill-Queen's University Press, 1989); Michael Gauvreau, *The Evangelical Century: College and Creed in English Canada from the Great Revival to the Great Depression* (Kingston, ON: McGill-Queen's University Press, 1991); Neil Semple, *The Lord's Dominion: The History of Canadian Methodism* (Kingston, ON: McGill-Queen's University Press, 1996); Scott McLaren, *Pulpit, Press, and Politics: Methodists and the Market for Books in Upper Canada* (Toronto, ON: University of Toronto Press, 2019).

United States.[21] Catholics in Quebec did experience considerable difficulties in recruiting a capable priesthood. At least until a revival of popular piety that began around 1840, Catholic officials regularly complained about the lax moral state of parish life. Viewed from the outside, however, it is impossible to find any Christian community in North American during this period where Christian rites, symbols, and standards did so much to organize the day-to-day life of an entire people as in Quebec.[22] Among the Protestants, Anglican expectations already exceeded actual performance. Methodist efforts begun slowly in Nova Scotia, the Eastern Townships, and Upper Canada but were picking up by the first decades of the nineteenth century.[23] Among Baptists in Nova Scotia, a more sober style of church practice, supported by considerable educational effort, grew out of Henry Alline's enthusiastic revivalism and was well on the way to creating solid community life.[24] Early Presbyterian immigration was injecting the perspective of Thomas Chalmers into selected locations in Nova Scotia, Prince Edward Island, and Upper Canada.[25] If Canadian churches devoted much more energy than their American counterparts to squabbling over the fruits of establishment, they shared with Americans major difficulties of understaffing, frontier hardship, and uncertain education. In both countries, clergy were being asked to superintend church life over immense

---

21 For a start, see John S. Moir, *The Church in the British Era: From the British Conquest to Confederation* (Toronto, ON: McGraw-Hill Ryerson, 1972); Nancy Christie, "'In these Times of Democratic Rage and Delusion': Popular Religion and the Challenge to the Established Order, 1760-1815," in *The Canadian Protestant Experience, 1760 to 1990*, ed. G. A. Rawlyk (Burlington, ON: Welch, 1990).

22 Lemieux, *Histoire du catholicisme québécois.*

23 Semple, *Lord's Dominion*, 27-70; and *The Contribution of Methodism to Atlantic Canada*, ed. Charles H. H. Scobie and John Webster Grant (Montreal, QC; Kingston, ON: McGill-Queen's University Press, 1992).

24 Daniel C. Goodwin, *Into Deep Waters: Evangelical Spirituality and Maritime Calvinist Baptist Ministers, 1790-1855* (Montreal, QC; Kingston, ON: McGill-Queen's University Press, 2010).

25 *The Contribution of Presbyterianism to the Maritime Provinces of Canada*, ed. Charles H. H. Scobie and G. A. Rawlyk (Montreal, QC; Kingston, ON: McGill-Queen's University Press, 1997).

areas with almost no parallel in Europe.

Through the 1790s, Canadian churches, with the exception of Catholicism in Quebec, shared the uncertainties that also prevailed in the United States. Canadian churches then experienced very substantial growth that lagged only slightly behind the explosive expansion of the American churches taking place from about 1800. This pattern of steady church expansion continued in Canada for at least the rest of the century (unlike the American situation where the rate of church growth began to slow after the Civil War). In other words, church expansion in Canada and the United States seems to have run roughly parallel during the first half of the nineteenth century, however much factors like the place of Quebec and the effects of immigration may have shaped church life differently in the two countries.

Recognizably Christian ideals exerted observable influence on the Canadian social order

Serious research would be required to make a comparative moral assessment of life on the ground in the two countries. A start might be made, however, with a few random observations. The first concerns the place of ethnic minorities. On the one hand, Canadians did not do particularly well in welcoming citizens of African descent. As Grant Gordon has shown, white Protestants made life difficult for David George and other Loyal, liberated slaves whom the British brought to Nova Scotia at the end of the Revolutionary War.[26] On the other hand, Canadian moral life was not compromised by the growth of slavery as was the case in the United States. Concerning engagement with Native Americans, Canadians did not do much better than Europeans elsewhere in the New World, even if the Delaware Indians converted through Moravian efforts did find a refuge in Upper Canada after having suffered murderous attacks, first in Pennsylvania during the colonial era and then in the Ohio Country during

---

26   Gordon, *From Slavery to Freedom*; and Simon Schama, *Rough Crossings: Britain, the Slaves and the American Revolution* (London: BBC Books, 2005).

the early years of the United States.[27] In another domain, popular use of the Bible in Canada continued to expand without the complication of the United States' increasingly strident polemics over whether the Scriptures allowed for slavery. Yet Canadian Bible distribution, dependent as it was on overseas support like the British and Foreign Bible Society, never took place as effectively as in the United States with the leading of the American Bible Society.

These fragments would require much more comprehensive evidence in order to make even a cautious comparative statement about the Christian character of Canadian and American society. Nonetheless, it is probably the case that Christian influence on family and community life in Canada was at least comparable to similar influences in the United States.

Several conclusions

We have come to the end of this simple, perhaps foolish exercise. But several conclusions may still be in order. First, it would take much more research than I have carried out to speak authoritatively about the domains of life that would have to be studied before drawing conclusions about the religious character of early Canada. Second, it would require a great deal of conceptual sophistication to adjudicate properly investigated historical information, since claims about the Christian character of entire societies are very difficult to make with clarity or precision. But, third, whatever might be said in absolute terms about the Christian character of Canadian society in the decades after the American Revolution, in comparative terms there is every reason to think that, despite what Americans like Abraham Keteltas claimed about the American War for Independence, Christianity was as alive and well in Nova Scotia, Quebec, and Upper Canada, as it was in the new United States of America.

---

27   More generally, see John Webster Grant, *Moon of Wintertime: Missionaries and the Indians of Canada in Encounter since 1534* (Toronto, ON: University of Toronto Press, 1984).

14

Pastoral vision: George MacDonald & his *Thomas Wingfold, Curate*

JONATHAN N. CLELAND

George MacDonald is well-known on account of the influence that he had on C. S. Lewis.[1] His novels like *Phantastes* and *Lilith* are also recognized as important works of fantasy literature. Although MacDonald is well-known today as a writer, he also served as a minister in a Congregationalist Church in Arundel from 1850–1853. This short stint was marked by controversy as his theology of Universalism ultimately led him to abandon his position.[2] Despite the brevity of this period in his life, he continued to see

---

1 This paper originated as a term paper that I wrote for David G. Barker's class "Pastoral Theology I" at Heritage Theological Seminary in the Fall of 2017. Dr. Barker's imprint on this paper is clear, and it is thanks to his encouragement in 2017 that I decided to turn to it again all of these years later. What is presented here is a revised and updated version of that same essay. It is my privilege to include this essay in this Festschrift for Grant A. Gordon. An essay on a historic pastoral vision seems fitting for a volume dedicated to a pastor-historian.

2 On MacDonald's Universalism as depicted in his novel *Lilith* (1895) and how MacDonald connects to Lewis and *The Great Divorce* (1945), see my short dictionary article, Jonathan N. Cleland, "Romanticism" in *The Essential Lexham Dictionary of Church History*, ed. Michael A. G. Haykin (Bellingham, WA: Lexham Press, 2022).

the importance of the pastorate. One sees a picture of what such a minister might look like in his lesser-known novel written in 1876 entitled *Thomas Wingfold, Curate*.[3]

Thomas Wingfold, Curate is a narrative that follows the development of a young curate.[4] Throughout the story, one sees MacDonald's vision for who a minister is to be as shaped through his portrayal of the life of Wingfold himself. This essay will briefly trace some of the main themes in MacDonald's novel. In doing so, this essay will not only highlight MacDonald's vision of the pastorate but will also depict potential points of contemporary application for ministers today.

The formation of Thomas Wingfold from death to doubt

The story begins with the introduction of two main characters: Helen Lingard, a young unmarried woman, niece of an entitled, widowed aunt; and Thomas Wingfold, a young curate who, while sitting out in the midst of nature, reflected on how he entered the church, what he considered "an ancient institution."[5] Everything in his life was bland and without passion; however, when he went over to Helen's aunt's for dinner, his life was presented with a challenge. Here he met George Bascombe, Helen's cousin, a self-proclaimed atheist. After dinner, Bascombe goes outside with Wingfold, and, while reflecting on the architectural work of a local church, Bascombe asks Wingfold, "Tell me honestly—do you believe one word of all that?"[6] This question startles Wingfold and catches him off guard. Later, the two depart company, and Wingfold goes his own way to the churchyard,

---

3   For a brief introduction to this work, see Leland Ryken, Philip Ryken, and Todd Wilson, *Pastors in the Classics: Timeless Lessons on Life and Ministry from World Literature* (Grand Rapids, MI: BakerBooks, 2012), 177–178. Numerous editions of *Thomas Wingfold, Curate* exist. In this chapter, I will cite from George MacDonald, *Thomas Wingfold, Curate* (Tyler, TX: Sparklight Press, 2012).

4   I will use the terms curate and pastor interchangeably.

5   MacDonald, *Thomas Wingfold, Curate*, 14.

6   MacDonald, *Thomas Wingfold, Curate*, 27.

sitting down on a gravestone to think further on what he was just asked.[7] In the midst of death, Wingfold seriously questions if he does indeed believe in God; or, on the other hand, is he simply just going through the motions of doing what a pastor does.[8]

In these opening chapters, Wingfold is confronted with the reality of his belief in God. Being a pastor, this is no doubt assumed by him; yet, has he ever been asked if he truly does believe? It is only by the crass questioning of the atheist Bascombe that Wingfold is led to sit amongst the dead and reflect on his own spiritual state. Here he has been, trying to teach others about God, when he himself is not even sure of what he believes. On a cold midnight of November, Wingfold leaves his gravestone chair with doubt.[9]

From doubt to hope

This doubt that Wingfold felt was further emphasized as the narrator points out that the sermons Wingfold had been preaching up to that point were not his own but were the work of his uncle.[10] Reading his uncle's sermons and reciting the prayers of the church's liturgy, Wingfold could safely stay in his unbelief. However, now aware of his own unbelief, he began to question his practices.[11]

Things got far worse, however, after being confronted with a letter from someone who had heard a recent sermon. In the letter, the man mentioned that he noticed a strong resemblance between the sermon that Wingfold had preached and that of one by Jeremy Taylor.[12] Beyond just preaching his uncle's sermons, then, Wingfold had been preaching his uncle's sermons that, some of which at least, were actually taken from the famous seventeenth-century preacher Jeremy Taylor. Wingfold responded to the letter

---

7   MacDonald, *Thomas Wingfold, Curate*, 31.
8   MacDonald, *Thomas Wingfold, Curate*, 33.
9   MacDonald, *Thomas Wingfold, Curate*, 34.
10 MacDonald, *Thomas Wingfold, Curate*, 55.
11 MacDonald, *Thomas Wingfold, Curate*, 57.
12 MacDonald, *Thomas Wingfold, Curate*, 65.

and asked its author if he would be willing to meet.[13]

This response led to his meeting of Joseph Polwarth, a person of strong faith. Although a simple gatekeeper, Polwarth discusses with Wingfold the true meaning and purpose of preaching.[14] In response to Polwarth's interaction, Wingfold states, "You are the only one of the congregation who has shown me any humanity, and I beg of you to be my friend and help me."[15] This honest statement by Wingfold is reflected in Jason Helopoulos' following comment about the life of a pastor: "Everyone in the church and many people in the community know you, and yet, no one *really* knows you."[16] Often the pastorate can be lonely. In the case of Wingfold, he was without a friend; and, in his doubt, unbelief, and copied sermons, he was alone. However, Polwarth stepped out and gave Wingfold hope, even offering to help him as a minister.[17]

In the life of the pastor, the hope offered by an older mentor is indeed quite necessary. Wingfold had tried to pastor on his own to no avail; it is only now through the friendship of Polwarth that things begin to change. The hope comes as Wingfold realizes he is not alone—he has someone to confide in, someone with whom to share his struggles. This is a must; the pastor needs someone who can offer advice, give reproach when needed, and offer an honest, listening ear. Whether it is received or sought, an older mentor is integral to helping a pastor become a pastor.

From hope to discipleship

Wingfold's relationship with Polwarth is instructive in how they engaged with each other. Wingfold brought his questions and ideas before

---

[13] MacDonald, *Thomas Wingfold, Curate*, 68.
[14] MacDonald, *Thomas Wingfold, Curate*, 72–75.
[15] MacDonald, *Thomas Wingfold, Curate*, 80.
[16] Jason Helopoulos, *The New Pastor's Handbook: Help and Encouragement for the First Years of Ministry* (Grand Rapids, MI: Baker Books, 2015), 90. Italics original.
[17] MacDonald, *Thomas Wingfold, Curate*, 77.

Polwarth.[18] From the very outset of Wingfold's doubt, Polwarth told Wingfold to learn about the person of Jesus. He counseled, "Take then your New Testament as if you had never seen it before, and read."[19] Such reading and thinking leads Wingfold to further conversation with Polwarth and others.[20]

From the seed of hope comes a budding mentorship, and from that mentorship comes discipleship. And although it began with unbelief, it progresses to belief; the doubt with which Wingfold began was not completely dispelled, but was used to further his seeking after Christ. Through reading scripture and interacting with Polwarth, Wingfold eventually came to say, "Even if there be no hereafter, I would live my time believing in a grand thing that ought to be true if it is not."[21]

From discipleship to a rethinking of nature

A recurring theme throughout the narrative is nature. In three major parts throughout the book, at the beginning, near the middle, and at the end, Wingfold is found in the midst of creation. At the beginning of the novel, he does not seem to have a strong affinity for creation. About halfway through the narrative, however, in the chapter entitled "A Review," Wingfold takes "delight in seeing the sky through the dark foliage of the yew."[22] At the beginning of the book, he sat on the gravestone questioning if he believed in God. Now, he sits on a stone, reflecting on creation. Before he questioned in doubt. Now he sits in contemplation and prayer, coming away with food for a sermon.[23] Why the change? "Whereas in former times the name Christ had been to him little more than a dull theological symbol, the thought of

---

18 For example, see MacDonald, *Thomas Wingfold, Curate*, 160.
19 MacDonald, *Thomas Wingfold, Curate*, 88.
20 See MacDonald, *Thomas Wingfold, Curate*, 265–270.
21 MacDonald, *Thomas Wingfold, Curate*, 348.
22 MacDonald, *Thomas Wingfold, Curate*, 303.
23 MacDonald, *Thomas Wingfold, Curate*, 303–306.

him and of his thoughts was now constantly with him."[24] At the end of the book, he seeks time off and he has "a day in a deep wood" with nothing more than his New Testament as a companion.[25] As Wingfold grew in his love for Christ, so too did he grow in his love for being in nature. With a renewed heart, Wingfold found refreshment in the Creator's creation.

In a world that is marketed by productivity, technology, and business, it is important to take time off and spend time away in creation. Like Wingfold, Eugene Peterson used to recommend the habit of being in creation. He has described it as a time spent reading Scripture, praying, and reflecting, all the while being immersed in God's handiwork.[26] Although being in nature may not be a viable option for every pastor each week, it is something that nonetheless seems to bring refreshment to many. In the same way that David looked to nature and reflected on God's beauty (Psalm 19:1–6), so too should believers, pastors especially. And perhaps, like Wingfold and Peterson, it will become a time of refreshment, when spending time away from technology and business, in communion with God, one can marvel at his handiwork.

What the Pastor does

In this story, the reader will learn much from what is not said. Wingfold is not once described as attending a meeting, nor is he described as leading his congregation toward a building campaign. Neither is he seen casting a vision for the church. His ministry, as presented by MacDonald, is really quite simple. His life as a pastor consists of three main things: preaching, praying, and visiting. The emphasis of the story is focused on who Wingfold is as a person, but from his development in his own personal life flows his development in these three areas of ministry.

---

24   MacDonald, *Thomas Wingfold, Curate*, 304.
25   MacDonald, *Thomas Wingfold, Curate*, 466.
26   Eugene Peterson, *The Pastor: A Memoir* (New York: HarperCollins, 2011), 220–221.

Preaching

As noted above, Wingfold begins his pastorate preaching his uncle's sermons, but after his confrontation with Polwarth, he begins preaching sermons of his own. Polwarth's advice to Wingfold is invaluable, and it attests to the fact that what one does as a pastor is grounded in who one is as a pastor.

In talking about one who preaches, Polwarth states, "If his own soul is unfed, he can hardly be expected to find food for other people, and has no business in any pulpit."[27] Polwarth's comment makes it clear that the spiritual health of the pastor is essential to the pastor's sermons. The pastor must, through his own study, prayer, and reflection, come up with a sermon that begins with himself. Only when a sermon is derived from one's own devotion and is lived out in experience can one then entertain the business of the pulpit. Bryan Chapell speaks to this when he states rightly, "The influence of a preacher's testimony on the acceptance of a sermon requires that one's life be under the rule of Scripture."[28]

In another place, when Wingfold is further along in his faith, he has another encounter with Bascombe. This time, however, he is far more prepared for the latter's attacks on theism. In a discussion with him, Wingfold comments, "my business is not to prove to any other man that there is a God, but to find him for myself. If I should find him, then will be time enough to think of showing him."[29] Wingfold here attests to a different response to attacks on the Christian faith. Contrary to the idea of presenting philosophical arguments to try and persuade his hearers, he rather tries to find God for himself; and, only from a place of having personally found God, does he then show God to others. This again speaks to the vital importance of the personal life of the pastor. The pastor simply cannot create sermons from nine to five. His sermonic output must come from a

---

27 MacDonald, *Thomas Wingfold, Curate*, 75.
28 Bryan Chapell, *Christ-Centered Preaching: Redeeming the Expository Sermon*, 2nd ed. (Grand Rapids, MI: Baker Academic, 2005), 37.
29 MacDonald, *Thomas Wingfold, Curate*, 200.

personal longing, thirst, and hunger for God. It is only from such a personal relationship, from a personal desire to seek God and live according to his commandments, that a pastor can then share what he has found with others.

Nevertheless, MacDonald is also careful to point out that the congregation will receive these sermons in a variety of different ways. For example, after Wingfold confessed to having read other people's sermonic material in one of his own sermons,[30] he had a variety of responses:

> A few in the congregation were disappointed because they had looked for a justification and enforcement of the confessional, thinking the change in the curate could only have come from that portion of the ecclesiastical heavens towards which they themselves turned their faces. A few others were scandalized at such an innovation on the part of a young man who was only a curate. Many, however, declared that it was the most interesting sermon they had ever heard in their lives—which perhaps was not saying much.[31]

Indeed, the plethora of responses displays a key element of ministry: one cannot make everyone happy. No matter what is said, no matter how well it is said, there will always be critics. Rather than trying to impress and make everyone happy, one must preach in a way that is faithful to Christ and his Word, knowing that there will always be people who find something to dislike. Yet when one is faithful to preach what is needed despite the criticism that follow, God can use those sermons to bring about change. Such transformation is seen in the narrative as the niece of Polwarth observes, "there are people in Glaston that are actually mending their ways because of Mr. Wingfold's teaching."[32]

---

30 MacDonald, *Thomas Wingfold, Curate*, 92.
31 MacDonald, *Thomas Wingfold, Curate*, 93.
32 MacDonald, *Thomas Wingfold, Curate*, 442.

A comment that MacDonald makes as the narrator before Wingfold begins a sermon reveals another key element of the preaching experience. MacDonald writes, "by the time he came to the sermon, [he] thought of nothing but human hearts, their agonies, and Him who came to call them to him."[33] When Wingfold preached, he did not do so in order to download information to a bunch of hearers; nor did he do so in order to gain the fame of a worldwide audience. Instead, he thought of the people in his congregation, their needs, their situations, and from that place, preached to them. The pastor must be one who knows and cares for his people. Moreover, he has to be one who knows Christ and desires to show his congregation what he has personally meditated on, learned, and implemented that week.

Praying

One way in which prayer is depicted in this novel, as mentioned above, is Wingfold spending time in nature. In the words of Eugene Peterson, this type of prayer is Kataphatic prayer, for it "uses icons, symbols, ritual, incense" and the created realm as "the way to the Creator." In Peterson's words, "Kataphatic prayer is 'praying with your eyes open.'"[34] For Wingfold, his time of praying amidst nature helped him immensely in his sermon preparation.[35] It helped him grow in his love and relationship with God. David Hansen also makes reference to praying thus in nature, claiming to even have what he calls "a prayer trail." On this trail he wanders and has time to reflect and talk to God about whatever comes to mind.[36]

Central to one's relationship with God is prayer. Out of this relationship the pastor is to pray for his congregation. In the time that he spends with people, Wingfold mentions that he prays for them.[37] MacDonald clearly

---

33 MacDonald, *Thomas Wingfold, Curate*, 307.
34 Eugene Peterson, *The Contemplative Pastor: Returning to the Art of Spiritual Direction* (Grand Rapids, MI: Eerdmans, 1989), 84.
35 MacDonald, *Thomas Wingfold, Curate*, 305.
36 David Hansen, *The Art of Pastoring: Ministry Without All the Answers*, Rev. ed. (Downers Grove, IL: InterVarsity Press, 2012), 118.
37 MacDonald, *Thomas Wingfold, Curate*, 257.

would have agreed with Peterson that this is a primary task for pastors—"to teach people to pray and to pray for them."[38]

Visiting

Finally, Wingfold spends a good portion of his time meeting with people. He visits with people in his church and those who are curious to learn about who God is. Other times he meets to give counsel and even exhortation. Wingfold is presented as one who is available and willing to meet whomever and whenever necessary.

One account that is especially fascinating concerns the time that Wingfold visited Polwarth's niece while she was sick. Confessing to him that she was in much pain, so much so that she could not even raise her hand to greet him, Wingfold responded accordingly: "The curate bowed reverentially, seated himself in a chair by her bedside, and, like a true comforter, said nothing."[39] Rather than immediately jumping to prayer, or flipping to a Bible verse to read to her, he was quiet, and sat beside her. In visiting people, it is often the case that one needs to remain silent. Counsel need not always be given in times of pain; often, all that is needed is a listening ear and a silent prayer.

Yet, when counsel is needed, it will sometimes go beyond the personal ability of the pastor. When he first meets Helen's brother, Leopold, the latter confessed to Wingfold that he was a murderer. On the run, he found himself back with his sister Helen at their aunt's house. After hearing the grave account of how Leopold had murdered his ex-girlfriend, Wingfold mentions to Helen that he was quite inexperienced to counsel Leopold. His first instinct was to bring his mentor Polwarth to see Leopold.[40] Evidently, Wingfold felt quite ill-equipped to counsel such a man. Polwarth's subsequent counsel ministered not only to Leopold, but also mentored Wingfold

---

38 Eugene Peterson, *Under the Unpredictable Plant: An Exploration in Vocational Holiness* (Grand Rapids, MI: Wm. B. Eerdmans, 1992), 111.
39 MacDonald, *Thomas Wingfold, Curate*, 185.
40 MacDonald, *Thomas Wingfold, Curate*, 261–262.

in how to counsel people like Leopold.

At other times, the counsel that is needed may be very much within the ability of the pastor, yet nonetheless difficult to give. In the case with Leopold and his sister, Helen, Wingfold is confronted with a difficult task. Helen, of course, does not want her brother to be convicted of murder; yet, Leopold, with a guilty conscience, wants to confess what he did to the authorities. Therefore, Wingfold had to confront Helen. And thus, the narrator writes, "Unless he is able to counsel a woman to the hardest thing that bears the name of duty, let him not dare give advice even to her asking."[41] Indeed, unless a person is willing to say what needs to be said, then a person should not say anything at all. This follows what Derek Prime and Alastair Begg call admonition, that is, the practice of warning and correction.[42] Sometimes in counseling, it is correction that is needed, even though it is not always easy to give. But, if it is needed, one needs to be prepared to give it; and, if one is not prepared, then, according to MacDonald, that person should not be willing to give any advice at all.

There will be other times when, in response to one's own confession, others are likewise led to confess. In response to Wingfold's sermon where he confessed to having read his uncle's sermons, the local liner-draper asked to meet with him. Once together, the draper pulled Wingfold aside and confessed to him that he had been ungodly in his business practices. Then he mentions, "But I should never have dared to confess it to you, sir, or, I believe, to any one, but for the confession you made in the pulpit some time ago."[43] Here, the draper confesses to Wingfold, because, as Jon Acuff once noted, Wingfold gave the gift of going second.[44] Wingfold, in confessing his sins first, opened the way for his congregation to confess their sins

---

41   MacDonald, *Thomas Wingfold, Curate*, 299.
42   Derek J. Prime and Alistair Begg, *On Being a Pastor: Understanding our Calling and Work* (Chicago, IL: Moody Publishers, 2004), 155.
43   MacDonald, *Thomas Wingfold, Curate*, 178.
44   Jon Acuff wrote about this in a blog entitled "Confessing 'Safe Sins.'" Regretfully, this post no longer seems to be available online.

as well. Wingfold modeled the way. Others could then follow him, seeing that it was acceptable, indeed necessary, to confess one's sins.

Finally, there are times when a pastor simply needs to be available to talk. In Leopold's last days, when he was slowly dying from a sickness, Wingfold spent as much time with him as he could.[45] And, in many conversations, Wingfold simply told Leopold what he was personally working through at the time, whether it had to do with the authenticity of the New Testament manuscripts[46] or had to do with the way Jesus spoke to women,[47] Wingfold simply made himself available to Leopold and spent time with him.

In some cases, pastors will have the privilege to talk to people about theological issues as Wingfold did. Other times, pastors will have the privilege to do, what Peterson calls, "the Ministry of Small Talk,"[48] where pastors minister in the ordinary, being "attentive to, immersed in, and appreciative of the everyday texture of people's lives."[49] Whether it is talking to others about the finer details of textual transmission or to do with something as simple as a grandson's baseball game, pastors need to be ready and available to talk. And this has to be seen, not as an intrusion, but as an integral part of being a pastor. Peterson writes, "What I intend is that we simply be present and attentive to what is there conversationally, as respectful of the ordinary as we are of the critical."[50]

Conclusion

This essay has sought to give the pastoral vision of George MacDonald in *Thomas Wingfold, Curate*. In this novel, MacDonald writes about romantic and familial relationships, death, irony, and doubt; yet through it all, he

---

45 MacDonald, *Thomas Wingfold, Curate*, 393.
46 MacDonald, *Thomas Wingfold, Curate*, 381–387.
47 MacDonald, *Thomas Wingfold, Curate*, 388–392
48 For his excellent chapter dedicated to this aspect of ministry, see Peterson, *Contemplative Pastor*, 111–116.
49 Peterson, *Contemplative Pastor*, 112.
50 Peterson, *Contemplative Pastor*, 115.

comments on how a young man develops from an unbelieving curate into one who loves God and displays that love to others. Far from a systematic textbook on being a pastor, this is a literary work that didactively portrays what a pastor is, shedding light on the topic in a unique and innovative way. This work by MacDonald has much to offer by way of reflection for the modern-day pastor. This vision may not resonate with some of the contemporary church's expectation, but perhaps that is exactly why it needs to be considered. And while MacDonald would not have regarded himself as an evangelical, the essence of this vision of pastoral ministry contains nothing that is contrary to the evangelical cure of souls (*cura animarum*).

15

"Can a Chinaman become a Christian?": World Christianity and Evangelicalism—An historian's reflection[1]

BAIYU ANDREW SONG

In the autumn of 1892, people on the west-coast United States could have read the following comments from a widely-circulated journal:

> The Chinese are irredeemably and irretrievably bad and vile, as a rule, and all the efforts to christianize them only make them greater hypocrites than ever. This is no slander, but a grave and solemn truth, and can be verified by the sad experience of men and women on this coast who have labored long and earnestly to convert them. It is utter folly to dream of the Chinese embracing the Christian religion, for it is alien to their disposition.[2]

---

1   Frederick J. Masters, "Can a Chinaman Become a Christian?," *Californian* 2 (October 1892): 622–632.
2   As quoted by Masters, "Can a Chinaman Become a Christian?," 622. Robert F. Mc-Clellan mistakenly assumed Masters to be the author of the above-quoted statement. A careful examination of Masters' article reveals that he held a radically different perspective and his purpose was to make a rebuttal against such a view. See Robert F.

CHAPTER FIFTEEN

Though William Milne (1785–1822), the second Protestant missionary to China, also complained about the slow production of Chinese converts seventy years earlier, the Scottish Congregationalist was, in comparison, more optimistic by stating that "several generations of time must roll away; and that we shall be long dead, and our bones and flesh undistinguishable from the mass of our mother earth" before "the actual 'turning of many to righteousness.'"[3] In other words, for Milne, China as a mission field required generations of collaborative labours under God's providence.

Opinions about the Chinese people and their culture, however, changed when thousands of Chinese flooded into the United States during the "California Gold Rush" (1848–1855).[4] In the decade prior to the Chinese Exclusion Act (1882), Protestants on the west coast welcomed the Chinese newcomers, as they believed that it was God who brought these morally-superior people to California to be Christianised. As James Eells (1822–1886), minister of First Presbyterian Church of Oakland, stated, Protestants expected to see "10,000 of the whole number ... converted to Christianity ... This would furnish 10,000 native missionaries to teach Christianity to their people," and would utilise significant American and Christian "influence upon their native land."[5] Nevertheless, Protestant

---

McClellan, "Missionary Influence on American Attitudes toward China at the Turn of This Century," *Church History* 38.4 (1969): 478; idem, *The Heathen Chinee: A Study of American Attitudes toward China, 1890–1905* (Columbus, OH: Ohio State University Press, 1971), 21.

3   William Milne, *A Retrospect of the First Ten Years of the Protestant Mission to China* (Malacca: Anglo-Chinese Press, 1820), 302.

4   On the statistics, see Pao-min Chang, *Continuity and Change: A Profile of Chinese Americans* (New York: Vantage, 1983).

5   James Eells, "The Chinese in America," *Presbyterian Review* 1 (April 1880): 261, 264, as quoted in Robert Seager, II, "Some Denominational Reactions to Chinese Immigration to California, 1856–1892," *Pacific Historical Review* 28.1 (1959): 50. Also see Wesley S. Woo, "Presbyterian Mission: Christianizing and Civilizing the Chinese in Nineteenth Century California," *American Presbyterians* 68.3 (1990): 167–178. On Eells, see Charles S. Pomeroy, *In Memoriam James Eells, D.D., LL.D. Memorial Discourse Delivered in the Second Presbyterian Church, Cleveland* (Cleveland, OH: W. W. Williams, 1886). On Canadian Christian outreach to the Chinese community, see Jiwu Wang, *"His Dominion" and the "Yellow Peril": Protestant Missions to Chinese

clergy soon found themselves in a battle with the Roman Catholics, Irish migrants, and labour unions, as the latter charged the Chinese migrants with being "an immoral, racially inferior, incurably heathen, crafty, low, lascivious, and generally debased race of people whose continued presence in the United States threatened the very structure of a well-ordered, moral, Christian society."[6] Thus, the Chinese aliens became an economic and moral threat, especially to the European migrants. As Diana L. Ahmad pointed out, "economic arguments dominated the call for Chinese exclusion," but moral arguments, especially "targeting opium use and Chinese prostitution constituted another side of the demands."[7] These verbal attacks also became violent, as riots against the Chinese community spread throughout California, Washington, Oregon, and even Wyoming. On October 24, 1871, about 500 white and Latino Americans attacked the Chinese residents in Los Angeles Chinatown. Appealing to mob "justice," nineteen Chinese were killed, of whom fifteen were lynched.[8] Unlike later incidents, such as the massacre in Rock Springs, Wyoming, in 1885, all of

---

Immigrants in Canada, 1859–1967 (Waterloo, ON: Wilfrid Laurier University Press, 2006).

6   Seager, "Some Denominational Reactions to Chinese Immigration to California," 53. Similar sentiments could also be found among Canadians in British Columbia, see W. Peter Ward, *White Canada Forever: Popular Attitudes and Public Policy toward Orientals in British Columbia*, 3rd ed. (Montreal, QC: McGill-Queen's University Press, 2002), 3–23.

7   Diana L. Ahmad, *The Opium Debate and Chinese Exclusion Laws in the Nineteenth-Century American West* (Reno, NV: University of Nevada Press, 2007), 3.

8   The lynching at Los Angeles Chinatown was the largest mob lynching case in the United States. See Scott Zesch, *The Chinatown War: Chinese Los Angeles and the Massacre of 1871* (Oxford: Oxford University Press, 2012); Livia Blackburne, *Dreams to Ashes: The 1871 Los Angeles Chinatown Massacre* (Minneapolis, MN: Carolrhoda, 2025). On racially-motivated lynching in the United States, see Christopher Waldrep, ed., *Lynching in America: A History in Documents* (New York; London: New York University Press, 2006); Manfred Berg, *Popular Justice: A History of Lynching in America* (Chicago, IL: Ivan R. Dee, 2011); Benjamin Fleury-Steiner, "Death in 'Whiteface': Modern Race Minstrels, Official Lynching, and the Culture of American Apartheid," in *From Lynch Mobs to the Killing State: Race and the Death Penalty in America*, ed. Charles J. Ogletree, Jr., and Austin Sarat (New York: New York University Press, 2006), 150–181.

the rioters in Los Angeles were freed after initial trials.[9] Worse, by 1879, west coast merchants, manufacturers, and clergy, who supported and defended the Chinese community began to have second thoughts, as many suspected that "gold rather than God had brought the troublesome Chinese to California in the first place," especially since there were only "some three hundred conversions [that] could be claimed by 1879 and many of these soon relapsed into paganism."[10]

Despite criticism from Protestant clergy, the U.S. Congress passed the Chinese Exclusion Act, which initially banned Chinese, except merchants, students, teachers, diplomats, and travellers, from entering the United States for a period of twenty years.[11] President Chester A. Arthur (1829–1886), however, vetoed it in April 1882, due to the bill's contradiction with the Burlingame Treaty, which had been signed between the U.S. and Qing China in 1868, and which particularly protected American missionaries in China from persecution and granted Chinese citizens certain privileges to become naturalised in the U.S.[12] Under enormous pressure, President Arthur finally approved a similar bill in May of that year, in which Congress

---

9   On violence against the Chinese community in the nineteenth century, see Beth Lew-Williams, *The Chinese Must Go: Violence, Exclusion, and the Making of the Alien in America* (Boston, MA: Harvard University Press, 2018); Roger Daniels, ed., *Anti-Chinese Violence in North America: An Original Anthology* (New York: Arno, 1979); Craig Storti, *Incident at Bitter Creek: The Story of the Rock Springs Chinese Massacre* (Ames, IA: Iowa State Press, 1990); Jean Pfaelzer, *Driven Out: The Forgotten War Against Chinese Americans* (Berkeley, CA: University of California Press, 2008).

10 Seager, "Some Denominational Reactions to Chinese Immigration to California," 60. In fact, by 1882, the pro-Chinese magazine *Christian Advocate* could find only one converted and ordained Chinese who had returned to China to preach the gospel.

11 For instance, one author wrote in the *Bulletin* of Providence, Rhode Island: "Some day, doubtless, we shall learn that by insulting a sensitive people who are essential to the development of our commerce on the Pacific, and who might have been made valuable customers, we have spited nobody so much as ourselves" (as quoted in *The Chinese Exclusion Act. Report and Resolutions Adopted by the Chamber of Commerce of the State of New York. December 5, 1889* [New York, 1889], 4).

12 On the Burlingame Treaty, see Frederick Wells Williams, *Anson Burlingame and the First Chinese Mission to Foreign Powers* (New York: Charles Scribner's Sons, 1912); Reuben Bert Magnuson, "Chino-American Relations from the Burlingame Treaty to the Chino-Japanese War" (MA thesis, University of Minnesota, 1932).

compromised with a ten-year exclusion clause. Later court decisions expanded the subject of exclusion to include American citizens of Chinese descent and the wives and children of Chinese merchants. By singling out only the Chinese people for exclusion, "the exclusion laws meant that Chinese, regardless of class, immigration, citizenship, or residency status, were treated differently from other immigrant groups."[13]

Nevertheless, the Chinese question was not settled.[14] As the Chinese Exclusion Act was set to expire in 1892, another round of public debates began to circulate in the public sphere. In October 1890, Addison Parker, a Baptist minister in Somerville, New Jersey (1889–1891), penned his opinion about the immigration problem, which was published in the *Baptist Quarterly Review*.[15] While condemning the U.S. government for breaking an international treaty with China and responding to common misconceptions about the Chinese migrants, Parker argued for the government's restriction on Chinese immigrants.[16] Despite placing Chinese and Euro-

---

13 Erika Lee, *At America's Gates: Chinese Immigration During the Exclusion Era, 1882–1943* (Chapel Hill, NC: University of North Carolina Press, 2003), 78. On Canadian legal decisions around the same era, see Sharryn J. Aiken, "From Slavery to Expulsion: Racism, Canadian Immigration Law, and the Unfulfilled Promise of Modern Constitutionalism," in *Interrogating Race and Racism*, ed. Vijay Agnew (Toronto, ON: University of Toronto Press, 2007); 55–111; James W. St. G. Walker, *"Race," Rights and the Law in the Supreme Court of Canada: Historical Case Studies* ([Toronto, ON]: Osgoode Society for Canadian Legal History; Wilfrid Laurier University Press, 1997).

14 From 1880 to 1885, many Chinese came to Canada from the United States to build the transnational railway. As the railway was being completed in November 1885, restrictions were introduced and a head tax was imposed upon every Chinese in Canada. The *Chinese Immigration Act* (1885) also limited the number of Chinese migrants in all vessels to one person per fifty tons of its tonnage. Later in 1923, under the government of William Lyon Mackenzie King (1874–1950), the *Chinese Immigration Act* (1923) was passed, which banned most forms of Chinese immigration to Canada. See Lily Cho, *Mass Capture: Chinese Head Tax and the Making of Non-Citizens* (Montreal, QC; Kingston, ON: McGill-Queen's University Press, 2021); John Price, *Orienting Canada: Race, Empire, and the Transpacific* (Vancouver, BC: University of British Columbia Press, 2011).

15 Addison Parker, "The Exclusion of the Chinese from the United States, and the Immigration Problem," *Baptist Quarterly Review* 12.48 (October 1890): 460–475.

16 Parker, "Exclusion of the Chinese from the United States, and the Immigration Problem," 474.

pean migrants on the same ground and repudiating assumptions of racial hierarchy, Parker secularised immigration by making it merely an economic and policy issue.[17] In comparison, Frederick J. Masters, a Methodist missionary among the Chinese in San Francisco, tackled the soteriological question, as critics believed that the Chinese by nature were incapable of experiencing conversion. Masters pointed out that "the question whether a Chinaman can be converted is often asked, not with cynical scorn, but in the spirit of sympathetic appreciation of the immense difficulties that confront the missionary in his work."[18] Nevertheless, the fundamental issue was one of ethnocentric stereotypes and a Eurocentric understanding of the Christian faith:

> The little credit a Chinaman gets on this coast for his Christian profession; the cold suspicion with which he is often treated, as if he must necessarily be a hypocrite; the anti-Chinese sentiment of the coast, shared even by some ministers of religion; the appalling immorality and godlessness of our cities, which a Chinaman is not slow to detect; the fresh memories of murdered kinsmen, of riots, boycotts and savage oppression; and the frequent hoodlum assaults made upon defenceless Chinese, even upon their women and children, as I have seen myself, do not make the white man's religion,

---

17   According to Joey S. Kim, "the belief in a hierarchy of human races was developed throughout the preceding centuries by white Christian Europeans. It was only through Christianity and the realm of the spirit that all people could overcome this chain" (Kim, "Christian Conversion through Racial Exclusion: The *Oriental; or, Tung-Ngai San-Luk*, the Second Chinese-Language Newspaper in the United States," *American Periodicals* 31.2 [2021]: 99–116). Also see Sylvester Johnson, "Religion, Race, and American Empire" in *The Oxford Handbook of Religion and Race in American History*, ed. Kathryn Gin Lum and Paul Harvey (Oxford: Oxford University Press, 2018), 61–78; Michael Altman, "Orientalism in Nineteenth-Century America" in *Oxford Handbook of Religion and Race in American History*, 123–140; Sarah Ruble, "American Missionaries and Race" in *Oxford Handbook of Religion and Race in American History*, 141–155; Kathryn Gin Lum, *Heathen: Religion and Race in American History* (Boston, MA: Harvard University Press, 2022).

18   Masters, "Can a Chinaman Become a Christian?," 622.

morals and social life particularly attractive to the average Chinese mind. In the face of such gigantic difficulties one can excuse the skepticism that underlies the question, "Can a Chinaman become a Christian?" The marvel is that any Chinaman will receive Christianity from a white man's lips.[19]

Nonetheless, Chinese people did not only believe the "white men's" message but also became preachers of the good news. To hammer it home, Masters mentioned ordained Chinese ministers of different denominations in both China and North America. To prove they were decent and real people, Masters also included photographs of eight of these Chinese Christian leaders, all dressed up as gentle scholars, among whom were Tong Ki-Hing (d. 1908), a significant Baptist leader in both San Francisco and Hong Kong, who was praised as "the Chinese Spurgeon for his ready wit, his luminous presentation of truth, and his subtle and searching application," and Sia Sek-Ong (1835–1893), a vital leader of the Methodist Episcopal Church in northern Fujian province, to whom Ohio Wesleyan University granted a Doctor of Divinity in 1888.[20]

---

19 Masters, "Can a Chinaman Become a Christian?," 623.
20 Masters, "Can a Chinaman Become a Christian?," 632.
     According to Masters, Xie (or Sia) was "a graduate of the Imperial University, who threw up a lucrative situation to become a Methodist preacher, itinerating from village to village and preaching the gospel, sometimes upon less than three dollars a month ... [He is also] the author of the prize tract, 'Who is Jesus?' a successful pastor and presiding elder and four years ago [1888] delegate to the last Methodist General Conference, [who] is worthy a place in the highest rank of the Methodist ministry" (Masters, "Can a Chinaman Become a Christian?," 632). In an article published in 1888, Xie was highly praised by a San Francisco journal. Xie was recognized as "a contributor to the Paris Exposition, and to the Centennial at Philadelphia. He is a man of extensive business relations and marked generosity. Before he became a Christian he gave ten thousand dollars to the Methodist mission, and another thousand in support of the Corean mission. As a heathen he also supported a founding asylum of one hundred girls. Furthermore, he is a helper to the distressed in all public calamities ... It is difficult, indeed, not to call such a man a Christian, whatever be the name of the masters he follows and imitates. To call him a heathen, were a compliment to his country men. Charity, the greatest of all Christian virtues, is his by gift of Nature. Aside from this, his learning and ministerial labors in Christian fields should secure him a seat in the Conference

Over one hundred years have passed since Frederick Masters voiced his defence of Chinese Christians. Yet, we still ask: Have we solved the problem? For Canadians, since Canada adopted multiculturalism as an official policy in 1971 and case laws since the Supreme Court's decision in *Baker* (1999), our society has abandoned concepts such as racial hierarchy and we have developed an international reputation for being an immigration-friendly country.[21] Despite recent debates over our current immigration system and policies, immigrants, especially Chinese immigrants, are no longer facing demands for exclusion or violent threats. Immigrant churches, on the other hand, are the most exuberant Christian groups across Canada. Nevertheless, we still see Christians of these groups being marginalised and silenced in our "mainstream" narratives.[22] Instead of asking, "Can a Chinaman become a Christian?," people today have learned to use less racially motivated terms to describe their dubiety over *their* doctrines and practices. On a practical level, multi-ethnic churches often encounter conflicts between white Canadians and the *Other* over cultural differences, such as parenting styles, when to come to church, and how much we should bring for refreshments. Though we behave with polite manners, it seems that this kind of "otherness" is impossible to overcome, even among Christians.

---

of the church he espouses" ("Good Heathen, Good Christian," *Golden Gate* 6.16 [May 5, 1888]: 4). While attending the Methodist General Conference at New York in 1888, Xia received an honorary degree of Doctor of Divinity from Ohio Wesleyan University ("Editorial Notes and Missionary News," *Chinese Recorder* [September 1888]: 441).

21   One of the criticisms of the Supreme Court's decision in *Baker* is its failure to address racial biases in decision making. See Roger Rowe, "'Baker' Revisited 2007," *Journal of Black Studies* 38.3 (2008): 338–345; Sania Chaudhry, "Bias and *Baker*," The Canadian Bar Association (https://www.cba.org/Sections/Administrative-Law/Articles/2024/Bias-and-Baker; accessed October 3, 2024). Also see Augie Fleras, "Canadian Exceptionalism: From a Society of Immigrants to an Immigration Society," in *Immigration, Racial and Ethnic Studies in 150 Years of Canada: Retrospects and Prospects*, ed. Shibao Guo and Lloyd Wong (Leiden: Brill, 2018), 301–324.

22   Renie Chow Choy followed Sang Hyun Lee's argument and described the experience as "the postcolonial condition of marginality (being excluded) and liminality (being located at the periphery or edge of a society)" (Choy, *Ancestral Feeling: Postcolonial Thoughts on Western Christian Heritage* [London: SCM Press, 2021], 56).

Instead of blaming cultural racism and colonialism and advocating affirmative action among evangelicals, this chapter aims to show that there are some fundamental problems with our imagination or meta-narrative of the Christian church.[23] As Étienne Balibar has pointed out, "Every social community reproduced by the functioning of institutions is imaginary," which is "based on the projection of individual existence into the weft of a collective narrative, on the recognition of a common name and on traditions lived as the trace of an immemorial past ... *only* imaginary communities are real."[24] The challenge comes from the Nicene Creed, which confesses: "I believe in one holy, catholic, and apostolic church." Nevertheless, before asking how should we imagine the church today, we need to take a historical detour and ask a historiographical question: Where is the "Chinaman" in our church history?

A brief survey of church history textbooks

Choosing a textbook is not easy; this is particularly true for courses in church history. Far too many evangelical schools do not have a high view of history and only require students to take one course in church history. Thus, a lecturer needs to pick a text that can cover the two-thousand-year history of the church and is not prolix or perplexing. Moreover, such a textbook also needs to help students obtain a larger picture of the Jesus

---

23 Cultural racism, according to Uri Ben-Eliezer, assumes that "certain groups are the genuine carriers of the national culture and the exclusive heirs of their history while others are potential slayers of its 'purity'" (Ben-Eliezer, "Becoming a Black Jew: Cultural Racism and Anti-Racism in Contemporary Israel," *Social Identities* 10.2 [2004]: 249). Also see Floya Anthias, "Cultural Racism or Racist Culture? Rethinking Racist Exclusions," *International Journal of Human Resource Management* 24.2 (1995): 279–301; Benjamin Bowser, "Racism: Origin and Theory," *Journal of Black Studies* 48.6 (2017): 572–590; J. M. Blaut, "The Theory of Cultural Racism," *Antipode: A Radical Journal of Geography* 24.4 (1992): 289–299; Pierre-André Taguieff, *The Force of Prejudice: On Racism and Its Doubles* (Minneapolis, MN: University of Minnesota Press, 2001); Étienne Balibar and Immanuel Wallerstein, *Race, Nation, Class: Ambiguous Identities*, trans. Chris Turner (London: Verso, 1991).
24 Etienne Balibar, "The Nation Form: History and Ideology," in Balibar and Wallerstein, *Race, Nation, Class*, 93.

movement, yet not overlapping with lecture content or losing sight of a particular theological tradition. According to Dyron B. Daughrity, there are five approaches to the discipline of church history, which are chronological, denominational, sociological, geographical, and biographical.[25] In addition, there is also the theological-topical approach. How have Chinese Christians been remembered according to these six approaches to church history?

Chronological approach

Chronological presentation is the classical approach to church history and has been used since Eusebius (c.260/5–339) in the fourth century. Unlike chroniclers, historians need to weigh historical data and choose significant matters from a given period. Historians, thus, are required to divide the meta-narrative into different periods or epochs, though they have the freedom to begin their narration from the creation of the world, the birth of Jesus, or the birth of the church.[26] The question then is how do historians divide the last two thousand years? One of the influential methods is to follow Leonardo Bruni (1370–1444) and Christoph Cellarius (1638–1707) by viewing history through the tripartite system: antiquity, medieval, and modernity.[27] Such a linear periodisation was first introduced in the Renaissance and assumed values in progression. Since periodisation is a

---

25   Dyron B. Daughrity, *Church History: Five Approaches to a Global Discipline* (New York: Peter Lang, 2012).

26   For instance, Eusebius began his *Ecclesiastical History* with a Christological treatise, where he went back to the Old Testament to argue for Jesus' incarnation and his two natures. Both Socrates Scholasticus (c.380–after 439) and Sozomen (c.400–c.450) picked up where Eusebius ended and began their works with Emperor Constantine's (c.272–337) conversion in 312. Also see William Adler, "Early Christian Historians and Historiography," in *The Oxford Handbook of Early Christian Studies*, ed. Susan Ashbrook Harvey and David G. Hunter (Oxford: Oxford University Press, 2009), 584–602.

27   See Donald R. Kelley, *Faces of History: Historical Inquiry from Herodotus to Herder* (New Haven, CT: Yale University Press, 1998); William G. Green, "Periodization in European and World History," *Journal of World History* 3.1 (1992): 13–53; Gary Ianziti, *Writing History in Renaissance Italy: Leonardo Bruni and the Uses of the Past* (Boston, MA: Harvard University Press, 2012).

morphological exercise, by which "all subdivisions of time inescapably reflect the values of the classifiers," the number of epochs or periods can vary.²⁸ For instance, the renowned church historian Jaroslav Pelikan (1923–2006) published his seminal work *The Christian Tradition: A History of the Development of Doctrine* in five volumes, by which the history of Christianity is divided into five periods: the emergence of the catholic tradition (100–600); the spirit of eastern Christendom (600–1700); the growth of medieval theology (600–1300); reformation of church and dogma (1300–1700); and Christian doctrine and modern culture (since 1700).²⁹ Kenneth Scott Latourette (1884–1968), Sterling Professor of Missions and Oriental History at Yale Divinity School, on the other hand, understood church history since Jesus in eight periods: "Christianity wins the Roman Empire and takes shape" (100–500); "the great recession" (500–950); centuries of "resurgence and advance" (950–1350); "geographic loss and internal lassitude, confusion, and corruption" (1350–1500); "reform and expansion" (1500–1750); "repudiation and revival" (1750–1815); "the great century" of growth (1815–1914); and "vigour amidst storm" (1914–).³⁰ Others, such as Tim Dowley (1946–), Bruce L. Shelley (1927–2010), Vivian H. H. Green (1915–2005), Diarmaid MacCulloch (1951–), Guy Bedouelle (1940–2012), Elizabeth Muir (1934–), Mark Noll (1946–), and even the *Oxford History of Christianity*, all followed a similar pattern.³¹ The problem is not the pe-

---

28 Green, "Periodization in European and World History," 13.
29 Jaroslav Pelikan, *The Christian Tradition: A History of the Development of Doctrine. Volume 1: The Emergence of the Catholic Tradition (100-600)* (Chicago, IL: University of Chicago Press, 1975); idem, *Volume 2: The Spirit of Eastern Christendom (600-1700)* (Chicago, IL: University of Chicago Press, 1977); idem, *Volume 3: The Growth of Medieval Theology (600-1300)* (Chicago, IL: University of Chicago Press, 1980); idem, *Volume 4: Reformation of Church and Dogma (1300-1700)* (Chicago, IL: University of Chicago Press, 1985); idem, *Volume 5: Christian Doctrine and Modern Culture (since 1700)* (Chicago, IL: University of Chicago Press, 1991).
30 Kenneth Scott Latourette, *A History of Christianity* (New York: Harper & Brothers, 1953), vii–x.
31 Tim Dowley, ed. *Introduction to the History of Christianity* (Berkhamsted, Hertfordshire: Lion Publishing, 1977; Minneapolis, MN: Fortress, 1995). As published by Fortress Press, Dowley's volume has gone through two further editions (2nd ed., 2013;

riodisation *per se*; instead, it is the attributed value for each period. For instance, we can observe from the various titles employed by Latourrette that he did not think of the late medieval era as a golden age.

It is also significant to mention Andrew F. Walls' (1928–2021) periodisation, which was not based on time or doctrine, but on culture. In his 1984 Finlayson lecture, Walls argued that Christian history should be divided into six phases––Jewish, Hellenistic-Roman, Barbarian, Western Europe, expanding Europe and Christian recession, and cross-cultural transmission––as "each phase represents its embodiment in a major culture area which has meant that in that phase [Christianity] has taken an impress from that culture."[32] Such a division was based on Walls' theory of "the gospel as prisoner and liberator of culture."[33] Since culture is the medium and context for communicating the gospel message, Walls stated that "all churches are culture churches."[34] Nevertheless, in his posthumous

---

3rd ed., 2018). Bruce L. Shelley, *Church History in Plain Language* (Dallas, TX: Word, 1995). Shelley's book was a popular textbook and went through five editions even after his death (2nd ed., Thomas Nelson, 1996; 3rd ed., Thomas Nelson, 2008; 4th ed., Thomas Nelson, 2013; 5th ed., Zondervan, 2021). Bradley P. Nystrom and David P. Nystrom, *The History of Christianity: An Introduction* (Boston, MA: McGraw-Hill, 2004); Vivian Green, *A New History of Christianity* (New York: Continuum, 1996); Diarmaid MacCulloch, *A History of Christianity: The First Three Thousand Years* (London: Penguin, 2009); Guy Bedouelle, *The History of the Church* (New York: Continuum, 2003); John McManners, ed., *The Oxford History of Christianity* (Oxford: Oxford University Press, 1990); Elizabeth Gillan Muir, *A Woman's History of the Christian Church: Two Thousand Years of Female Leadership* (Toronto, ON: University of Toronto Press, 2019); Mark A. Noll, *Turning Points: Decisive Moments in the History of Christianity* (Grand Rapids, MI: Baker, 1997). Noll's volume has gone through four editions, and the fourth edition is co-written by Noll, David Komline, and Han-Luen Kantzer Komline in 2022. Noll's book also became a model for other writers, such as Alice T. Ott, *Turning Points in the Expansion of Christianity: From Pentecost to the Present* (Grand Rapids, MI: Baker, 2021); Heath W. Carter and Laura Porter, *Turning Points in the History of American Evangelicalism* (Grand Rapids, MI: Eerdmans, 2017).

32 Andrew F. Walls, "Culture and Coherence in Christian History: The Finlayson Lecture for 1984," *Scottish Bulletin of Evangelical Theology* 3.1 (1985): 1–9. It is also published with the same title in *Evangelical Review of Theology* 9.3 (1985): 214–225; and in Walls, *The Missionary Movement in Christian History: Studies in the Transmission of Faith* (Maryknoll, MY: Orbis; Edinburgh: T&T Clark, 1996), 16–25.

33 See Walls, *Missionary Movement in Christian History*, 3–15.

34 Walls, *Missionary Movement in Christian History*, 8.

work, *The Missionary Movement from the West: A Biography from Birth to Old Age*, Walls divided Western mission history into four stages.[35] Much like a human, Western missions experienced an early age till the eighteenth century. It then moved to middle age in the nineteenth century but faced midlife crises in the late nineteenth and early twentieth centuries. Since the Second World War, Western missions have moved on to an old age, having lost their former vitality.[36]

Overall, the chronological approach provides a convenient birds-eye view of the trajectory and changes of the Christian church over time. However, historians have to be selective and generic in presentation, and thus sometimes miss important details and nuances. By examining some of these volumes, it is a surprise to find out that Chinese Christians are immensely under-represented, if not completely ignored, in their narratives. For instance, in Thomas S. Kidd's recent work, only nine Chinese Christians are mentioned, among whom are John Hu (b. 1681) and Bishop Luo Wenzao (c.1610s–1691), who were Chinese Catholic converts in the seventeenth century, and Dora Yu (1873–1931), a mentor of Watchman Nee (1903–1972) and the only female Chinese Christian.[37] Others, such as John D. Woodbridge and Frank A. James III, Mark Noll, Robert Bruce Mullin, Vivian Green, and Tim Dowley, have even lesser numbers of Chinese Christians in their works.[38] Curiously, in MacCulloch's gigantic

---

35 Andrew F. Walls, *The Missionary Movement from the West: A Biography from Birth to Old Age*, ed. Brian Stanley (Grand Rapids, MI: Eerdmans, 2023).

36 Notice how Walls ends with hope in world Christianity, as he believed that Christianity is always global. Thus, for Walls, while Western missions are now marked by old age, the Christian Church can and should return to its global nature and find new energy in a global age.

37 Thomas S. Kidd, *Christian History, Volume 2: From the Reformation to the Present* (Nashville, TN: B&H, 2024). The Chinese Christians mentioned in Kidd's presentations include Dora Yu, Watchman Nee, Hong Xiuquan (1814–1864), John Hu, Liang Fa (1789–1855), Luo Wenzao, Xi Shengmo (1836–1896), Wang Mingdao (1900–1990), and Wang Yi (1973–).

38 Woodbridge and James only mentioned Chiang Kai-Shek (1887–1975), Hong Xiuquan, Liang Fa, Cai Gao (1788–1818), and Taiwanese theologian C. S. Song (1929–) in their *Church History, Volume Two: From Pre-Reformation to the Present Day*. The

CHAPTER FIFTEEN

presentation, there are only four Chinese Christians mentioned in his 72-page index. Of these, three were political leaders and the only clergy person was Florence Li (1907–1992), who was the first woman to be ordained to the priesthood in the Anglican Communion, and who primarily ministered outside of mainland China.[39] Nevertheless, for authors such as David and Bradley Nystrom, Martin Marty (1926–), Clyde Manschreck (1917–), George Herring, Guy Bedouelle, O.P. (1940–2012), Jakob Balling, and Bruce Shelley (1927–2010), no Chinese Christian can be found in their histories of Christianity.[40]

Denominational approach

The situation is even more dire when it comes to the denominational approach. To use Baptist history as an example, if more work needs to be done on English Baptist life in the long eighteenth century or the Canadian Baptist experience, Chinese Baptist history is like a piece of moorland rarely cultivated, as even Baptist historians can seldomly name any Chinese Baptist. For instance, in *The Baptist Story: From English Sect to*

Rise and Growth of the Church in Its Cultural, Intellectual, and Political Context (Grand Rapids, MI: Zondervan, 2013). Mark Noll, in his *Turning Points*, only mentioned T. C. Chao (1888–1979). Robert Bruce Mullin only mentioned Xu Guangqi (1562–1633), the Chinese politician and Catholic convert (Mullin, *A Short World History of Christianity* [Louisville, KY: Westminster John Knox, 2008]). Vivian Green mentioned Cardinal Tie Ken-sin (1903–2011), Sun Yat-sen (1866–1925), and Florence Li. Tim Dowley's edited volume only mentioned Bishop K. H. Ting (1915–2012), Luo Wenzao, and Chiang Kai-Shek. In McManners' *Oxford History of Christianity*, Chinese Christians such as T. C. Chao, Y. T. Wu (1895–1979), K. H. Ting, Sun Yat-Sen, Luo Wen-zao, Florence Li, and Watchman Nee are mentioned. It is curious to see that in Latourette's *History of Christianity*, he only mentioned Cheng Jing-yi (1881–1939) and Chiang Kai-Shek.

39 The other Chinese Christians mentioned in MacCulloch's work were Sun Yat-san, Hong Xiuquan, and Hong Ren-gan (1822–1864).

40 Nystrom and Nystrom, *The History of Christianity*; Martin Marty, *The Christian World: A Global History* (New York: Modern Library, 2007); Clyde L. Manschreck, *A History of Christianity in the World* (Englewood Cliffs, NJ: Prentice-Hill, 1974); George Herring, *Introduction to the History of Christianity* (New York: New York University Press, 2006); Bedouelle, *History of the Church*; Jakob Balling, *The Story of Christianity from Birth to Global Presence* (Grand Rapids, MI: Eerdmans, 2003). Even in the fifth edition, the recently updated edition, of Shelley's *Church History in Plain Language*, no Asian Christians are mentioned.

Global Movement, the authors did not mention any Chinese Baptist by name, despite a concise and general description of the Baptist mission in China.[41] Even with David Bebbington (1949–) and H. Leon McBeth (1931–2013), only one or two Chinese Baptists' names can be found in their works and their lives were only casual remarks in passing.[42] In his *A Global Introduction to Baptist Churches*, Robert E. Johnson mentioned eight to nine Chinese Baptists. Specifically, Johnson talked about Gong Dong (c.1850–c.1900), a Chinese migrant who was later called to minister at the First Baptist Church, Portland, Oregon, and who became the first fully ordained Asian-American Baptist in 1875. Moreover, Johnson mentioned these Chinese names without referring to their life stories. Furthermore, Johnson also mistakenly put Jitsuo Morikawa (1912–1987) under the category of a Chinese-American Baptist preachers. This kind of ignorance about Chinese Baptists is incredible.

It is curious to observe that Chinese Baptist leaders such as Yang Ching (or Yong Seen Sang, d. 1882), who was the first Chinese Baptist minister and probably studied at Richmond Seminary in Virginia; Huang Pin-San (1823–1890), the first Chinese minister of Shanghai Old Gate Baptist Church; Tong Ki-Hing, "China's Spurgeon;" Yang Hai-feng (1860–1927), a significant author and preacher in southern China; Dong Jing-an (1875–1944), the president of Shanghai University; Chang Wen-kai (1871–1931),

---

41 Anthony L. Chute, Nathan A. Finn, and Michael A. G. Haykin, *The Baptist Story: From English Sect to Global Movement* (Nashville, TN: B&H, 2015). The same can be said about Gordon L. Heath, Dallas Friesen, and Taylor Murray, *Baptists in Canada: Their History and Polity* (Hamilton, ON: McMaster Divinity College Press, 2020); Bill J. Leonard, *Baptists in America* (New York: Columbia University Press, 2005); William H. Brackney, *Historical Dictionary of the Baptists* (Lanham, MD: Scarecrow Press, 2009). In fact, a recent history of a Canadian Baptist seminary did not include anything about their Chinese student body.

42 David W. Bebbington, *Baptists Through the Centuries: A History of a Global People* (Waco, TX: Baylor University Press, 2010); H. Leon McBeth, *The Baptist Heritage: Four Centuries of Baptist Witness* (Nashville, TN: B&H, 1987). Bebbington mentioned Fook Lough (1841–1884), a Chinese barber who sold himself as a slave after conversion and shared the gospel with the Chinese people in Guyana and established a Chinese Baptist church in 1860/1 at Peter's Hall, East Bank, Demerara.

CHAPTER FIFTEEN

editor of the *True Light* magazine and defender of the Christian faith during Chinese anti-Christian movements; and Wang Peizhen (1899–1971), an outstanding co-worker of Watchman Nee, did not have any space in the larger Baptist story.[43] Sadly, more discussions about the Southern Baptist missionary Lottie Moon (1840–1912) and Canadian fundamentalist T. T. Shields (1873–1955) are found in denominational histories than these *other* Baptists.

Sociological approach

Scholars such as Émile Durkheim (1858–1917) and Max Weber (1864–1920) have provided significant insights for historians from a sociological perspective.[44] Later sociologists such as Rodney Stark (1934–2022) and Danièle Hervieu-Léger (1947–) primarily view Christianity as a living

---

43   The first Chinese Baptist minister was Yang Ching (or Yong Seen Sang, or Yeung Chin Sam, 1811–1882), who came to faith through the influence of Jehu Lewis Shuck and was baptised by the latter in 1844. In October 1845, Yang went to the United States with Shuck to study theology. Upon their return, Yang and Shuck went to Shanghai to plant First Baptist Church in Shanghai. Yang was later sent back to Canton. See H. A. Tupper, *A Decade of Foreign Missions, 1880–1890* (Richmond, VA: Foreign Board of the Southern Baptist Convention, 1891), 128–129, 265–266; Princeton S. Hsu, *A History of Chinese Baptist Churches* (Hong Kong: Baptist Press, 1972), 5:13–15; Thomas G. Oey, "Yang, Qing (Yong Seen Sarng) (1811–1882)," in *Asian Americans: An Encyclopedia of Social, Cultural, Economic, and Political History*, ed. Xiaojian Zhao and Edward J. W. Park (New York: Bloomsbury, 2013), 228–229. On Huang Pin-san, see Baiyu Andrew Song, "Huang Pin-san (1823–1890) and Early Baptists in Shanghai," *Bulletin of Canadian Baptist Historical Society* 3 (2024): 19–55; Yang Zhonghua, "'On Practicing Virtue': A Study of Huang Pin-San's (1823–1890) Contextualised Theology" (MDiv thesis, Toronto Baptist Seminary, 2025). On Chang Wen-kai, see Baiyu Andrew Song, "Jesus Christ in the 'Chinese Enlightenment': A Case Study of Chang Wan-Kai's (1871–1931) Christology," *Midwestern Journal of Theology* 20.1 (2021): 52–71; Jue Wang, *Zhang Yijing (1871–1931) and the Search for a Chinese Christian Identity* (Cumbria, UK: Langham, 2021).

44   See Max Weber, *The Protestant Ethic and the Spirit of Capitalism*, trans. Stephen Kalberg (Chicago, IL: Fitzroy Dearborn, 2013); idem, *Sociology of Religion*, ed., Talcott Parsons (Boston, MA: Beacon, 1993); idem, *The Religion of China: Confucianism and Taoism* (Charlottesville, VA: University of Virginia Press, 1968); Émile Durkheim, *The Elementary Forms of Religious Life*, trans., Carol Cosman (Oxford: Oxford University Press, 2008); W. S. F. Pickering, ed., *Durkheim on Religion: A Selection of Readings with Biographies and Introductory Remarks* (Edinburgh: James Clarke, 2011).

movement and social phenomenon.⁴⁵ By collecting and analysing data, sociologists challenge stereotypical assumptions and present a larger cultural picture of Christianity. Christian scholars such as Sam Reimer of Crandall University and Gina A. Zurlo of Gordon-Conwell Seminary have adopted such a methodology.⁴⁶ With interviews and quantitative research, specific questions were asked about the Christian experience in different communities.

Besides Stark's *A Star in the East: The Rise of Christianity in China*, in which he challenged the framework of calculating the Christian population in China, researchers such as Li Ma, Jin Li, Jie Kang, Aminta Arrington, and Mark McLeister have also done both sociological and anthropological studies of contemporary Chinese Christianity, especially among marginalised communities, such as Chinese ethnic minority groups and disabled Chinese Christians.⁴⁷

---

45 See Rodney Stark and Xiuhua Wang, *A Star in the East: The Rise of Christianity in China* (West Conshohocken, PA: Templeton, 2016); Danièle Hervieu-Léger, *Religion as a Chain of Memory*, trans. Simon Lee (New Brunswick, NJ: Rutgers University Press, 2000); idem, *Religion, utopie et mémoire* (Paris: Éditions EHESS, 2021).

46 See Sam Reimer, *Evangelicals and the Continental Divide: The Conservative Protestant Subculture in Canada and the United States* (Montreal, QC; Kingston, ON: McGill-Queen's University Press, 2003); idem, *Caught in the Current: British and Canadian Evangelicals in an Age of Self-Spirituality* (Montreal, QC; Kingston, ON: McGill-Queen's University Press, 2023); Gina A. Zurlo, *Global Christianity: A Guide to the World's Largest Religion from Afghanistan to Zimbabwe* (Grand Rapids, MI: Zondervan, 2022); idem, *Women in World Christianity: Building and Sustaining a Global Movement* (Hoboken, NJ: John Wiley & Sons, 2023).

47 See Li Ma and Jin Li, *Surviving the State, Remaking the Church: A Sociological Portrait of Christians in Mainland China* (Eugene, OR: Pickwick, 2017); Jie Kang, *House Church Christianity in China: From Rural Preachers to City Preachers* (New York: Palgrave Macmillan, 2016); Aminta Arrington, *Songs of the Lisu Hills: Practicing Christianity in Southwest China* (University Park, PA: Penn State University Press, 2020); Mark McLeister, "Worship, Technology and Identity: A Deaf Protestant Congregation in Urban China," *Studies in World Christianity* 25.2 (2019): 220–237; idem, "Popular Christianity, Sensation and Ling'en Authority in Contemporary China," *Asian Ethnology* 78.1 (2019): 127–153. Also see Paul Freston, "Globalization, Religion, and Evangelical Christianity: A Sociological Meditation from the Third World," in *Interpreting Contemporary Christianity: Global Processes and Local Identities*, ed. Ogbu U. Kalu and Alaine Low (Grand Rapids, MI: Eerdmans, 2008), 24–51.

CHAPTER FIFTEEN

Geographical and biographical approaches
As world Christianity has developed into a field of study, an increasing number of works have adopted a geographical or biographical approach.[48] For instance, scholars such as Kwame Bediako (1945–2008), Sebastian and Kirsteen Kim, Dana L. Robert, Emma Wild-Wood, and Scott W. Sunquist, have focused on both the locality and globality in their studies and significantly contributed to studies of Christianity in Africa and Asia.[49] Regarding Chinese Christianity, besides the pioneering efforts of Daniel H. Bays (1942–2019) and R. G. Tiedemann (1941–2019), recent scholarship by Chlöe Starr, Daryl R. Ireland, Lian Xi, Jonathan A. Seitz, Marina Xiaojing Wang, Christopher Payk, Melissa Wei-Tsing Inouye (1979–2024), John Sampson, and Jue Wang reflect the increasing demand to study Chinese churches and their indigenous leaders in depth and to seriously consider their theological contributions.[50] They have challenged popular hagiog-

---

48   On a history of the development, see Dana L. Robert, "World Christianity as a Revitalization Movement," in *World Christianity: History, Methodologies, Horizons*, ed. Jehu J. Hanciles (Maryknoll, NY: Orbis, 2021), 3–22.

49   See Kwame Bediako, *Jesus in Africa: The Christian Gospel in African History and Experience* (Yaoundé, Cameroon: Editions Clé; Carlisle, Cumbria: Regnum, 2000); idem, *Theology and Identity: The Impact of Culture upon Christian Thought in the Second Century and in Modern Africa* (Eugene, OR: Wipf & Stock, 2011); idem, *Christianity in Africa: The Renewal of a Non-Western Religion* (Edinburgh: Edinburgh University Press, 1995); Sebastian C.H. Kim and Kirsteen Kim, *A History of Korean Christianity* (Cambridge: Cambridge University Press, 2015); Enoch Jinsik Kim and Sebastian Kim, eds., *The Identity and Mission of the Korean American Church* (Minneapolis, MN: Fortress, 2024); Kirsteen Kim, *Mission in the Spirit: The Holy Spirit in Indian Christian Theologies* (London: SPCK, 2009).

50   Daniel H. Bays, *A New History of Christianity in China* (Malden, MA; Oxford: Wiley-Blackwell, 2011); idem, ed., *Christianity in China: From the Eighteenth Century to the Present* (Stanford, VA: Stanford University Press, 1996); R. G. Tiedemann, *Reference Guide to Christian Missionary Societies in China: From the 16th to the 20th Century* (Armonk, NY; London: Sharpe, 2009); idem, ed., *Handbook of Christianity in China, Vol. Two: 1800–Present* (Leiden: Brill, 2010); Daryl R. Ireland, *John Song: Modern Chinese Christianity and the Making of a New Man* (Waco, TX: Baylor University Press, 2020); Christopher Payk, *Following Christ and Confucius: Wang Mingdao and Chinese Christianity* (Notre Dame, IN: University of Notre Dame Press, 2024); John Sampson, "Chinese Theology in Countercultural Perspective: Contextualization and the Contribution of T. C. Chao" (PhD dissertation, University of Toronto, 2022); Chlöe Starr, ed., *Modern Chinese Theologies: Independent and Indigenous, Volume 2* (Minneapolis,

raphies and laboured in archival research, and produced balanced and contextualised presentations of significant leaders of Chinese Christianity, such as Liang Fa, John Song (1901–1944), Wang Mingdao (1900–1991), T. C. Chao (1888–1979), Jia Yuming (1880–1964), Zhang Wen-kai (1871–1931), Paul Wei (1879–1919), and K. H. Ting (1915–2012).

Nevertheless, geographical and biographical approaches also have significant weaknesses, as scholars can easily miss the larger picture and fail to make connections between the West and the indigenous world being studied. In addition, there is still a significant need for scholars to transcend continental divisions and draw attention to diasporic studies by asking questions such as, how did Chinese Christians manage the cultural differences and pressure for assimilation in foreign lands? In this regard, Alexander Chow, Alison R. Marshall, Jiwu Wang, and Joshua Paddison have done some pioneering labours.[51]

MN: Fortress, 2023); Xi Lian, *Redeemed by Fire: The Rise of Popular Christianity in Modern China* (New Haven, CT: Yale University Press, 2010); Li Ma, *Christian Women and Modern China: Recovering a Women's History of Chinese Protestantism* (Lanham, MD: Lexington, 2021); Melissa Wei-Tsing Inouye, *China and the True Jesus: Charisma and Organization in a Chinese Christian Church* (Oxford: Oxford University Press, 2018); Marina Xiaojing Wang, "Church Unity Movement in Early Twentieth-Century China: Cheng Jingyi and the Church of Christ in China" (PhD dissertation, Edinburgh University, 2013); *idem*, "The Chinese Home Missionary Society: An Early Attempt at Shaping an Interdenominational and Indigenised Chinese Christianity (1918–1955)," *Yearbook of Chinese Theology 2017*, ed. Paulos Z. Huang (Leiden: Brill, 2017), 75–96; Jin Meng, "Christian Embodiment of Neo-Confucian Active Mysticism: A Study on Jia Yuming's Spirituality" (PhD dissertation, Edinburgh University, 2023); Jia Ma and Suyun Liao, *Incorruptible Love: The K.H. Ting Story* (New York: Peter Lang, 2018).

51 Alexander Chow has recently worked in this area and produced pioneering works, including "From Takeaway to British Chinese: Christianity among Overseas Chinese in the United Kingdom," in *Journeys of Asian Diaspora: Mapping Originations and Destinations*, ed. Sam George (Minneapolis, MN: Fortress, 2021), 9–24; *idem*, "British Immigration Policies and British Chinese Christianity," in *Ecclesial Diversity in Chinese Christianity*, ed. Alexander Chow and Easten Law (New York: Palgrave Macmillan, 2021), 99–120; *idem*, "Urbanisation, Diaspora, and the Tenacity of Chinese Evangelicalism," in *Ecumenism and Independency in World Christianity: Historical Studies in Honour of Brian Stanley*, ed. Alexander Chow and Emma Wild-Wood (Leiden: Brill, 2020), 329–346. Also see Alison R. Marshall, *Cultivating Connections: The Making of Chinese Prairie Canada* (Vancouver, BC: University of British Columbia Press, 2014); Wang, *"His Dominion" and the "Yellow Peril"*; Joshua Paddison, *American*

CHAPTER FIFTEEN

Theological and topical approaches

The theological and topical approaches to church history are a unique blend of theological inquiries and the history of doctrinal development. Despite using a propositional approach to history, when executed effectively, it can offer profound insights. For instance, in his *Jesus Through the Centuries* and *Mary Through the Centuries*, Jaroslav Pelikan used Jesus and Mary as points of connection to explore how Christian doctrines evolved in diverse cultural contexts.[52] Similarly, contemporary scholars like R. S. Sugirtharajah and Kwok Pui-lan have integrated postcolonial and feminist frameworks into their study of doctrines such as Christology, hermeneutics, and the Bible.[53] Bruce Gordon's recent work, *The Bible: A Global History*, is a prime example of this approach, as he narrates a global history of the Bible, from its formation to its impact in the Global South.[54] Regarding Chinese Christianity, scholars such as Alexander Chow, Chloë Starr, and Daniel Qin have produced monographs and edited volumes on doctrinal topics, such as public theology, soteriology, hermeneutics, and Christology.[55] In addition, under the editorship of Roman Malek, five volumes of collected essays and primary sources are published under the title *The Chinese Face*

Heathens: Religion, Race, and Reconstruction in California (Berkeley, CA: University of California Press; San Marino: Huntington Library, 2012).

52   Jaroslav Pelikan, *Jesus Through the Centuries: His Place in the History of Culture* (New Haven, CT: Yale University Press, 1999); idem, *Mary Through the Centuries: Her Place in the History of Culture* (New Haven, CT: Yale University Press, 1996).

53   See R. S. Sugurtharajah, *The Bible and Asia: From the Pre-Christian Era to the Postcolonial Age* (Boston, MA: Harvard University Press, 2013); idem, *Jesus in Asia* (Boston, MA: Harvard University Press, 2018); idem, *Hindus and Their Christian Bible* (New York: Bloomsbury, 2024); idem, *The Brahmin and His Bible: Rammohun Roy's Precepts of Jesus 200 Years On* (New York: Bloomsbury, 2019).

54   Bruce Gordon, *The Bible: A Global History* (New York: Basic Books, 2024).

55   Alexander Chow, *Chinese Public Theology: Generational Shifts and Confucian Imagination in Chinese Christianity* (Oxford: Oxford University Press, 2018); Carl S. Kilcourse, *Taiping Theology: The Localization of Christianity in China, 1843–64* (New York: Palgrave Macmillan, 2016); Daniel Qin, "Evolution of Evangelical Socio-Political Approaches in Contemporary China (1980s–2010s)" (PhD dissertation, Edinburgh University, 2020); Chloë Starr, ed., *Reading Christian Scriptures in China* (London; New York: T&T Clark, 2008).

of Jesus Christ, examining the Christological presentation and reception in Chinese language and among Chinese audience.

By reviewing current scholarship through these six approaches to church history, it can be observed that there is a tendency for Chinese Christianity to remain within a cultural and disciplinary ghetto. In other words, as someone once told me, a course on Chinese church history should only be offered to Chinese students and those training for missions. Christians of Chinese and other non-European backgrounds are, thus, not treated as equal guests at the Lamb's table.

Conclusion: World Christianity for Evangelicalism

Almost twenty-five years ago, Alister E. McGrath examined evangelical theological method and reflected on the futures of evangelical theology.[56] By the end of his essay, McGrath briefly addressed what he called "challenges from Africa and Asia." Responding to Wolfhart Pannenberg (1928–2014), who argued that "Western theology has been shaped by its engagement with the rise of the natural sciences and the secular critique of authority," McGrath argues that evangelicals insist that "theology arises from Scripture and is not derived from a series of philosophical presuppositions."[57] Thus, "the success of the movement rests on its willingness to correlate Scripture with the context in which it finds itself, rather than simply reaching backward into evangelical history to draw out past correlations, such as the way in which a text was applied by Calvin in his sixteenth-century Genevan context."[58] Nevertheless, it seems that McGrath has only partially addressed the issue here, as his argument appears to be built upon an East-West dualism. The precise problem is not why Chinese Christians need to read John Calvin (1509–1564), or how relevant is

---

56   Alister E. McGrath, "Evangelical Theological Method: The State of the Art," in *Evangelical Futures: A Conversation on Theological Method*, ed. John G. Stackhouse, Jr. (Grand Rapids, MI: Baker; Leicester: Inter-Varsity; Vancouver, BC: Regent College Publishing, 2000), 35–37.
57   McGrath, "Evangelical Theological Method," 37.
58   McGrath, "Evangelical Theological Method," 37.

evangelical theology in Nairobi. The confidence of evangelical theology, if centred on the incarnate God as revealed in the biblical canon, should be for our believing and teaching the catholic faith, despite being intrinsically influenced by modernity. The challenge for evangelicals today is not only reconsidering our epistemology, such as abandoning foundationalism and critiquing modernistic assumptions; it also requires us to adjust our orientation, which involves our imagination of the *ecclesia catholica*. To borrow Andrew F. Walls' words: evangelicals need to understand that "the crucial fact is, African, Asian, and Latin American Christian history are not a matter of mere local significance; they are simply church history, the story of God's dealings with humanity. They belong to the whole church, and none of us can afford to be without them. Christianity has always been in principle global."[59] Thus, as a *narrative community*, the Christian church, and particularly evangelicals today, need to re-imagine our meta-narrative, as even Immanuel Kant (1724–1804) observed that we need to imagine ourselves as a "world family" beyond nation and denominational identity. In this family, no one is a refugee, and every Christian should enjoy "unlimited hospitality."[60] The problem is we have disintegrated into "private narratives, models of self-realization," instead of remembering what the Creed states: *we* are "one holy, catholic, and apostolic church."[61] Therefore, evangelicals need to seriously consider if our imagination of the church is big or catholic enough to be the body of Christ, which is intrinsically marked by its unity in diversity through consanguineous love. Furthermore,

---

59 Andrew F. Walls, *Missionary Movement from the West*, 239–240.

60 Byung-Chul Han, *The Crisis of Narration*, trans. Daniel Steuer (Hoboken, NJ: Polity, 2024), 63. According to Kant, "all men are entitled to present themselves in the society of others by virtue of their right to communal possession of the earth's surface. Since the earth is a globe, they cannot disperse over an infinite area, but must necessarily tolerate one another's company. And no-one originally has any greater right than anyone else to occupy any particular portion of the earth" (Immanuel Kant, *Perpetual Peace: A Philosophical Sketch* [Cambridge University Press, 1991], 106).

61 Han, *Crisis of Narration*, 64. Also see Scott W. Sunquist, *The Shape of Christian History: Continuity and Diversity in the Global Church* (Downers Grove, IL: InterVarsity, 2022); Stephen T. Pardue, *Why Evangelical Theology Needs the Global Church* (Grand Rapids, MI: Baker, 2023).

the question—"where is the Chinaman?"—should not only be asked by historians, but every evangelical scholar in their respective disciplines.

Coda

I first met Dr Grant Gordon at the sixth annual conference of the Andrew Fuller Centre in Louisville, KY, in 2012, where he presented a paper on John Ryland, Jr. (1753–1825). Being a freshman to Baptist history, I had much to learn at my first academic conference. With knowing Gordon, a fellow Canadian, I also purchased his *Wise Counsel* (2009), which was a collection of letters from John Newton (1725–1807) to Ryland.[62] On a personal level, Gordon's *Wise Counsel* has deeply impacted me, especially Newton's rebuke to the young Ryland: "I believe it not more impossible to find a humble Arminian, than a proud and self-sufficient Calvinist."[63] For a young and restless Calvinist, Newton's words were a blow to the head. Getting to know Dr. Gordon personally, I have developed enormous respect for his dedication to the Christian church and his ability in historical research. Nevertheless, what turned my respect to deep admiration was Gordon's *From Slavery to Freedom*, which was a pioneering work on the life of David George (1743–1810).[64] Writing in 1992, Gordon acknowledged the scarcity of resources and studies on this Black Baptist preacher.[65] Nevertheless, with tireless research and a detective-like mind, Gordon was able to provide precise details about George's life story and to extend it to a book of more than 350 pages.[66] Despite recent scholarship, Black Baptists, such as David

---

62 Grant Gordon, ed., *Wise Counsel: John Newton's Letters to John Ryland, Jr.* (Edinburgh: Banner of Truth, 2009).
63 Gordon, ed., *Wise Counsel*, 15.
64 Grant Gordon, *From Slavery to Freedom: The Life of David George, Pioneer Black Baptist Minister* (Hantsport, NS: Lancelot, 1992).
65 Gordon, *From Slavery to Freedom*, xiii.
66 The only account of David George's life was his autobiographical note published as "An Account of the Life of Mr. David George, from Sierra Leone in Africa; given by himself in a conversation with Brother Rippon of London, and Brother Pearce of Birmingham," in the *Baptist Annual Register*, ed. John Rippon (London, 1793), 473–483.

CHAPTER FIFTEEN

George, are still marginalised in the Baptist meta-narrative.[67] Gordon's *From Slavery to Freedom*, though focused on David George, was an exemplary attempt to address a significant gap in Baptist history. Despite his efforts, though, Gordon's *From Slavery to Freedom* is not well known. And worse even for historians of the long eighteenth century, only a few have heard of the name David George. There is a desperate need for evangelical scholars to learn from Dr Gordon's example, to get their hands dirty in the archives and to reconstruct a new meta-narrative of the catholic church, all for the love of Christ.

---

67   For instance, Harvey Amani Whitfield, *Biographical Dictionary of Enslaved Black People in the Maritimes* (Toronto, ON: University of Toronto Press, 2022); Noel Leo Erskine, *Black Missionary in an Age of Enslavement: The Life and Times of George Liele* (Lanham, MD: Rowan & Littlefield, 2024); 2024); Hannah Lane, "Revisiting Accounts of the Life of Mr. David George" in *The Black Baptist Experience in Canada*, ed. Gordon L. Heath and Dudley A. Brown (Eugene, OR: Pickwick, 2025), 266–296.

www.ingramcontent.com/pod-product-compliance
Lightning Source LLC
Chambersburg PA
CBHW020520080526
44583CB00013B/674